A guide to the
BIRDS OF PUERTO RICO
and the
VIRGIN ISLANDS

HERBERT A. RAFFAELE

Illustrated by
Cindy J. House
John Wiessinger

Single plates by
Cynthie Fisher
Alejandro Grajal
John Yrizarry

Revised Edition

PRINCETON UNIVERSITY PRESS

Library of Congress Cataloging in
Publication Data will be found on the last
printed page of this book

This book has been composed in Baskerville

Maps:

Places to Bird by Art Ciccone
Puerto Rico and the Virgin Islands by Diane Naylor

Editorial and production services by
Fisher Duncan, 10 Barley Mow Passage,
London W4 4PH, UK

Printed in the United Kingdom

Contents

**Vagrants, Unestablished Exotics and Hypothetical
Species   199**

Places to Bird

To my parents, Thomas and Florence Raffaele,
the people of Puerto Rico and the Virgin Islands,
and to an improved future for the wildlife of the region.

Preface to the Revised Edition

Updating this guide has taken far more effort than I ever expected considering only seven years have transpired since drafting the first edition. However, I am very pleased that this extra effort was necessary because it indicates that the number of people actively birding in the region has increased dramatically and this situation is all for the good.

I was also extremely pleased with the prompt and generous response of the many observers now active in the region in providing me with new records. I did not have the pleasure of meeting many of these contributors nor in some cases did I even contact them directly, thus their responsiveness is that much more appreciated.

However, before acknowledging these contributors I must first make up for a serious oversight in the first edition by crediting J. Phillip Angle, Ralph Browning and the staff of the Division of Birds of the Smithsonian Institution for their generosity in loaning bird specimens to Cindy House for her work in preparing many of the plates. Such loans make substantial demands on the museum staff and are something of a risk to the specimens, consequently I regret not having expressed the appreciation of Cindy and myself earlier in the first edition.

Significant input to the second edition was provided by: Paul Baicich, Thelma Douglas, Barbara Dowell, Dr Michael Gochfeld, Enrique Hernandez-Prieto, Jorge Moreno, David Pashley, Sue Rice, Dr Chan Robbins, Jorge Saliva, Dr Fred Schaffner, Dr Cindy Staicer, the St Croix Environmental Association, Francisco Vilella, and Ro Wauer.

Special thanks are also due to Rob Norton who has done an outstanding job over the last decade in generating new data and compiling the sundry notes on new bird records from throughout the West Indies and particularly the Virgin Islands. This is an arduous task much appreciated by all those interested in Caribbean birds.

Furthermore, the efforts of Fred Sladen must be highlighted for his impressive contributions during this decade to our knowledge of the birds of St Croix and specifically for his thorough and unflagging assistance in documenting many new records presented in this edition.

Finally I must thank the person behind—albeit not very far behind—the scenes—my wife Jan. Jan was relentless in performing many of the most tedious aspects of the revisions and were it not for her the reissuing of this book might certainly have been delayed. Beyond that, her companionship and support during this period were highly appreciated.

Overall, this new edition presents eleven new bird species, now well documented from the region, as well as significantly updating the status of birds in the Virgin Islands. It also includes plate to text cross-referencing which was an unfortunate oversight in the first edition.

May this guide serve you well.

H.A.R.
July, 1989

Preface

I first visited Puerto Rico in 1963 and subsequently returned to the island on a number of occasions, including a residency there of six and a half years, during which I served as a wildlife biologist for the Commonwealth of Puerto Rico. The information in this guide is primarily based on intensive field work during this period.

Many people have generously contributed to this book. I must begin with my parents who strongly supported my early interest in birds and Nilda Iris Aponte who encouraged me and lent support during the initial, difficult stages of undertaking this task. In Puerto Rico I must thank Mr and Mrs Raphael Aponte for their kind hospitality during portions of my residency on the island. To Mr Rubén Freyre in particular as well as Mr Gabriel del Toro, Emilio Colón and Ariel Lugo, my immediate supervisors during the six years I worked for the Department of Natural Resources, I offer my gratitude for the confidence they had in me and the support they gave me. Joan Duffield, Mitch Fram, Melvin Ruiz, and Valentín Santana were my field assistants on the job, and I owe much to all of them. It is with the greatest pleasure that I recognize Noel Snyder and Jim Wiley, two indefatigable ornithologists with whom I had the good fortune of working closely for several years. Both reviewed most of the manuscript offering valuable criticisms and were companions par excellence in the field. Roy Thomas established important contacts for me in the Virgin Islands and accompanied me on a trip among the islands. Jim Riddle and Robert Norton generously contributed the write-up of the birds of Mary Point Pond, St John. Robert Norton also wrote up Mangrove Lagoon, St Thomas and thoroughly reviewed and updated the manuscript with respect to the Virgin Islands. Storrs Olson updated the section on fossil birds.

Others who have contributed significantly to this book include: Paul and Fran Beach, Bedford Brown, Barbara Cintrón, Melín Díaz, Eugene Eisenmann, Donald Erdman, Sean Furniss, Morty Henríquez, Mary Hickman, Cameron and Kay Kepler, Douglas Kraus, Elizabeth Litovich, the National Park Service — St John, The Natural History Society of Puerto Rico, Richard Philibosian, Lillian Pope, the Queens County Bird Club, William B. Robertson Jr, Rowan Roy, Lúis Manuel Santos Ramos, Fritz Scheider,

George Seaman, James Sedgwick, Robert Smolker, Helen Snyder, Karin Steinhoefer, Bill Truesdell, Iván Vélez, Frank Wadsworth, Beth Wiley, Roy Woodbury, and John Yntema.

Of course, I must applaud my two children, Nildita and Herby, for their tolerance of my regularly being away in the field or sequestered behind my desk.

I expect to publish detailed documentation supporting comments I have made on the region's birdlife in appropriate scientific journals.

Introduction

Aims

This guide is the first self-contained source for the field identification of birds (other than fossil forms) known to occur or have occurred in Puerto Rico and the Virgin Islands. The book also attempts to foster an appreciation of the uniqueness of the region's wildlife and enhance awareness of conservation issues. The section 'Places to Bird' will help make the stay of short-term visitors more productive. Finally, the book substantially updates the data on avian distribution and abundance in the region. It covers records through November 1988.

Species Categories

The main text contains accounts covering 284 living species of birds. The first edition included species for which there were at least one collected specimen (or an adequate photograph), or three separate sight records by reliable observers. Additions to this edition were based on a minimum of three reliable records. Two exceptions include the American Robin and White-throated Sparrow, for which I personally have single sight records. Full dates (when known) are given for birds recorded just once, while only the month is included for other accidentals.

Fossil birds (7 species) are discussed in the 'Conservation' section. The section starting on p. 10 covers vagrants, unestablished exotics and hypothetical species. Birds known from the region by only one or two sight records fall into either of the first two categories. 'Vagrants' (51 species) include birds that stray to the region without having been intentionally brought by humans. 'Unestablished exotics' (22 species) are imported birds which have escaped in very small numbers, or which were intentionally released and became extirpated. The total number of birds in the region including vagrants, unestablished exotics and fossil forms sums to 364 species. A 'hypothetical' listing (6 species) includes dubious published reports. Data from some published accounts have been totally omitted due to their spurious nature.

Species Accounts

The status terms are defined below and are based on an observer visiting a suitable locality and habitat in the appropriate season. For birds that roost communally (e.g. herons), I give their status under normal field conditions and not for watching flocks flying to or from a roost.

Very common: 20 or more in a single day

Common: 5—20 in a single day

Uncommon: not seen on every trip, but at least twice per year

Rare: fewer than twice per year, but at least once every 5 years

Very rare: generally one every 5—10 years

Extremely rare: generally one every 10—15 years

Accidental: 1—5 records and generally no more than one every 15 years

There are always difficulties in classifying some birds, such as the Broad-winged Hawk, which can regularly be seen only at a couple of localities; however, I have tried to clarify these cases in the text. A few species, such as the Golden-winged Warbler, were virtually unknown from the region a few years ago, but there have been a number of recent sightings. In cases similar to the Goldenwing's, where it is more likely the bird was overlooked than that its status changed, I have weighed my assessment of its status accordingly. I have attempted to refrain from using the term 'irregular' for species that appear to fluctuate in abundance from year to year because, in general, the regularity with which bird observations have been made in the region has probably fluctuated much more widely than have bird populations.

Descriptions of plumages, calls and nests refer to what is familiar in the region.

Common Spanish names have been selected to eliminate some local misnomers, such as by substituting Paloma Perdiz for Perdiz, and to bring the local names more in line with those used internationally (e.g. Garrapatero instead of Judío). To avoid confusion, several local names are sometimes presented.

Definitions

♀	female
♂	male
Antilles	the West Indies excluding the Bahamas. The Greater and the Lesser Antilles combined.
Central America	from Guatemala to Panama.
Crepuscular	active at dawn and dusk.
Endemic	confined to a specific region and found nowhere else in the world. Used here primarily for birds known only from Puerto Rico and the Virgin Islands.
Extinct	an organism which no longer has living representatives.
Extirpated	an organism that has been eliminated from a particular area, but not its worldwide range.
Greater Antilles	Puerto Rico, the Virgin Islands, Jamaica, Hispaniola, and Cuba.
Lesser Antilles	the islands east and southeast of the Virgin Islands excluding Trinidad, Tobago and other islands near the coast of South America.
Migrant	passes through the region in spring and/or fall. The terms spring and fall are used somewhat loosely (for example, the 'fall' migration of shorebirds actually begins in August).
Pelagic	pertaining to the open ocean.
Possible breeders	no evidence of breeding, but some undetected reproduction possible.
Probable breeders	no direct evidence of breeding, but changes in distribution or population size suggest that breeding must occur.
Region	Puerto Rico and the American and British Virgin Islands.
Transient	a migrant.
Visitor	resident in the region for part of the year, but does not breed in the region.
West Indies	Greater and Lesser Antilles and Bahamas.

Composition of the Avifauna

Of the region's 284 bird species 276 occur in Puerto Rico and 210 in the Virgin Islands. These birds are divided into various groups in the following table:

The Region's Avifaunal Composition

Status	Puerto Rico	Virgin Islands	Region
Native, breeding permanent residents	94	60	97
Breed and then leave	11	10	11
Nonbreeding migrants and visitors	134	129	139
Introduced — permanent or probable breeders	31	6	32
Introduced — possible breeders	5	5	5
Recently extirpated	1	0	1

It is important to keep in mind that migrant and visiting species play a major role in the ecology of the region, as do the permanent residents. The term 'visitor' has been used for brevity rather than the more accurate, but lengthy phrase, 'nonbreeding fall to spring resident'. The sole recently extirpated bird is the White-necked Crow. The Greater Flamingo and birds of similar status could well have been included in this category, but are placed under visitors because though they no longer breed in the region wanderers still occur.

Causes of the Avifaunal Increase

As a result of the large increase in breeding exotics in Puerto Rico the island now supports 85 species of breeding land birds (from pigeons to finches), the greatest number of any West Indian island. Puerto Rico, with its 284 species, also harbors the second largest total avifauna, surpassed only by Cuba. It will be interesting to see whether the island can sustain this diversity, or whether a new equilibrium will be reached only after the extirpation or extinction of several species.

An intriguing question is why Puerto Rico and the Virgin Islands have experienced such a large influx of birds. The explanation appears to be twofold. The economic status of the residents of the region has improved substantially over the past few decades, making possible a large expansion in the pet trade, especially of caged birds. As has happened in various other localities with warm climates, many of these birds escape and establish themselves. That this sequence of events explains the high incidence of wild exotics is supported by the fact that ten out of the eleven exotic birds most frequently imported into the USA from 1968—71 (excluding the Common Canary, which is captively bred) are now wild in Puerto Rico.

The second reason is that most of the natural habitat of the region has been substantially altered since the European colonization, thus increasing certain habitats, such as grassy edges and scrub thickets. Because of their previous scarcity, these habitats supported a limited indigenous avifauna and their sudden increase apparently provided more niches than could be filled by native birds. This probably serves to explain invasions from adjacent islands in the last 100 years by the White-winged Dove, Mourning Dove, Caribbean Elaenia, Lesser Antillean Bullfinch, and the Northern Mockingbird (from Puerto Rico to the Virgin Islands), not to mention the profusion of seed-eating exotics.

The potential problems of niche competition, crop damage and disease transmission are severe, and the Puerto Rican government has begun to reduce the chances of future introductions.

Field Hazards

The natural habitats of Puerto Rico and the Virgin Islands are probably as safe as those anywhere in the world, although there are a few hazards of which the zealous field observer should be aware. Many freshwater bodies are infected with a fluke (*Shistosoma*) which causes the disease Bilharzia. While some waters are uninfected they might not always remain so, thus it is best to avoid contact with the fresh water of swamps, streams and lakes. Piped drinking water is normally safe at all localities. There are few poisonous organisms, the most significant ones being scorpions and centipedes. The one mildly poisonous snake, *Alsophis*, is rarely encountered.

Biogeography

Barriers to Dispersal

Puerto Rico and the Virgin Islands are oceanic islands that formed beneath the sea. As they are not known to have been connected to a continental landmass by a land bridge, the first organisms to inhabit these islands had to arrive by crossing open ocean. The sea is one of the most effective barriers in limiting the movement of terrestrial and freshwater life from one locality to another. Consequently, only a very small number of continental organisms have ever succeeded in reaching this region and becoming established. (Once having arrived, these animals can speciate through local geographical isolation, certainly the main cause of the development of the region's organisms, though not its birds, but this is beyond the scope of this discussion.)

There are several mechanisms by which animals are believed to have reached these islands. Many species are carried on flotsam which are driven by the currents or blown by the wind. Others are no doubt lifted by the powerful winds of hurricanes, or travel within the eye, only to be dropped later some distance from their native land. Very few of these individuals have the good fortune to be deposited near a remote island where there is a niche available in which they can survive. It is hypothesized, however, that this happened when the American Kestrel and the Smooth-billed Ani first reached Mona Island as a result of being carried there by a hurricane that struck the southeast corner of Hispaniola in 1930. Also, the Lesser Antillean Bullfinch was apparently transported to the Virgin Islands by Hurricane Donna in 1960.

In addition to the effects of the water barrier, a second factor limiting animal diversity on oceanic islands is the reduced number of niches. The niche of an animal refers to the specific set of environmental conditions that the species needs to survive. If the proper conditions for the species are not available over a broad spectrum of variables (resource dimensions) the creature is doomed. For example, looking at food resources, are foods of the proper size present in the habitat? If so, are they obtainable? A seed may have too thick a husk or an insect may be too elusive. Even if present and obtainable, are the foods available all year round and do they provide proper nutrition? Since birds eat either plant or animal foods, the antecedents of these creatures, too, had to have succeeded in crossing a major water barrier. As a result, the food resource spectrum for birds invading islands is generally much smaller than for their counterparts on continents. Not only are food resources less diverse on islands, but the same is true of other important variables such as habitat types, nesting sites, forms of cover, and so on.

The size of the island, its form and its distance from major landmasses with source organisms all play significant roles in the success of a colonizing species in reaching the island, the diversity of niches that will be present on the island, and the ultimate success of the colonization attempt.

A question that arises in studying the avifauna of this region is why Puerto Rico should support 14 endemic species while the Virgin Islands share only two of these and have none of their own. Difficulty of dispersal is not the reason as the islands are close to one another; certainly almost any bird arriving on one could ultimately spread to the other. The apparent cause for the low number of avian endemics and other forms on the Virgin Islands seems to be a consequence of their small size and their limited habitat diversity. Puerto Rican endemics do reach the Virgin Islands at times, as evidenced by the Puerto Rican Lizard-Cuckoo specimen from St Thomas, but apparently there is not enough suitable habitat for their continued survival.

Diversity versus Uniqueness

As a consequence of the region being oceanic, its fauna is not very diverse. The best illustration of this is the region's non-aquatic mammalian fauna, which totals only 13 living and nine extinct forms. Of these 22 species, 16 are bats which, with their ability to fly, have an obvious advantage in their ability to disperse.

What the fauna of the region lacks in diversity it more than makes up for in uniqueness. This inverse relationship of diversity to uniqueness is generally the case for oceanic islands, such as Puerto Rico and most other West Indian islands. This is to say that the greater the distance an island is formed from a continent (assuming islands are of somewhat equal size and elevation), the fewer plant and animal species it will support, but the greater the distinctiveness of those species.

This concept can be clarified by comparing various islands. Trinidad and Tobago, two sister islands lying only 32 km (20 miles) from South America, were once connected to that continent by a land bridge. Their combined landmass is little more than half of that of Puerto Rico, but their avifauna totals approximately 400 species, well over 100 more than occur in Puerto Rico including its introduced species. However, all the bird species on Trinidad and Tobago, with the sole exception of an endemic guan, are found either on South America proper or elsewhere. Though Puerto Rico's native avifauna (excluding extinctions and introductions) is only 239 species, 14 of these (6%) are endemic to this island (including two also occurring on the Virgin Islands). Puerto Rico also supports one avian genus (*Nesospingus*) not found anywhere else, and one family (Todidae) found on other West Indian islands, but not known from living representatives on any continent.

At the other extreme, we might look at New Caledonia and the Society Islands in the Pacific Ocean. New Caledonia is separated from the east coast of Australia by approximately 1126 km (700 miles) of ocean. As a result, and though it is nearly twice the size of Puerto Rico, its avifauna totals a mere 68 species. However, 16 of these (24%) are endemic forms, one being the famous Kagu (*Rhynochetos jubatus*) which is the sole representative of an avian family endemic to the island. The Society Islands, isolated near the center of the Pacific Ocean, support only 17 species of birds, but of these, all except one are not found anywhere else in the world.

Uniqueness: Its Values

The uniqueness of island forms is of particular interest to humankind. The simplicity of island ecosystems, and the distinctive differences between organisms on adjacent islands, provide ideal conditions for the study of the evolutionary process. Indeed, the theory of evolution was crystallized in the mind of Charles Darwin following his study of the finches on the Galapagos Islands off the coast of Ecuador.

In addition to providing excellent examples of the evolutionary process at work, organisms on islands serve as invaluable tools for understanding portions of the past biological history of the earth. As species on continents evolve, the less adaptable forms are generally replaced. A few relic species such as the crocodile survive, but for the most part scientists must be content with fossil records of this evolutionary process. In unusual circumstances, however, some of these ancient forms may be preserved as 'living fossils' through their isolation on islands.

The marsupials of Australia are a vast assemblage of such relic species preserved through isolation on a large island. Early during the evolution of mammals, when pouched forms were much more broadly distributed, Australia and South America drifted away from the great, main landmass with their marsupial populations intact. Placentals evolved and dominated the rest of the world, ultimately crossing into South America by way of a new land connection formed several million years ago, and almost all of its marsupials were driven to extinction. By virtue of isolation, however, the marsupials of Australia survived and remain today as one of science's most precious tools in understanding the evolutionary past.

Puerto Rico and the Greater Antilles, to a lesser extent, play a similar role in the Western Hemisphere. It is known that, with the reconnection of North and South America, much of the original fauna of Central America became extinct and was replaced. It is generally believed that some of the fauna of Puerto Rico and the other islands are relic populations of what once existed in Central and even North America. The endemic Puerto Rican Tody is one of the most outstanding living examples of such a relic species. Presently only five species survive of the endemic West Indian family, Todidae, all of these being confined to the Greater Antilles. However, new fossil evidence indicates that this family was once fairly widespread on the continent having ranged at least to Wyoming in central North America. The period of this family's continental distribution dates to the mid-Oligocene, 30 million years ago.

Conservation

The Problem

As humankind has come to dominate most habitats of the world, new pressures have been placed on wild animals, causing the rate of extinction of vertebrate forms to increase alarmingly in the last few centuries. Of the approximately 8600 species of birds in the world no fewer than 78 have become extinct since 1681. Of particular significance in this region is the fact that of the 78 species, 69, or 88%, were inhabitants of islands.

Island species are particularly vulnerable for two reasons. Their limited range leaves them no peripheral habitat for escape, and in many cases they have developed in isolation from predators with the result that they have no mechanisms with which to defend themselves against humans and their beasts.

Principal Causes of Extinction and Endangerment

Extinction and endangerment can result from natural causes, or may be induced by humans. There are three principal methods by which humankind has prompted the extinction of animals. These are: 1) hunting, 2) habitat destruction and human disturbance, and 3) introduction of predators and other animals. In this region, as in the rest of the world, habitat destruction is easily the principal cause of endangerment, with hunting the next most important factor (see the table on p. 16).

Fossil Birds

To date, seven birds are known in the region only from fossil or subfossil remains (though this number will be substantially increased as the analysis of a large new collection of fossil bones from Puerto Rico is completed). One of these birds, DeBooy's Rail (*Nesotrochis debooyi*), may have succumbed because of human pressures. This was a flightless ground-dwelling bird of tasty flesh, as evidenced by the accumulations of its bones in the relatively recent midden deposits of the Amerindians. Though unproven, it is quite likely that, as has happened with a number of flightless birds on other islands, the introduced predators and vermin of

10

the settlers such as pigs, dogs, cats, and rats made a quick end of this defenseless bird. The name 'Carrao', used by many country people to describe a flightless, edible bird, is almost certainly referable to the Limpkin, and not DeBooy's Rail as most authors have suggested.

A parakeet (*Aratinga maugei*), endemic to Puerto Rico, expired in the nineteenth century and was never collected by scientists; thus it is known only from fossil bones and the tales of country people. The cause of its demise is unknown, but it would not be surprising if deforestation and hunting played significant roles. The parakeet survived on Mona Island until the late 1890s, and may have been eliminated there as a result of hunting or the devastating hurricane of 1899.

A macaw (*Ara autocthones*), reputedly endemic to St Croix, is known only from a single bone dug from a midden; although this appears to be from a species no longer extant, it is probable that Amerindians transported these birds from island to island, so it may be doubted that this macaw was really native to St Croix. Two other endemic fossil birds were from Puerto Rico and include an endemic barn-owl (*Tyto cavatica*) and woodcock (*Scolopax anthonyi*). The three remaining fossil forms were the quail-dove (*Geotrygon larva*) which is probably a representative of *G. caniceps* of Hispaniola and Cuba, the Cuban Crow (*Corvus nasicus*), and a caracara (*Polyborus 'latebrosus'*), which is known from such fragmentary specimens that it is uncertain whether these belong to the living species *P. plancus* or to an extinct form. The extinction of these birds was apparently pre-Columbian and most probably due to natural causes.

Recent Extinctions and Extirpations

Five other birds have been eliminated more recently as breeding residents from the region. One of these was an endemic subspecies that is now extinct. The other four forms have fortunately survived and currently breed elsewhere. Three of these continue to occur as extremely rare or accidental vagrants in Puerto Rico. The Culebra race of the Puerto Rican Parrot (*Amazona vittata gracilipes*) is the local subspecies to have become extinct. The cause of its demise is not known, but this was probably due to excessive hunting. The parrot was reported as being common on Culebra in 1899 where it was said to cause damage to local crops. Extinction is believed to have occurred prior to 1912.

In the 1700s, the White-necked Crow (*Corvus leucognaphalus*) was abundant, but its numbers and range gradually declined in Puerto Rico through the nineteenth century; by the early part of the twentieth century it appeared to be confined to the Luquillo Mountains. The last sighting in the wild was of two birds high up on El Yunque in 1963. Now extirpated from Puerto Rico, and St Croix where it is known only from midden deposits, the species is now also declining on its last remaining island — Hispaniola. The White-necked Crow was reputed to have delicious flesh, but it is questionable whether overhunting was the principal cause of its demise. Certainly the destruction of the native forests in which it lived was partially responsible.

The three other avian species that have been extirpated from the region as breeding residents, but which still occur as rare vagrants or accidentals, include the Greater Flamingo, the Black Rail, young of which were reported to have been taken in the late 1800s, and the Black-bellied Whistling-Duck, which is believed to have bred in the vicinity of Cartagena Lagoon in the early part of this century. Hunting was doubtless a major factor in the demise of the Greater Flamingo and Black-bellied Whistling-Duck. The introduction of the mongoose may have been responsible for the elimination of the Black Rail as a breeding bird.

Endangered and Threatened Species

The number of bird species that are endangered or to some degree threatened in this region far outnumber those already extinct. A full 51 species or 21% of the local avifauna (excluding exotics), fall into this category. In many cases, the threat is to the status of the bird, which may be significantly altered, though the species may not be totally extirpated. For example, the Magnificent Frigatebird is seen commonly over protected bays and islets the year round, while Audubon's Shearwater occurs regularly offshore, but there is a danger that the last remaining breeding colonies of these species will soon disappear from the region. The number of regularly active frigatebird rookeries here has dwindled to four, and the largest of these, on Monito Island, was until recently being considered for an air-to-ground bombing target. Audubon's Shearwater is similarly threatened. While both species might persist as visitors to this region subsequent to the destruction of these nesting colonies, they will be dependent on islets belonging to neighboring governments for suitable nesting conditions. Consequently, the frigatebirds and shearwaters would not be self-sustaining within this territory, making them subject to elimination by factors totally outside local control. Three former breeding species, eliminated as such in recent times and now exceedingly rare, include the Greater Flamingo, Black Rail and Black-bellied Whistling-Duck, all discussed earlier. The plight of the frigatebirds and shearwaters illustrate the continuation of this trend which is, in their cases, at a dishearteningly advanced stage. Unfortunately, a number of other bird species are being subjected to the same treatment by the human hand and may be prone to the same fate if effective conservation practices are not undertaken.

Of greatest concern are the endemic species and subspecies directly faced with total extinction. The endemic species are discussed in turn under the individual species accounts, while the subspecies are so marked in the table dealing with causes of endangerment. On p.16 is a table of the 51 bird species which are presently threatened or endangered within this region. The degree of endangerment of each is listed, as well as the cause of endangerment. Interestingly, all appear to be suffering from human activities, and none, with the exception of the Yellow-shouldered Blackbird, primarily as a result of natural causes.

Habitat Destruction and Disturbance

No fewer than 49 of the 51 species in the table are to some degree being detrimentally affected by disturbance or destruction of their habitat (the term disturbance is used to include poaching, but not hunting *per se*). The draining and filling of the region's limited freshwater swamps is having the greatest single impact with a negative effect on 22 species. This, coupled with hunting, which during the waterfowl season is concentrated in the freshwater swamps, has endangered all six species of breeding ducks and has caused the dramatic decline of many other swamp-dwelling forms. Disturbances to offshore islets vary greatly in form, from increased boat traffic around them and poaching to their use as bombing targets or for tourist developments. In any case, 14 avian species, dependent on islets as remote refuges on which to breed, are threatened as a result. The destruction of mangroves and their adjacent mudflats is having a detrimental impact on 11 species, while the cutting of forests has affected nine. For birds, the most critical remaining forests, excluding mangroves, include those which are best developed vegetationally and least disturbed by human activities. Among these are the surviving virgin forests located primarily on peaks, ridges, and higher valleys of mountains, and the most remote forested haystack hills, dry scrub forests, and dense coastal woodlands, particularly near lagoons or marshes. Large tracts that can sustain viable populations of animals are generally superior to small ones.

Hunting

Hunting is a traditional pastime practiced for many years, virtually everywhere, without adequate controls. As a result, many native breeding game birds have been decimated and it is a difficult struggle to raise their reduced populations to a less precarious level. The British Virgin Islands have eliminated hunting totally and the effects are quite noticeable in the unusual tameness of all the local birds. The American Virgin Islands strictly regulate hunting. More recently Puerto Rico has followed suit, taking a number of endangered native game birds such as the Ruddy Duck, White-crowned Pigeon and Purple Gallinule off the list of huntable species. Unfortunately, striking birds from the hunting list, though a critical first step, does not suffice as a remedy for reducing the degree of endangerment. Effective enforcement is a fundamental element of a sound conservation policy. Until recently it had been virtually lacking in Puerto Rico though it was somewhat better in the Virgin Islands. In 1977 Puerto Rico took a major step towards improving its enforcement capability by forming a corps of natural resource wardens but regrettably, indications are that this group has not been particularly effective. An additional complicating factor in regulating hunting is that the breeding seasons of many birds in the subtropics are extended and often erratic. For example, there is evidence of the White-cheeked Pintail breeding in the region during every month of the year and the Ruddy Duck breeding through the peak of Puerto Rico's hunting season. This means that there is no season of the year when hunting could occur without risking disruption of reproduction of the species. There is no easy way around this problem, yet it is one that must be dealt with. To date it has been basically ignored in Puerto Rico.

Predation

The mongoose (*Herpestes auropunctatus*), introduced to the region between 1877 and 1879 to control the depredations of rats on sugar cane, is the most detrimental wild predator on birds, while cats and rats, also play a role. The mongoose was very probably the major cause of endangerment of the Puerto Rican Nightjar, Short-eared Owl, Black Rail, Key West Quail-Dove and Bridled Quail-Dove, all ground nesters. Fortunately, indications are that all of these, with the exception of the Black Rail, have rebounded since the turn of the century when most were thought extinct in the region. In fact, the Short-eared Owl is seen regularly in Puerto Rico and the Bridled Quail-Dove is now fairly common in more heavily wooded portions of the Virgin Islands. Consequently, neither species is presently endangered. Apparently these birds have reached something of an equilibrium with the mongoose after suffering heavily when that creature was at peak numbers over half a century ago. Unfortunately, other factors such as habitat destruction are also threatening some of these birds.

Chemicals

Pesticides and other chemicals are not known to have endangered any species in the region. The Brown Pelican, which has been severely affected by pesticides along the Gulf and west coasts of the USA, is a breeding resident in the region. Judging from sightings of active nests with young and from the percentage of juveniles within flocks, it appears that the local birds are not suffering in any conspicuous way from pesticide overdoses.

Proposed Conservation Measures

Since the first edition of this book was printed five years ago, conservation in the region has seen some advances and some setbacks. One important new development is the growth of several active conservation groups in both Puerto Rico and the Virgin Islands. While five years ago there was only a single organization, now there are at least five — quite a dramatic change in such a short period of time. Furthermore, several of these focus heavily on specific conservation activities and not just on the enjoyment of nature. Potentially the efforts of such groups can play a major role in countering the trend towards uncontrolled development and monitor the sometimes lethargic efforts of governmental agencies responsible for environmental matters.

The first positive steps in many years have recently occurred with respect to the conservation of new natural areas. The creation of the Humacao Wildlife Refuge that will help sustain Puerto

Causes of Endangerment

Key
E – endemic species
ES – endemic subspecies

Degree of endangerment
A – very endangered: These species are practically extinct (or extirpated). In most cases active steps must be taken to insure their survival and in some cases extirpation may have already occurred.
B – endangered: The species is so rare or its habitat so restricted that any increase in the pressure on it will move it to category A.
C – threatened: Species that are surviving reasonably well, but which depend on habitats under great pressure by developers.

Degree	Species	Habitat disturbance or destruction				Hunting	Mongoose, rats
		Freshwater swamps	Forest	Small islets	Mangroves, lagoons		
A	Puerto Rican Parrot (E)		*			*	
A	Puerto Rican Nightjar (E)		*				*
A	Yellow-shouldered Blackbird (E)**						
A	Plain Pigeon (ES)		*				
A	Puerto Rican Screech-Owl (ES)†		*			*	
A	Audubon's Shearwater			*			*
A	Masked Booby			*			
A	Greater Flamingo				*	*	
A	West Indian Whistling-Duck	*				*	
A	Black-bellied Whistling-Duck	*				*	

	Species	1	2	3	4	5	6
A	Masked Duck		*				*
A	Limpkin	*	*				*
A	Black Rail						*
A	Snowy Plover			*			
B	Sharp-shinned Hawk (ES)					*	
B	Broad-winged Hawk (ES)				*		*
B	Least Grebe					*	
B	Red-billed Tropicbird				*		
B	Red-footed Booby				*		
B	Magnificent Frigatebird				*		
B	Great Blue Heron			*			
B	Black-crowned Night-Heron						*
B	Glossy Ibis						*
B	Fulvous Whistling-Duck		*				*
C	White-cheeked Pintail		*				*
C	Ruddy Duck		*				*
C	Yellow-breasted Crake		*				*
C	Caribbean Coot						*
C	Common Tern		*		*		
C	Roseate Tern				*		
C	Royal Tern				*		
C	Sandwich Tern				*	*	
C	White-crowned Pigeon		*	*	*	*	
C	Key West Quail-Dove	*					

(continued)

(continued)

Degree	Species	Habitat disturbance or destruction				Hunting	Mongoose, rats
		Freshwater swamps	Forest	Small islets	Mangroves, lagoons		
C	Elfin Woods Warbler (E)		*				
C	Brown Pelican			*			
C	Reddish Egret	*			*		
C	Great Egret	*		*			
C	Snowy Egret	*		*			
C	American Bittern	*					
C	Northern Pintail	*				*	
C	American Wigeon	*				*	
C	Northern Shoveler	*				*	
C	Ring-necked Duck	*				*	
C	Purple Gallinule	*			*		
C	Whimbrel				*		
C	Willet				*		
C	Short-billed Dowitcher						
C	Marbled Godwit	*			*		
C	Hudsonian Godwit	*			*		
C	Least Tern			*	*		
Totals:	51	22	9	14	11	16	4

**Nest parasitism by Glossy Cowbird.
†Only the Virgin Islands subspecies is endangered.

Rico's dwindling populations of native White-cheeked Pintails, West Indian Whistling-Ducks and Ruddy Ducks was an impressive achievement. The same is true for the imminent protection of Cartagena Lagoon, another of Puerto Rico's prime wetland areas. Considering that the majority of Puerto Rico's endangered and threatened species occur in wetlands and that wetlands protection was identified in the earlier edition of this guide, as the number one need, the conservation of these two areas is of particular significance.

Despite the creation of these wildlife reserves and other important protected areas, the problem of managing already-existing reserves continues to plague Puerto Rico specifically. Despite the fact that the Department of Natural Resources is now over 15 years old and has grown dramatically during that period of time, it has very little to show in the way of improved management of the numerous areas under its jurisdiction. Specifically, the management of key species as well as the development of public use and environmental education programs have advanced little within these natural areas.

This raises a point that is just as applicable now as it was in the first edition of this book. Namely, in the long run, conservation measures will not succeed without education. The term 'education' is used in the broadest sense meaning not only the teaching in the classroom of students about the importance and beauty of wildlife and nature, but also training hunters and fishermen, law enforcement officers and the public in general.

It remains true that an important aspect of environmental education is to inform citizens how they can help avoid misuse of valuable local natural resources. The Endangered Species Act and the National Environmental Protection Act, among others, are powerful tools in the hands of any person interested in the environment. Yet, surprisingly few people in the region, even in local government, are aware of the existence of these laws, not to mention the potential powers they grant. There are indications that this situation is changing, but the transition is not fast enough.

The problem of training local personnel in wildlife and resources management remains significant. Though the situation is improving in that local biologists have increasingly sought higher degrees in these fields at universities in the USA, there has been little advancement in the development of local or regional training programs which could focus much more sharply on the specifics of resources management on subtropical islands. With the institutional resources available in Puerto Rico and the Virgin Islands, the opportunity exists to develop training programs in order to supply natural resources specialists to meet local needs. Furthermore, these might also serve the needs of islands lacking such institutional resources elsewhere in the Caribbean.

Finally, the drive to develop beachfront property in Puerto Rico and the Virgin Islands is probably more intense now than ever before. Everyone would like to cash in on the tourist's dollar. That is all well and good, but the reason why tourists come to resorts in the region should be remembered. Local agencies must be concerned with how to keep waters clean for swimming, how to keep reefs alive for snorkeling and even how to maintain white sand on the beaches for sunbathing. On my last visit to the region the beaches of the hotel where I stayed had just been reopened after being closed due to excessive levels of sewage in the coastal waters. Neither local inhabitants nor visitors like this, but tourists have a choice to go elsewhere.

Increasingly there are other alternative sites that one can visit with beautiful beaches, palm trees, and coral reefs — and there will be even more. Increasingly other countries of the Caribbean and the Gulf of Mexico are attempting to attract tourists. What must be realized by local developers is that tourists have an ever-increasing choice of where to go and that it takes but one bad experience to prompt a tourist to go elsewhere. Ultimately, only those localities that best manage their natural resources — beaches, reefs, offshore waters, sand, mangroves and even their upland forests which play a significant role in sustaining the quality of these other resources — shall be able to benefit from tourism over the long term. In sum, effective resource conservation is in the best long-term interests of the tourist industry.

This contention is not farfetched. In fact it should be obvious to anyone who looks at local development with anything more than the most short-sighted and self-interested view. Unfortunately, far-sightedness is not a typical trait of governmental agencies. Nevertheless, until this becomes the case and local agencies take a realistic approach towards resources management, the local wildlife and other delicate natural resources of the region shall remain in jeopardy.

Plates

Descriptive Parts of a Bird

Accidentals

Flying Seabirds

Large, Long-legged Birds (Mostly Waders)

Medium and Small, Long-legged Birds (Mostly Waders)

Swimming Birds

Descriptive Parts of a Bird

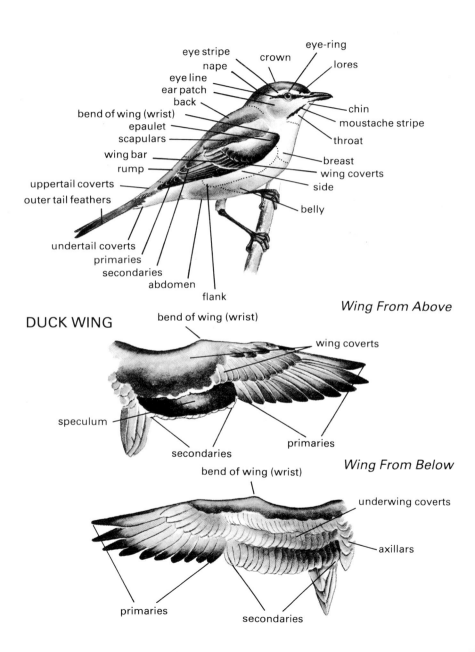

eye stripe
crown
eye-ring
nape
lores
eye line
ear patch
back
chin
bend of wing (wrist)
moustache stripe
epaulet
throat
scapulars
wing bar
breast
rump
wing coverts
uppertail coverts
side
outer tail feathers
belly
undertail coverts
primaries
secondaries
abdomen
flank

Wing From Above

DUCK WING
bend of wing (wrist)
wing coverts
speculum
secondaries
primaries

Wing From Below
bend of wing (wrist)
underwing coverts
axillars
primaries
secondaries

Plate 1: Accidentals

NORTHERN ROUGH-WINGED SWALLOW *Stelgidopteryx serripennis* 12.5−14 cm (5−5.5″)
White underparts blend into pale brown on throat, brown upperparts. **(p. 147)**

CHIMNEY SWIFT *Chaetura pelagica* 12.5 cm (5″)
Medium size; long, fluttering wings; 'flying cigar' appearance; pale throat visible under ideal conditions. **(p. 130)**

RUBY-THROATED HUMMINGBIRD *Archilochus colubris* 8−9.5 cm (3−3.75″)
Male: Red throat. **Female:** Light underparts, small white spot behind eye. **(p. 135)**

BLUE-WINGED WARBLER *Vermivora pinus* 12.5 cm (5″)
All yellow body, dark stripe through eye and white wing bars. **(p. 158)**

SWAINSON'S WARBLER *Limnothlypis swainsonii* 15 cm (6″)
Rusty crown, conspicuous white eye stripe, body olive-brown above and pale below. **(p. 160)**

BAIRD'S SANDPIPER *Calidris bairdii* 18−19 cm (7−7.5″)
Flight: White of rump divided into two lateral patches. **Habit:** Picks food rather than probes. **(p. 82)**

GRAY-CHEEKED THRUSH *Catharus minimus* 18 cm (7″)
Pale underparts with fine spots on breast and throat, gray cheek, lacks eye-ring. **(p. 150)**

LESSER BLACK-BACKED GULL *Larus fuscus* 53−63 cm (21−25″)
Adult: Large size, black mantle and *yellow* legs. **Immature:** Very similar to immature Herring Gull. **(p. 89)**

GREATER SHEARWATER *Puffinus gravis* 48 cm (19″)
Large size, limited white on rump and hindneck, lacks white on forehead. **(p. 25)**

ARCTIC TERN *Sterna paradisaea* 35−39 cm (14−15.5″)
Short legs, tail extends to wing tips when sitting, red bill. Winter: Bill dark. **(p. 94)**

CINNAMON TEAL *Anas cyanoptera* 38−40 cm (15−16″)
Male: Cinnamon-colored head and underparts. **Female:** Similar to female Blue-winged Teal. **(p. 52)**

NORTHERN ROUGH-WINGED SWALLOW

CHIMNEY SWIFT

spread tail ♂

RUBY-THROATED HUMMINGBIRD

SWAINSON'S WARBLER

BLUE-WINGED WARBLER

BAIRD'S SANDPIPER

GRAY-CHEEKED THRUSH

winter

LESSER BLACK-BACKED GULL

imm. (1st winter)

GREATER SHEARWATER

winter

ARCTIC TERN

CINNAMON TEAL

JOHN C. YRIZARRY

Plate 2: Boobies, Tropicbirds, Frigatebirds and Pelicans

RED-FOOTED BOOBY *Sula sula* 66–76 cm (26–30″)
   Adult: *Brown Phase* – Brown with white hindparts. *White Phase* – White including tail. **Immature** (not depicted): Sooty brown, paler below, sometimes with a slightly darker band across breast. **(p. 31)**

BROWN BOOBY *Sula leucogaster* 71–76 cm (28–30″)
   Adult: Brown head and upperparts, white belly and abdomen. **Immature** (not depicted): Like adult, but light brown on belly and abdomen. **(p. 30)**

MASKED BOOBY *Sula dactylatra* 81–91 cm (32–36″)
   Adult: White with *black* tail. **Immature** (not depicted): Brownish-gray head and upperparts, whitish below and on upper back and rump. **(p. 29)**

RED-BILLED TROPICBIRD *Phaethon aethereus*
   91–107 cm (36–42″) with tail plumes
   46–51 cm (18–20″) without tail plumes
   Red bill, black barring on back (see imm. White-tailed Tropicbird), long tail plumes.
   (p. 28)

WHITE-TAILED TROPICBIRD *Phaethon lepturus*
   18 cm (32″) with tail plumes;
   37–40 cm (15–16″) without tail plumes
   Adult: Black markings on mantle, long tail. **Immature** (not depicted): Barred back with *short* tail (Adult Redbilled has *long* tail). **(p. 28)**

MAGNIFICENT FRIGATEBIRD *Fregata magnificens* 94–104 cm (37–41″)
   Long, forked tail; long, slender wings with crook at wrist. **Adult Male:** Appears all black. **Adult Female:** Black with white breast. **Immature** (not depicted): Black with white head and breast. **(p. 35)**

AMERICAN WHITE PELICAN *Pelecanus erythrorhynchos* 125–165 cm (50–65″)
   Large white bird, large orange-yellow bill. **(p. 32)**

BROWN PELICAN *Pelecanus occidentalis* 107–137 cm (42–54″)
   Large dark bird, unusual bill. **Breeding:** Back of head and nape reddish-brown.
   Immature: Grayish-brown plumage. **(p. 32)**

Pelicans not to scale.

RED-FOOTED BOOBY
adult (brown phase)
adult (white phase)

BROWN BOOBY
adult

MASKED BOOBY
adult

RED-BILLED TROPICBIRD

WHITE-TAILED TROPICBIRD

MAGNIFICENT FRIGATEBIRD
♂
♀

AMERICAN WHITE PELICAN
nonbreeding

imm.

BROWN PELICAN
breeding
nonbreeding

Plate 3: Pelagics

AUDUBON'S SHEARWATER *Puffinus lherminieri* 30 cm (12″)
Rounded tail, rapid wingbeats between glides. **(p. 25)**

BLACK-CAPPED PETREL *Pterodroma hasitata* 35−40 cm (14−16″)
White rump patch, white hindneck and forehead. **(p. 26)**

LEACH'S STORM-PETREL *Oceanodroma leucorhoa* 20 cm (8″)
Long pointed wings, sharply angled; pale brown wing band; notched tail; feet *do not* extend beyond tail; flight bounding and erratic; divided rump patch. **(p. 26)**

WILSON'S STORM-PETREL *Oceanites oceanicus* 18−19 cm (7−7.5″)
Blacker than Leach's; rounded wrist joints; flight fluttery, but direct with brief glides; feet extend beyond tail; rump patch undivided; tail square. **(p. 27)**

SKUA *Catharacta 'skua'* 51−61 cm (20−24″)
Massive build, white patch at base of primaries (see text for details on species). **(p. 99)**

POMARINE JAEGER *Stercorarius pomarinus* 53−56 cm (21−22″)
White patch at base of primaries. **Adult:** Blunt, twisted central tail feathers. *Light Phase* − Whitish throat and belly. *Dark Phase* − Entirely dark brown. **Immature** (not depicted): Similar to dark phased adult, but central tail feathers are *not* extended. **(p. 99)**

Wilson's Storm-Petrel
(top of tail)

AUDUBON'S
SHEARWATER

BLACK-
CAPPED
PETREL

Leach's Storm-Petrel
(top of tail)

WILSON'S
STORM-
PETREL

LEACH'S
STORM-
PETREL

SKUA

POMARINE JAEGER

J NIESSANGER

Plate 4: Gulls and Skimmers

GREAT BLACK-BACKED GULL *Larus marinus* 69–79 cm (27–31″)
Adult: Large size, black mantle, flesh-colored legs. **Immature:** Whiter head, rump, tail and underparts than immature Herring Gull. **(p. 89)**

RING-BILLED GULL *Larus delawarensis* 46–51 cm (18–20″)
Adult: Ring on bill. **Immature:** Narrow black band on tail. **(p. 90)**

HERRING GULL *Larus argentatus* 56–66 cm (22–26″)
Adult: Gray mantle, flesh-colored legs, red spot on bill. **Immature:** *1st winter* — Plumage uniformly brown, dark head and tail. *2nd winter* — Paler plumage; broad ill-defined tail band. **(p. 89)**

COMMON BLACK-HEADED GULL *Larus ridibundus* 39–43 cm (15.5–17″)
Adult: White uppersides and dusky undersides of primaries. *Summer* — Brown head; thin, dark red bill. *Winter* — Black spot behind eye. **Immature:** Black band on tail, black spot behind eye, ochre bill with black tip, *dusky* undersides of primaries. **(p. 90)**

BLACK SKIMMER *Rynchops niger* 43–51 cm (17–20″)
Adult: Long orange bill tipped with black; black above, white below. **Immature:** Brown above, flecked with white. **(p. 100)**

LAUGHING GULL *Larus atricilla* 38–43 cm (15–17″)
Adult: Black head. *Winter* — Head white with dark markings. **Immature:** Black tail band. *1st winter* — Dark head, breast and mantle. *2nd winter* — Paler head and breast. **(p. 91)**

GREAT
BLACK-BACKED
GULL

imm.
(1st winter)

imm.
(1st winter)

adult
(summer)

RING-BILLED
GULL

imm.
(1st winter)

adult
(summer)

HERRING
GULL

adult
(summer)

imm.

COMMON
BLACK-
HEADED
GULL

adult
(winter)

adult
(winter)

adult
(summer)

BLACK
SKIMMER

imm.

imm.
(1st winter)

adult
(summer)

adult

adult
(winter)

LAUGHING
GULL

Plate 5: Terns I

CASPIAN TERN *Sterna caspia* 48–58 cm (19–23″)
Large size, blood-red bill. **Winter:** Black flecks on forehead. **(p. 97)**

ROYAL TERN *Sterna maxima* 46–53 cm (18–21″)
Large size, brilliant, fire-orange bill. **Winter:** White forehead. **(p. 96)**

CAYENNE TERN *Sterna eurygnatha* 40 cm (16″)
Large size, dull yellow bill. **(p. 96)**

SANDWICH TERN *Sterna sandvicensis* 35–40 cm (14–16″)
Slender black bill with yellow tip. **(p. 97)**

ROSEATE TERN *Sterna dougallii* 35–39 cm (14–15.5″)
Very long, deeply forked tail; pale mantle and primaries; tail extends beyond wing tips when sitting. **Summer:** Bill black with some red. **(p. 93)**

FORSTER'S TERN *Sterna forsteri* 35–38 cm (14–15″)
Winter: Black mark behind eye *does not* continue across nape. **Summer:** Orange bill with black tip. **(p. 92)**

COMMON TERN *Sterna hirundo* 33–40 cm (13–16″)
Deeply forked tail, dark outer primaries, tail does not extend beyond wing tips when sitting. **Summer:** Redder bill than Roseate's. **(p. 92)**

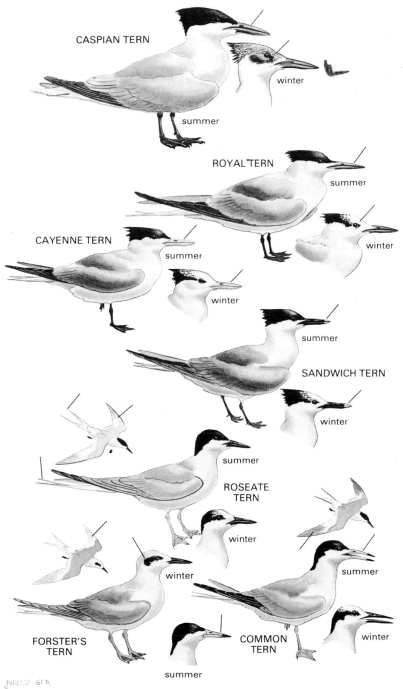

CASPIAN TERN

winter

summer

ROYAL TERN

summer

winter

CAYENNE TERN

summer

winter

SANDWICH TERN

summer

winter

ROSEATE
TERN

summer

winter

summer

FORSTER'S
TERN

winter

winter

COMMON
TERN

summer

winter

J.WEISSINGER

Plate 6: Terns II

SOOTY TERN *Sterna fuscata* 38−43 cm (15−17″)
Adult: Black above, white below. **Immature** (not depicted): Entirely dark brown flecked with white, white undertail coverts. **(p. 95)**

BROWN NODDY *Anous stolidus* 38 cm (15″)
Dark brown, white cap. **(p. 98)**

BRIDLED TERN *Sterna anaethetus* 35−38 cm (14−15″)
Adult: Deep brownish-gray back, white line above and *behind* eye, white nape. **Immature** (not depicted): Similar to adult, but flecked with white. **(p. 94)**

GULL-BILLED TERN *Sterna nilotica* 33−38 cm (13−15″)
Summer: Thick, black bill. **Winter:** Gray spot behind eye. **(p. 91)**

BLACK TERN *Chlidonias niger* 23−25 cm (9−10″)
Winter: Dark upperparts, unusual head markings. **Summer:** All black. **(p. 98)**

LEAST TERN *Sterna antillarum* 21.5−24 cm (8.5−9.5″)
Adult in Summer: Small size, yellow bill and feet, white forehead. **Winter and Immature:** Yellowish feet. **(p. 95)**

SOOTY TERN
adult

BROWN NODDY

BRIDLED TERN
adult

GULL-BILLED TERN
summer
winter

BLACK TERN
winter
summer

LEAST TERN
adult
(summer)
winter

Plate 7: Herons and Egrets

SNOWY EGRET *Egretta thula* 51–71 cm (20–28″)
Black legs with yellow feet, black bill, yellow lores. **(p. 40)**

CATTLE EGRET *Bubulcus ibis* 48–64 cm (19–25″)
Short, thick yellowish bill; small size. **Breeding:** Feet and bill pinkish; tan wash on crown, breast and back. **(p. 38)**

LITTLE BLUE HERON *Egretta caerulea* 56–71 cm (22–28″)
Adult: Uniform dark gray body, brownish-red head and neck. **Immature:** White plumage, base of bill pale gray, greenish legs. **(p. 37)**

TRICOLORED HERON *Egretta tricolor* 61–71 cm (24–28″)
Gray appearance, white belly and undertail coverts. **(p. 40)**

GREAT EGRET *Casmerodius albus* 89–107 cm (35–42″)
Large size, yellow bill, black legs. **(p. 39)**

GREAT BLUE HERON *Ardea herodias* 107–132 cm (42–52″)
Dark Phase: Large, blue-gray bird. **White Phase:** Large size, yellowish legs. **(p. 36)**

REDDISH EGRET *Egretta rufescens* 69–81 cm (27–32″)
Flesh-colored bill with black tip is conspicuous in either dark or white phase birds, ruffled neck feathers, 'dances' when feeding. **(p. 39)**

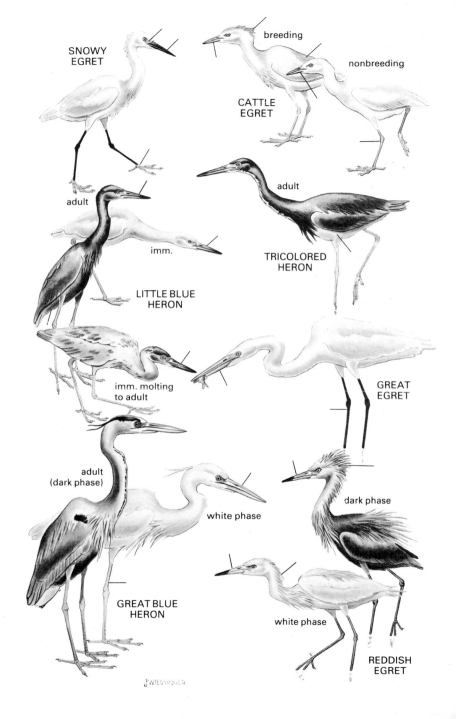

SNOWY
EGRET

breeding

nonbreeding

CATTLE
EGRET

adult

adult

imm.

TRICOLORED
HERON

LITTLE BLUE
HERON

imm. molting
to adult

GREAT
EGRET

adult
(dark phase)

white phase

dark phase

GREAT BLUE
HERON

white phase

REDDISH
EGRET

J WIESSINGER

Plate 8: Herons and Bitterns

BLACK-CROWNED NIGHT-HERON *Nycticorax nycticorax* 58—71 cm (23—28″)
   Adult: Black crown and back; white face, underparts and head plumes. **Immature:** Mottled brown like immature Yellowcrowned, but thinner bill, browner, larger white flecks. **Flight:** Only its *feet* extend beyond tail. **(p. 41)**

YELLOW-CROWNED NIGHT-HERON *Nycticorax violaceus* 56—71 cm (22—28″)
   Adult: Gray underparts, black and whitish head markings. **Immature:** Like immature Blackcrowned, but heavier bill, grayer plumage, smaller white flecks. **Flight:** Its longer *legs* extend beyond tail. **(p. 42)**

LEAST BITTERN *Ixobrychus exilis* 28—35 cm (11—14″)
   Small size, rusty coloration, cream-colored patch on upper wing. **(p. 42)**

GREEN-BACKED HERON *Butorides striatus* 40—48 cm (16—19″)
   Small size, short neck, dark coloration, orangish legs. **(p. 36)**

AMERICAN BITTERN *Botaurus lentiginosus* 58—61 cm (23—24″)
   Black neck mark, often points bill upwards. **Flight:** Black wing tips. **(p. 43)**

BLACK-CROWNED
NIGHT-HERON

adult

imm.

adult

imm.

YELLOW-CROWNED
NIGHT-HERON

LEAST
BITTERN

adult

GREEN-BACKED
HERON

imm.

adult

AMERICAN
BITTERN

adult

Plate 9: Ibises, Spoonbills, Flamingos and Limpkins

WHITE IBIS *Eudocimus albus* 56–71 cm (22–28″)
Long, decurved bill. **Adult:** White plumage. **Flight:** Outstretched neck, black wing tips. **Immature:** Uniform brown plumage, white belly and rump. **(p. 44)**

GLOSSY IBIS *Plegadis falcinellus* 56–64 cm (22–25″)
Dark coloration; long, decurved bill. **(p. 44)**

ROSEATE SPOONBILL *Ajaia ajaja* 66–81 cm (26–32″)
Spatulate bill. **Adult:** Pink coloration. **Immature:** White plumage. **(p. 44)**

GREATER FLAMINGO *Phoenicopterus ruber* 107–122 cm (42–48″)
Rosy coloration, long legs and neck, curved bill. **(p. 45)**

LIMPKIN *Aramus guarauna* 69 cm (27″)
Plumage brown with white streaks; long neck and legs; long, slightly decurved bill. **(p. 69)**

imm.

adult

WHITE IBIS

imm.

adult

GLOSSY IBIS

imm.

adult

ROSEATE SPOONBILL

adult

GREATER FLAMINGO

LIMPKIN

Plate 10: Plovers

PIPING PLOVER *Charadrius melodus* 18 cm (7″)
Short, heavy bill; pale, gray upperparts. **Flight:** White rump. **Summer:** Light orange legs and base of bill. **Winter:** Legs and bill dark. **(p. 71)**

SEMIPALMATED PLOVER *Charadrius semipalmatus* 18.5 cm (7.25″)
Brown upperparts, light orange legs and base of bill, breast band may be incomplete. **Winter:** Bill dark. **(p. 70)**

SNOWY PLOVER *Charadrius alexandrinus* 14−15 cm (5.5−6″)
Small size; slender, black bill; pale coloration; dark legs. **Summer:** Dark ear patch. **(p. 71)**

BLACK-BELLIED PLOVER *Pluvialis squatarola* 26−34 cm (10.5−13.5″)
Flight: White rump, black axillars. **Winter:** Stocky build, short bill, light gray coloration. **Summer:** Black underparts except for tail coverts. **(p. 73)**

WILSON'S PLOVER *Charadrius wilsonia* 18−20 cm (7−8″)
Single breast band, thick black bill. **(p. 72)**

NORTHERN LAPWING *Vanellus vanellus* 30 cm (12″)
Crest, black and white pattern. **Flight:** Wing tips rounded. **(p. 70)**

LESSER GOLDEN PLOVER *Pluvialis dominica* 26 cm (10.5″)
Flight: No black in axillars. **Winter:** Plumage browner and darker than Blackbellied, rump and tail are dark. **Summer:** Black extends to undertail coverts. **(p. 73)**

KILLDEER *Charadrius vociferus* 25 cm (10″)
Two black breast bands. **(p. 72)**

PIPING
PLOVER

winter

summer

SEMIPALMATED
PLOVER

winter

summer

SNOWY
PLOVER

BLACK-
BELLIED
PLOVER

winter

summer

WILSON'S
PLOVER

♂

♀

NORTHERN
LAPWING

winter

summer

LESSER
GOLDEN
PLOVER

KILLDEER

Plate 11: Sandpipers I

RUDDY TURNSTONE *Arenaria interpres* 20.5—23 cm (8—9″)
Winter: Dark breast markings, orange legs. **Summer:** Unusual facial markings, ruddy back. **(p. 76)**

PECTORAL SANDPIPER *Calidris melanotos* 20—24 cm (8—9.5″)
Medium size, yellowish-green bill and legs, sharp demarcation between streaked breast and white belly. **(p. 83)**

STILT SANDPIPER *Calidris himantopus* 20—21.5 cm (8—8.5″)
White rump; greenish legs; long bill, thick at base, slight droop at tip. **Summer:** Rust-colored cheek and crown. **(p. 86)**

RUFF (female: REEVE) *Philomachus pugnax* ♂ 30 cm (12″) ♀ 23—28 cm (9—11″)
Female and Winter Male: Chunky build, erect posture; yellow base of bill; buff-colored breast, scaly in appearance; legs light (varying in color). **Summer Male:** Variably colored and elaborately plumed breast and head feathers. **(p. 87)**

SHORT-BILLED DOWITCHER *Limnodromus griseus* 26—30 cm (10.5—12″)
Long, straight bill. **Flight:** White rump patch extends well up back. **Winter:** From Longbilled by voice. **Summer:** Breast rust-colored, flanks spotted rather than barred. **(p. 85)**

LONG-BILLED DOWITCHER *Limnodromus scolopaceus* 28—32 cm (11—12.5″)
Long, straight bill. **Flight:** White rump patch extends well up back. **Winter:** From Shortbilled by voice. **Summer:** Underparts rust-colored to lower belly, flanks barred. **(p. 85)**

RED KNOT *Calidris canutus* 25—28 cm (10—11″)
Medium size, chunky build, greenish legs, short bill. **Summer:** Breast rusty-red. **(p. 81)**

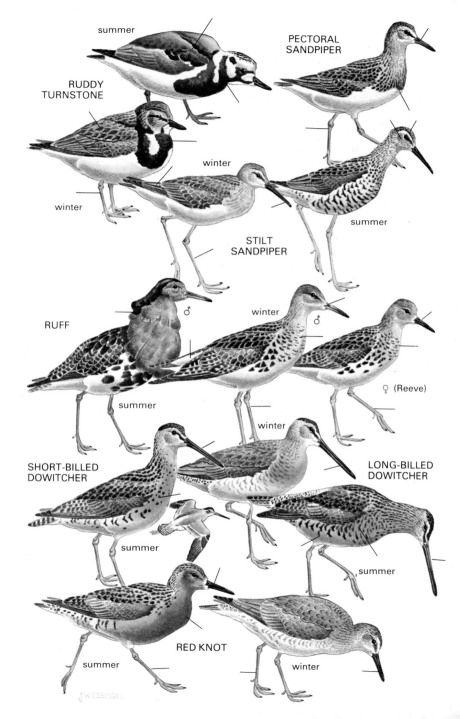

summer

PECTORAL
SANDPIPER

RUDDY
TURNSTONE

winter

winter

STILT
SANDPIPER

summer

RUFF

winter ♂

♀ (Reeve)

summer

winter

SHORT-BILLED
DOWITCHER

LONG-BILLED
DOWITCHER

summer

summer

RED KNOT

summer

winter

J.WIESSINGER

Plate 12: Sandpipers II

SEMIPALMATED SANDPIPER   *Calidris pusilla*   14−16.5 cm (5.5−6.5″)
Small size, black legs, medium-length black bill. **(p. 83)**

LEAST SANDPIPER   *Calidris minutilla*   12.5−16.5 cm (5−6.5″)
Small size, yellowish legs, brown coloration. **(p. 82)**

WESTERN SANDPIPER   *Calidris mauri*   15−18 cm (6−7″)
Bill heavy at base, decurved at tip and longer than Semipalmated's; scapulars may
remain rust-colored into fall. **(p. 84)**

WHITE-RUMPED SANDPIPER   *Calidris fuscicollis*   18−20 cm (7−8″)
Larger than Semipalmated and Western Sandpipers. **Flight:** White uppertail coverts.
Winter: Darker gray than other 'peeps'. **Summer:** Darker brown than other 'peeps'.
(p. 83)

SANDERLING   *Calidris alba*   18−21.5 cm (7−8.5″)
Flight: White wing stripe. **Winter:** Light gray upperparts, white underparts. **Summer:**
Rust-colored head and breast. **(p. 84)**

SPOTTED SANDPIPER   *Actitis macularia*   18−20 cm (7−8″)
Walk: Teetering. **Flight:** Shallow, rapid wingbeats. **Winter:** White underparts, orangish
base of bill. **Summer:** Dark spots on underparts. **(p. 78)**

SOLITARY SANDPIPER   *Tringa solitaria*   19−23 cm (7.5−9″)
White eye-ring, dark upperparts, black barring on outer tail feathers. **Flight:** Wingbeats
deep and distinctive. **(p. 79)**

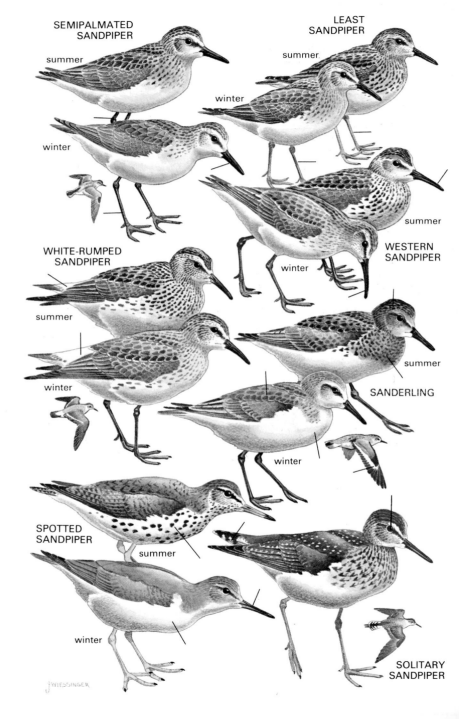

SEMIPALMATED
SANDPIPER

summer

winter

LEAST
SANDPIPER

summer

winter

WESTERN
SANDPIPER

summer

winter

WHITE-RUMPED
SANDPIPER

summer

winter

SANDERLING

summer

winter

SPOTTED
SANDPIPER

summer

winter

SOLITARY
SANDPIPER

J WIESSINGER

Plate 13: Sandpipers and Oystercatchers

HUDSONIAN GODWIT *Limosa haemastica* 33–40 cm (13–16″)
Long, slightly upturned bill; black tail with white at base. **(p. 87)**

WILLET *Catoptrophorus semipalmatus* 38–40 cm (15–16″)
Large size, light gray coloration, dark legs, thick bill. **Flight:** Black and white wing pattern diagnostic. **(p. 80)**

MARBLED GODWIT *Limosa fedoa* 40–51 cm (16–20″)
Large size; long, slightly upturned bill; no white on rump. **(p. 86)**

ESKIMO CURLEW *Numenius borealis* 30–35 cm (12–14″)
Smaller than Whimbrel with shorter and straighter bill, cinnamon underwings, unbarred primaries. **(p. 77)**

WHIMBREL *Numenius phaeopus* 38–46 cm (15–18″)
Large size; long, decurved bill; striped crown. **(p. 77)**

DUNLIN *Calidris alpina* 20–23 cm (8–9″)
Heavy bill, decurved at tip; chunky build. **Winter:** Gray wash on breast, head and upperparts. **Summer:** Black belly, rust-colored back. **(p. 81)**

AMERICAN OYSTERCATCHER *Haematopus palliatus* 48 cm (19″)
Black hood, long orange-red bill. **(p. 74)**

HUDSONIAN
GODWIT

winter

summer

WILLET

winter

summer

MARBLED
GODWIT

WHIMBREL

ESKIMO
CURLEW

summer

winter

DUNLIN

AMERICAN
OYSTERCATCHER

PW ESSENGER

Plate 14: Sandpipers, Phalaropes, Stilts and Avocets

WILSON'S PHALAROPE *Phalaropus tricolor* 23 cm (9″)
Thin straight bill. **Habit:** Spins in water. **Winter:** White breast, faint dark mark through eye. **Summer Male:** Tan wash on neck. **Summer Female:** Chestnut band from shoulder blending to black eye stripe. **(p. 87)**

GREATER YELLOWLEGS *Tringa melanoleuca* 33–38 cm (13–15″)
Large size; yellow legs; long straight bill, slightly upturned. **(p. 79)**

LESSER YELLOWLEGS *Tringa flavipes* 25–28 cm (10–11″)
Medium size, yellow legs, bill thinner and shorter than that of Greater Yellowlegs. **(p. 79)**

COMMON SNIPE *Gallinago gallinago* 27–29 cm (10.5–11.5″)
Long bill, striped head and back. **(p. 77)**

UPLAND SANDPIPER *Bartramia longicauda* 28–32 cm (11–12.5″)
Short bill, small head, long neck and tail. **Flight:** Wingbeats shallow. **(p. 78)**

AMERICAN AVOCET *Recurvirostra americana* 40–51 cm (16–20″)
Large size, sharply upturned bill, black and white coloration. **Summer:** Head and neck cinnamon. **Winter:** Head and neck gray. **(p. 75)**

BLACK-NECKED STILT *Himantopus mexicanus* 34–39 cm (13.5–15.5″)
Large size; black upperparts; white underparts; long, red legs. **(p. 75)**

WILSON'S
PHALAROPE

♀
breeding

♂
breeding

winter

GREATER
YELLOWLEGS

LESSER
YELLOWLEGS

UPLAND
SANDPIPER

COMMON
SNIPE

summer

AMERICAN
AVOCET

winter

BLACK-NECKED STILT

Plate 15: Rails, Gallinules and Coots

CLAPPER RAIL *Rallus longirostris*   35.5 cm (14″)
Gray, chicken-like, long bill, barred flanks. **(p. 65)**

BLACK RAIL *Laterallus jamaicensis*   14 cm (5.5″)
Tiny size, black bill, white spots on back, rust-colored nape. **(p. 66)**

YELLOW-BREASTED CRAKE *Porzana flaviventer*   14 cm (5.5″)
Tiny size, tawny yellow appearance, blackish crown, white line above eye, short bill.
(p. 66)

SORA *Porzana carolina*   22 cm (8.75″)
Gray-brown plumage; stubby, yellow bill; black face and throat. **Immature:** Lacks
black on face and throat. **(p. 65)**

COMMON MOORHEN *Gallinula chloropus*   34 cm (13.5″)
Adult: Red bill and frontal shield, white flank stripe. **Immature:** Gray and brown,
white flank stripe, bill lacks red. **(p. 67)**

PURPLE GALLINULE *Porphyrula martinica*   33 cm (13″)
Adult: Bluish-purple coloration, yellow legs, bluish-white frontal shield. **Immature:**
Golden brown, yellow legs, lacks flank stripe. **(p. 67)**

AMERICAN COOT *Fulica americana*   38–40 cm (15–16″)
Adult: Black appearance, white bill and undertail coverts, lacks large white frontal
shield on crown. **Immature:** Gray. **(p. 68)**

CARIBBEAN COOT *Fulica caribaea*   38–40 cm (15–16″)
Adult: Black appearance, white frontal shield extending to crown. **Immature:** Gray.
(p. 68)

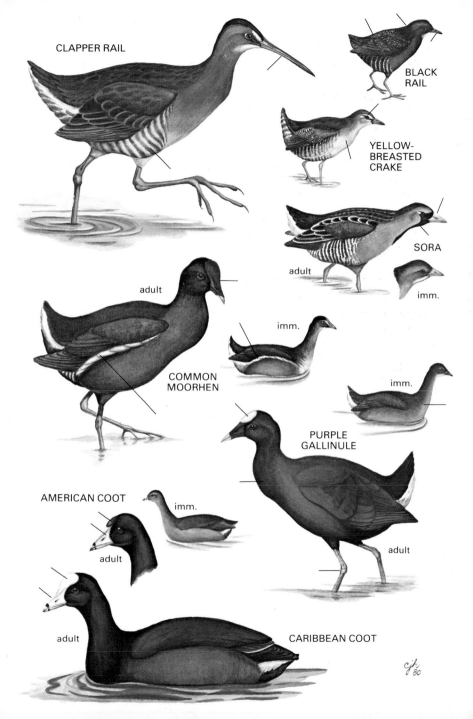

CLAPPER RAIL

BLACK RAIL

YELLOW-BREASTED CRAKE

SORA
adult
imm.

COMMON MOORHEN
adult

imm.

imm.

PURPLE GALLINULE
adult

AMERICAN COOT
imm.
adult

CARIBBEAN COOT
adult

Plate 16: Grebes, Cormorants and Large Waterfowl

DOUBLE-CRESTED CORMORANT *Phalacrocorax auritus* 74–89 cm (29–35″)
Blackish appearance, orange throat pouch, hooked bill, sits with wings spread. **(p. 33)**

OLIVACEOUS CORMORANT *Phalacrocorax olivaceus* 63–69 cm (25–27″)
Difficult to distinguish from Double-crested Cormorant; smaller bulk, duller throat pouch, thinner bill. **(p. 34)**

PIED-BILLED GREBE *Podilymbus podiceps* 30–38 cm (12–15″)
Conical bill. **Breeding:** Black throat and band on bill. **(p. 24)**

LEAST GREBE *Tachybaptus dominicus* 23–26 cm (9–10.5″)
Small size, blackish coloration, thin bill, yellow-orange iris, white wing patch (not always visible). **(p. 23)**

SNOW GOOSE *Chen caerulescens* 58–71 cm (23–28″)
White Phase: White with black primaries. **Dark Phase:** Bluish-gray with white head. **(p. 47)**

TUNDRA SWAN *Cygnus columbianus* 122–140 cm (48–55″)
Large white bird. **(p. 47)**

imm.

DOUBLE-
CRESTED
CORMORANT

adult
(breeding)

drying
wings

OLIVACEOUS CORMORANT

adult
(breeding)

nonbreeding

LEAST
GREBE

breeding

nonbreeding

PIED-BILLED
GREBE

breeding

adult
dark phase
("Blue" Goose)

TUNDRA
SWAN

SNOW GOOSE

adult
white phase

Plate 17: Waterfowl

FULVOUS WHISTLING-DUCK *Dendrocygna bicolor* 46–51 cm (18–20")
Tawny coloration, white stripe on side, white rump. **(p. 47)**

WEST INDIAN WHISTLING-DUCK *Dendrocygna arborea* 48–56 cm (19–22")
Deep brown coloration, black and white markings on side. **(p. 48)**

NORTHERN PINTAIL *Anas acuta* ♂ 69–74 cm (27–29") ♀ 54–56 cm (21.5–22")
Speculum rust-colored. **Male:** Brown head; white stripe down neck; long, pointed tail. **Female:** Mottled brown; pointed tail; long, slender neck. **(p. 50)**

WHITE-CHEEKED PINTAIL *Anas bahamensis* 38–48 cm (15–19")
Red bill mark, white cheek, green speculum. **(p. 50)**

AMERICAN WIGEON *Anas americana* 46–56 cm (18–22")
Male: Light blue bill, white crown, white patch on forewing, green speculum. **Female:** Similar to male but has grayish head and grayish-white patch on forewing. **(p. 52)**

NORTHERN SHOVELER *Anas clypeata* 43–53 cm (17–21")
Large bill, green speculum, blue patch on forewing. **Male:** Green head, white breast, rufous sides. **Female:** Mottled brown. **(p. 52)**

GREEN-WINGED TEAL *Anas crecca* 33–39 cm (13–15.5")
Small size, green speculum, lacks blue in forewing. **Male:** Green eye patch, brown head, white vertical bar in front of wing. **Female:** Mottled brown. **(p. 51)**

LESSER SCAUP *Aythya affinis* 38–46 cm (15–18")
Male: Dark head, breast and tail; whitish back and flanks. **Female:** Brown with large white mark behind bill. **(p. 54)**

BLUE-WINGED TEAL *Anas discors* 38–40 cm (15–16")
Small size, blue forewing. **Male:** White crescent on face. **Female:** Mottled brown. **(p. 51)**

RING-NECKED DUCK *Aythya collaris* 40–46 cm (16–18")
Male: Bill pattern, black back, white vertical bar in front of wing. **Female:** Brown coloration, eye-ring, bill pattern. **(p. 53)**

MASKED DUCK *Oxyura dominica* 30–36 cm (12–14")
White wing patch, erect tail. **Male:** Black face, ruddy coloration. **Female:** Brown with two stripes on face below eye. **(p. 55)**

RUDDY DUCK *Oxyura jamaicensis* 35–43 cm (14–17")
Erect tail. **Male:** Ruddy coloration, white cheek patch, blue bill. **Female:** Brown with single stripe below eye. **(p. 55)**

See also Plate 18.

WEST INDIAN
WHISTLING-DUCK

♀

FULVOUS
WHISTLING-DUCK

NORTHERN
PINTAIL

♂

WHITE-
CHEEKED
PINTAIL

♀

♂

AMERICAN
WIGEON

♀

NORTHERN
SHOVELER

♂

GREEN-
WINGED
TEAL

♀

♀

♂

BLUE-
WINGED
TEAL

LESSER
SCAUP

♀

♂

♂

RING-
NECKED
DUCK

♀

♀

RUDDY
DUCK

MASKED
DUCK

♀

♂

breeding

♂ nonbreeding

ojh
81

Plate 18: Waterfowl (flying)

FULVOUS WHISTLING-DUCK *Dendrocygna bicolor* 46–51 cm (18–20″)
White rump, tawny underparts. **(p. 47)**

WEST INDIAN WHISTLING-DUCK *Dendrocygna arborea* 48–56 cm (19–22″)
Dark, unmarked wings and rump. **(p. 48)**

BLUE-WINGED TEAL *Anas discors* 38–40 cm (15–16″)
Small size, blue forewing, dark belly. **(p. 51)**

GREEN-WINGED TEAL *Anas crecca* 33–39 cm (13–15.5″)
Small size, green speculum, lacks blue in forewing, light belly. **(p. 51)**

NORTHERN SHOVELER *Anas clypeata* 43–53 cm (17–21″)
Large bill, blue forewing, green speculum. **Male:** Dark belly, dark green head. **Female:**
Brown. **(p. 52)**

NORTHERN PINTAIL *Anas acuta* ♂ 69–74 cm (27–29″) ♀ 54–56 cm
(21.5–22″)
   Male: Long, pointed tail; long, slender neck; brown head with white throat and neck.
   Female: Mottled brown; pointed tail; long, slender neck. **(p. 50)**

AMERICAN WIGEON *Anas americana* 46–56 cm (18–22″)
White patch on forewing, green speculum. **(p. 52)**

WHITE-CHEEKED PINTAIL *Anas bahamensis* 38–48 cm (15–19″)
White cheek patch, green speculum. **(p. 50)**

LESSER SCAUP *Aythya affinis* 38–46 cm (15–18″)
White wing stripe. **(p. 54)**

RING-NECKED DUCK *Aythya collaris* 40–46 cm (16–18″)
White wing stripe, dark back. **(p. 53)**

MASKED DUCK *Oxyura dominica* 30–36 cm (12–14″)
   Male: Dark head, white wing patch. **Female:** Striped head, white wing patch. **(p. 55)**

RUDDY DUCK *Oxyura jamaicensis* 35–43 cm (14–17″)
   Chunky build, white cheek patch. **Flight:** Uneven and with rapid wingbeats. **(p. 55)**

See also Plate 17.

Dabbling or Diving Duck	Whistling-Duck	Stiff-tailed Duck	Merganser
Body angled slightly upward	Head and feet droop	Stocky build	Horizontal body axis

FULVOUS
WHISTLING-
DUCK

WEST INDIAN
WHISTLING-DUCK

BLUE-
WINGED
TEAL

♂

♀

NORTHERN
SHOVELER

GREEN-
WINGED
TEAL

♂

♀

♂

♀

AMERICAN
WIGEON

♂

NORTHERN
PINTAIL

♀

♂

♀

WHITE-
CHEEKED
PINTAIL

RING-
NECKED
DUCK

LESSER
SCAUP

♂

♀

♂

♀

MASKED
DUCK

♂

♀

RUDDY
DUCK

♂

♀

J WIESSINGER

Plate 19: Accidental Waterfowl

MALLARD *Anas platyrhynchos* 51—71 cm (20—28")
Male: Green head, white neck ring. **Female:** Mottled brown, blue speculum with white borders. **(p. 49)**

AMERICAN BLACK DUCK *Anas rubripes* 53—64 cm (21—25")
Dark brown body, purple speculum. **Flight:** White wing linings. **(p. 49)**

BLACK-BELLIED WHISTLING-DUCK *Dendrocygna autumnalis* 46—53 cm (18—21")
Black belly, white wing patch. **Flight:** Upper side of wing principally white. **(p. 48)**

WOOD DUCK *Aix sponsa* 43—51 cm (17—20")
Male: Crest, iridescent coloration. **Female:** Crest, white eye patch. **(p. 53)**

BUFFLEHEAD *Bucephala albeola* 33—38 cm (13—15")
Male: White head patch. **Female:** Browner than ♂, white facial stripe. **(p. 54)**

CANVASBACK *Aythya valisineria* 51—61 cm (20—24")
Sloping forehead profile. **Male:** Rust-colored head and neck. **Female:** Grayish plumage. **(p. 54)**

HOODED MERGANSER *Lophodytes cucullatus* 40—48 cm (16—19")
Crest, hooked bill. **Male:** Crest has large white patch. **Female:** Dark face, bill and back. **(p. 56)**

RED-BREASTED MERGANSER *Mergus serrator* 51—64 cm (20—25")
Crest, hooked bill. **Male:** Dark breast, white collar. **Female:** Rust-colored head and neck, gray body. **(p. 56)**

MALLARD ♂ ♀

AMERICAN BLACK DUCK

BLACK-BELLIED WHISTLING-DUCK ♂

WOOD DUCK ♂ ♀

CANVASBACK ♀ ♂

BUFFLEHEAD ♀ ♂

HOODED MERGANSER ♂ ♀

RED-BREASTED MERGANSER ♀ ♂

Plate 20: Raptors

AMERICAN KESTREL *Falco sparverius* 23–30 cm (9–12″)
Small size, light brown back, red tail with terminal black band, distinctive facial pattern.
Male: Blue wings. **(p. 61)**

PEREGRINE FALCON *Falco peregrinus* 38–51 cm (15–20″)
Large size, mask-like head pattern. **Flight:** Pointed wings; long, narrow tail; rapid, pigeon-like flight. **Adult:** Dark slate above, cream with dark bars below. **Immature:** Brown, heavy streaking below. **(p. 60)**

MERLIN *Falco columbarius* 25–34 cm (10–13.5″)
Medium size, heavy barring underneath, banded tail. **Flight:** Pointed wings; long, narrow tail; great speed and agility. **Male:** Slate gray above. **Female:** Brown above. **(p. 61)**

SHARP-SHINNED HAWK *Accipiter striatus* 28–33 cm (11–13″)
Flight: Short, rounded wings; narrow tail; flies alternately flapping and gliding. **Adult:** Slate gray above, barred rufous underparts. **Immature** (not depicted): Brown above, heavily streaked below. **(p. 58)**

BROAD-WINGED HAWK *Buteo platypterus* 39 cm (15.5″)
Adult: Tail banded with black and white, rufous breast. **Immature** (not depicted): Dark bars on breast, lacks distinctive tail bands. **(p. 59)**

RED-TAILED HAWK *Buteo jamaicensis* 48–64 cm (19–25″)
Adult: Large size, red tail, white breast, streaked belly. **Immature** (not depicted): Tail grayish-brown and finely barred. **(p. 58)**

NORTHERN HARRIER *Circus cyaneus* 46–61 cm (18–24″)
White rump, long wings and tail. **Flight:** Low over ground, wings held above horizontal.
Male: Grayish-blue. **Female:** Brown. **(p. 59)**

OSPREY *Pandion haliaetus* 53–61 cm (21–24″)
White head with black line through eye. **Flight:** White below with black wrist patch. **(p. 60)**

TURKEY VULTURE *Cathartes aura* 69–76 cm (27–30″)
Large size, dark coloration. **Flight:** Wings two-toned and held above horizontal in broad V. **(p. 57)**

AMERICAN
KESTREL

PEREGRINE
FALCON

adult

MERLIN

BROAD-
WINGED
HAWK

SHARP-
SHINNED
HAWK

adult

RED-TAILED
HAWK

adult

♂

NORTHERN HARRIER

adult

OSPREY

TURKEY
VULTURE

J WESSINGER

Plate 21: Cuckoos, Ani and Owls

YELLOW-BILLED CUCKOO *Coccyzus americanus* 28–32 cm (11–12.5″)
White underparts; long, black tail with white spots. **Flight:** Rufous patch on wing.
(p. 119)

MANGROVE CUCKOO *Coccyzus minor* 28–30 cm (11–12″)
Underparts buff-colored; black ear patch; long, black tail with white spots. **Flight:**
Lacks rufous on wing. **(p. 118)**

SMOOTH-BILLED ANI *Crotophaga ani* 30–33 cm (12–13″)
Entirely black plumage; heavy, parrot-like bill; long tail. **(p. 120)**

COMMON BARN-OWL *Tyto alba* 30–43 cm (12–17″)
Light face and underparts, dark eyes, long legs. **(p. 121)**

SHORT-EARED OWL *Asio flammeus* 35–43 cm (14–17″)
Streaking on breast, yellow eyes, dark facial disk. **Flight:** Irregular; light underwing
with black wrist patch, large buff-colored patch on upperwing. **(p. 123)**

PUERTO RICAN SCREECH-OWL *Otus nudipes* 23–25 cm (9–10″)
Small size, gray-brown to rusty upperparts, white underparts with heavy brown streaks,
no ear tufts. **(p. 122)**

Blue background highlights endemic species.

YELLOW-BILLED CUCKOO

MANGROVE CUCKOO

SMOOTH-BILLED ANI

COMMON BARN-OWL

SHORT-EARED OWL

PUERTO RICAN SCREECH-OWL

cjh
81

Plate 22: Puerto Rican Lizard-Cuckoo

PUERTO RICAN LIZARD-CUCKOO *Saurothera vieilloti* 40–48 cm (16–19″)
Large size; very long tail; two-toned underparts (gray chin and breast, cinnamon belly and undertail coverts). **Immature** (not depicted): Like adult, but light cinnamon rather than gray breast. **(p. 119)**

Plate 23: Miscellaneous

YELLOW-BELLIED SAPSUCKER *Sphyrapicus varius* 20–21.5 cm (8–8.5″)
White facial stripes, large white patch on wing. **Male:** Red throat. **Female:** White throat. **Immature** (not depicted): Brown plumage. **(p. 139)**

HELMETED GUINEAFOWL *Numida meleagris* 53 cm (21″)
Slate gray plumage with white spots, naked head and neck. **(p. 64)**

RED JUNGLEFOWL *Gallus gallus* ♂ 71 cm (28″) ♀ 43 cm (17″)
Comb on head. **(p. 63)**

NORTHERN BOBWHITE *Colinus virginianus* 25 cm (10″)
Chunky, brown bird. **Male:** White throat and eye stripe. **Female** (not depicted):
Buff-colored throat and eye stripe. **(p. 62)**

BELTED KINGFISHER *Ceryle alcyon* 28–35.5 cm (11–14″)
Crest, slate blue and white plumage, large bill. **Female:** Two breast bands, upper blue, lower rusty-orange. **Male:** One blue breast band. **(p. 137)**

CEDAR WAXWING *Bombycilla cedrorum* 18–18.5 cm (7–7.25″)
Crest, brown plumage, yellow band on tip of tail. **Immature:** Streaked underparts.
(p. 152)

WHITE-VENTED MYNA *Acridotheres javanicus* 25 cm (10″)
Crest; yellow bill and legs; white undertail coverts, tail tip and wing patch. **(p. 153)**

HILL MYNA *Gracula religiosa* 30 cm (12″)
Brilliant orange bill, yellow wattle on hind neck, white wing patch. **(p. 154)**

WHITE-NECKED CROW *Corvus leucognaphalus* 48–51 cm (19–20″)
Large size, black plumage. **(p. 148)**

EUROPEAN STARLING *Sturnus vulgaris* 21.5 cm (8.5″)
Flight: Straight, wings swept back. **Breeding:** Glossy black, yellow bill. **Nonbreeding:**
Underparts heavily flecked with white, dark bill. **Immature** (not depicted): Brownish-gray with fine stripes on breast. **(p. 152)**

Plate not to scale.

YELLOW-
BELLIED
SAPSUCKER

♂

♀

adult

RED
JUNGLEFOWL

♂

HELMETED
GUINEAFOWL

NORTHERN
BOBWHITE

♂

♂

♀

BELTED
KINGFISHER

adult

imm.

CEDAR
WAXWING

WHITE-
VENTED
MYNA

HILL MYNA

nonbreeding

WHITE-
NECKED
CROW

breeding

EUROPEAN
STARLING

Plate 24: Puerto Rican Woodpecker

PUERTO RICAN WOODPECKER *Melanerpes portoricensis* 23–27 cm (9–10.5″)
Black upperparts, red throat and breast, white rump and forehead, unbarred back
and wings. **Female and Immature:** Less red than adult male. **(p. 138)**

~cindy house~
81

Plate 25: Pigeons and Doves

SCALY-NAPED PIGEON *Columba squamosa* 35.5–40 cm (14–16″)
Slate gray body, upper body with wine tint (at close range). **Immature** (not depicted):
More ruddy. **(p. 101)**

ROCK DOVE *Columba livia* 33–35.5 cm (13–14″)
Variable coloration, white rump and black tail band (wild birds). **(p. 103)**

PLAIN PIGEON *Columba inornata* 38–40 cm (15–16″)
Paler than other pigeons, more brown in plumage, white band on leading edge of
wing, wine color on wings and belly. **Flight:** Thin white line transversing wing.
Immature (not depicted): Darker than adults, more brown in plumage. **(p. 102)**

WHITE-CROWNED PIGEON *Columba leucocephala* 33–35.5 cm (13–14″)
Slate gray body. **Male:** White crown. **Female and Immature** (not depicted): Crown
grayish-white. **(p. 100)**

WHITE-WINGED DOVE *Zenaida asiatica* 28–30 cm (11–12″)
Large white wing patches, white on tail at corners. **(p. 105)**

ZENAIDA DOVE *Zenaida aurita* 25–28 cm (10–11″)
White band on trailing edge of secondaries, rounded tail with white terminal band
nearly complete. **(p. 104)**

RINGED TURTLE-DOVE *Streptopelia risoria* 28–30 cm (11–12″)
Light tan plumage, black band around nape. **(p. 106)**

SPOTTED DOVE *Streptopelia chinensis* 30 cm (12″)
Black band spotted with white on nape, long tail tipped with white, light gray bend
of wing. **Immature** (not depicted): Lacks the neck pattern. **(p. 106)**

MOURNING DOVE *Zenaida macroura* 28–33 cm (11–13″)
Long, wedge-shaped tail fringed with white, no white on wings. **(p. 103)**

COMMON GROUND-DOVE *Columbina passerina* 15–18 cm (6–7″)
Tiny size. **Flight:** Rufous wing patch. **Female** (not depicted): Paler, duller than male.
(p. 107)

BRIDLED QUAIL-DOVE *Geotrygon mystacea* 30 cm (12″)
White line under eye, brown back, throat white, rufous limited to patch on wing,
underparts buffy-brown. **(p. 109)**

KEY WEST QUAIL-DOVE *Geotrygon chrysia* 28–30 cm (11–12″)
White line under eye, ruddy back and wings, whitish underparts. **(p. 108)**

RUDDY QUAIL-DOVE *Geotrygon montana* 25 cm (10″)
Rusty coloration, buff-colored stripe below eye, rufous underparts. **Female:** Less rusty.
(p. 107)

SCALY-NAPED PIGEON

ROCK DOVE

PLAIN PIGEON

WHITE-CROWNED PIGEON

WHITE-WINGED DOVE

ZENAIDA DOVE

RINGED TURTLE-DOVE

SPOTTED DOVE

MOURNING DOVE

COMMON GROUND-DOVE

KEY WEST QUAIL-DOVE

RUDDY QUAIL-DOVE

♂

♀

BRIDLED QUAIL-DOVE

AGrajaL

Plate 26: Parrots and Parakeets

BUDGERIGAR *Melopsittacus undulatus* 18 cm (7″)
Usually green underparts (may be blue, yellow or white), yellow head and back barred with black. **(p. 110)**

CANARY-WINGED PARAKEET *Brotogeris versicolurus* 23 cm (9″)
Green plumage, white and yellow wing patch, ivory bill. **(p. 113)**

ORANGE-FRONTED PARAKEET *Aratinga canicularis* 23–24 cm (9–9.5″)
Medium size, orange forehead, white eye-ring, blue primaries. **(p. 110)**

BROWN-THROATED PARAKEET *Aratinga pertinax* 23–28 cm (9–11″)
Yellowish-orange patch on face; throat and breast brown; primaries blue. **(p. 111)**

HISPANIOLAN PARAKEET *Aratinga chloroptera* 28–30 cm (11–12″)
White eye-ring, red bend of wing. **Flight:** Red underwing coverts; long, pointed tail. **(p. 112)**

MONK PARAKEET *Myiopsitta monachus* 28 cm (11″)
Large parakeet; crown, breast, belly gray; upperparts green; flight feathers blue. **(p. 112)**

RED-CROWNED PARROT *Amazona viridigenalis* 30–33 cm (12–13″)
Red crown, cheeks bright green. **Flight:** Orange-red patch on wing, blue primaries. **(p. 113)**

ORANGE-WINGED PARROT *Amazona amazonica* 32 cm (12.5″)
Yellow on cheek and crown, lores and eye stripe blue. **Flight:** Orange-red patch on wing, blue primaries. **(p. 114)**

HISPANIOLAN PARROT *Amazona ventralis* 28–30 cm (11–12″)
White eye-ring and forehead, black mark behind eye, maroon belly, blue primaries. **(p. 115)**

BLACK-HOODED PARAKEET *Nandayus nenday* 35.5 cm (14″)
Large parakeet, black head, red thighs, long tail. **(p. 117)**

YELLOW-CROWNED PARROT *Amazona ochrocephala* 35.5 cm (14″)
Large green parrot, yellow head (variable in extent). **Flight:** Red patch on wing, blue primaries. **(p. 114)**

BUDGERIGAR

CANARY-WINGED PARAKEET

ORANGE-FRONTED PARAKEET

BROWN-THROATED PARAKEET

HISPANIOLAN PARAKEET

MONK PARAKEET

RED-CROWNED PARROT

ORANGE-WINGED PARROT

HISPANIOLAN PARROT

BLACK-HOODED PARAKEET

YELLOW-CROWNED PARROT

Plate 27: Puerto Rican Parrot

PUERTO RICAN PARROT   *Amazona vittata*   30 cm (12″)
  Green plumage, white eye-ring, red forehead, blue primaries. **(p. 116)**

Plate 28: Goatsuckers and Swifts

ANTILLEAN NIGHTHAWK *Chordeiles gundlachii* 20−25 cm (8−10″)
White wing patch, erratic flight. **Call:** *Que-re-que-qué.* **(p. 127)**

BLACK SWIFT *Cypseloides niger* 15−18 cm (6−7″)
Large size; long, fluttering wings; 'flying cigar' appearance; appears black. **(p. 129)**

COMMON NIGHTHAWK *Chordeiles minor* 20−25 cm (8−10″)
Identical to West Indian Nighthawk. **Call:** *Ñeet.* **(p. 127)**

SHORT-TAILED SWIFT *Chaetura brachyura* 10 cm (4″)
Small size; long, fluttering wings; 'flying cigar' appearance; light gray rump, tail and
undertail coverts. **(p. 129)**

CHUCK-WILL'S-WIDOW *Caprimulgus carolinensis* 28−33 cm (11−13″)
Dark mottled black, brown and buff-colored plumage; large size; outer tail feathers
show white in male. **(p. 125)**

PUERTO RICAN NIGHTJAR *Caprimulgus noctitherus* 21.5 cm (8.5″)
Comparison to Chuck-will's-widow: Smaller size, plumage less ruddy, more white
on tail of male. **(p. 125)**

Blue background highlights endemic species.

ANTILLEAN
NIGHTHAWK

BLACK SWIFT

COMMON
NIGHTHAWK

SHORT-
TAILED
SWIFT

CHUCK-
WILL'S-
WIDOW

tail of ♀

♂

tail of ♀

♂

PUERTO RICAN
NIGHTJAR

J. WIESSINGER

Plate 29: Hummingbirds

GREEN-THROATED CARIB *Eulampis holosericeus* 11—12.5 cm (4.5—5")
Large size, slightly decurved bill, green breast. **(p. 133)**

ANTILLEAN CRESTED HUMMINGBIRD *Orthorhyncus cristatus*
8—9.5 cm (3.25—3.75")
Tiny size. **Male:** Crest. **Female:** Light underparts, tail *not* forked. **(p. 134)**

GREEN MANGO *Anthracothorax viridis* 11—14 cm (4.5—5.5")
Large size, emerald green underparts. **(p. 132)**

PUERTO RICAN EMERALD *Chlorostilbon maugaeus* 9—10 cm (3.5—4")
Small size, forked tail, *lacks* crest. **Male:** Green, black tail, flesh-colored lower mandible.
Female: Light underparts, black bill, outer tail feathers tipped with white. **(p. 130)**

ANTILLEAN MANGO *Anthracothorax dominicus* 11—12.5 cm (4.5—5")
Large size, light yellowish-green upperparts. **Male:** Black on breast. **Female:** Light
below, white tips on tail feathers (except on the central pair). **(p. 131)**

Blue background highlights endemic species.

ANTILLEAN
CRESTED
HUMMINGBIRD

♂

♀

GREEN-
THROATED
CARIB

GREEN MANGO

♀

PUERTO RICAN
EMERALD

♂

♂

♀

ANTILLEAN
MANGO

Plate 30: Puerto Rican Tody

PUERTO RICAN TODY   *Todus mexicanus*   11 cm (4.5″)
Small and chunky; bright green upperparts; red throat and lower mandible; long, broad bill; yellow flanks on white underparts. **Immature** (not depicted): Red throat lacking. **(p. 136)**

Plate 31: Flycatchers, Thrushes and Mimic Thrushes

LESSER ANTILLEAN PEWEE   *Contopus latirostris*   15 cm (6″)
Ochre-colored underparts, light colored lower mandible. **(p. 142)**

GREATER ANTILLEAN PEWEE   *Contopus caribaeus*   16 cm (6.25″)
Underparts grayish-buff, light colored lower mandible. **(p. 143)**

LOGGERHEAD KINGBIRD   *Tyrannus caudifasciatus*   23.5–26 cm (9.25–10.25″)
Dark upperparts, blackish on crown, white underparts, large bill, distinctly two-toned plumage. **(p. 140)**

GRAY KINGBIRD   *Tyrannus dominicensis*   23–24 cm (9–9.5″)
Gray upperparts, pale gray-white underparts, black ear coverts. **(p. 139)**

CARIBBEAN ELAENIA   *Elaenia martinica*   16.5–18 cm (6.5–7″)
Two whitish wing bars. **(p. 143)**

PUERTO RICAN FLYCATCHER   *Myiarchus antillarum*   18.5–20 cm (7.25–8″)
Dark back and head, light underpart. **(p. 141)**

PEARLY-EYED THRASHER   *Margarops fuscatus*   28–30 cm (11–12″)
White iris, brown upperparts, white underparts with brown markings, white on tail. **(p. 151)**

NORTHERN MOCKINGBIRD   *Mimus polyglottos*   25 cm (10″)
Gray upperparts, white underparts, white markings on wings and tail. **(p. 150)**

RED-LEGGED THRUSH   *Turdus plumbeus*   28 cm (11″)
Gray coloration, red bill and legs. **(p. 149)**

AMERICAN ROBIN   *Turdus migratorius*   24 cm (9.5″)
Reddish breast and belly, dark gray back, outer tail feathers tipped with white. **(p. 149)**

Blue background highlights endemic species.

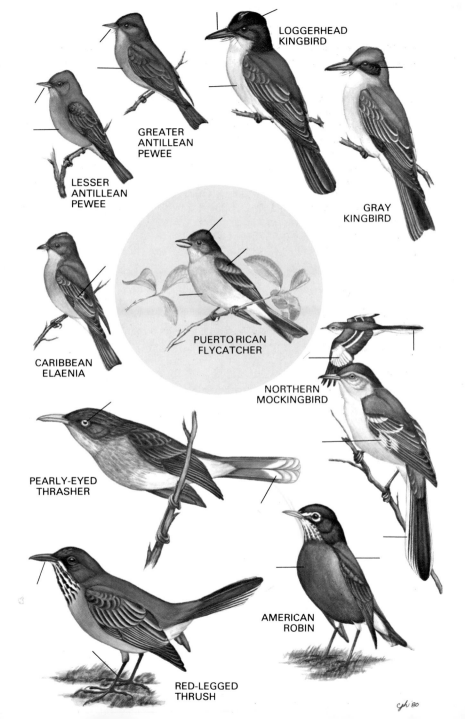

LOGGERHEAD
KINGBIRD

GREATER
ANTILLEAN
PEWEE

LESSER
ANTILLEAN
PEWEE

GRAY
KINGBIRD

CARIBBEAN
ELAENIA

PUERTO RICAN
FLYCATCHER

NORTHERN
MOCKINGBIRD

PEARLY-EYED
THRASHER

AMERICAN
ROBIN

RED-LEGGED
THRUSH

Plate 32: Swallows

BARN SWALLOW *Hirundo rustica* 15–19 cm (6–7.5″)
Deeply forked tail with white tail spots, dark blue upperparts, buff-colored underparts. **(p. 146)**

CLIFF SWALLOW *Hirundo pyrrhonota* 12.5–15 cm (5–6″)
Chestnut chin, throat, sides of face; buff-colored forehead and rump; only slight notch in tail. **(p. 146)**

CAVE SWALLOW *Hirundo fulva* 12.5–14 cm (5–5.5″)
Rust-colored rump, light throat, underparts washed with rufous, chestnut forehead, only slight notch in tail. **(p. 146)**

TREE SWALLOW *Tachycineta bicolor* 12.5–15 cm (5–6″)
White underparts, dark blue-green back. **Immature** (not depicted): Brown back, white underparts. **(p. 144)**

BANK SWALLOW *Riparia riparia* 12.5–14 cm (5–5.5″)
Dark band across white breast, brown upperparts. **(p. 145)**

CARIBBEAN MARTIN *Progne dominicensis* 19–21 cm (7.5–8.25″)
Large size. **Male:** Dark head and throat, white belly. **Female and Immature:** Brownish wash on breast blends into white (not depicted). **(p. 145)**

PURPLE MARTIN *Progne subis* 19–20 cm (7.5–8″)
Large size. **Male:** Dark underparts. **Female and Immature:** Scaled pattern on gray-brown breast, gray patches on sides of neck, fairly distinct border between breast and belly coloration. **(p. 144)**

CLIFF
SWALLOW

BARN SWALLOW

CAVE SWALLOW

TREE
SWALLOW

BANK
SWALLOW

CARIBBEAN
MARTIN

PURPLE
MARTIN

Plate 33: Vireos and Warblers

WHITE-EYED VIREO   *Vireo griseus*   12.5 cm (5″)
Yellow 'spectacles', whitish throat, white iris, white wing bars. **Immature:** Brown iris.
(p. 155)

YELLOW-THROATED VIREO   *Vireo flavifrons*   12.5 cm (5″)
Bright yellow 'spectacles' and throat, white wing bars, olive-colored upperparts.
(p. 154)

PUERTO RICAN VIREO   *Vireo latimeri*   12.5 cm (5″)
Incomplete white eye-ring; underparts two-toned: grayish throat and breast, light yellow
on belly. **(p. 155)**

BLACK-WHISKERED VIREO   *Vireo altiloquus*   16.5 cm (6.5″)
Black moustache stripe, buffy-white eye stripe bordered with black. **(p. 157)**

RED-EYED VIREO   *Vireo olivaceus*   15 cm (6″)
Very similar to Black-whiskered Vireo, but greener above, whiter below, *lacks* black
moustache stripe. **Immature:** Brown iris. **(p. 156)**

BANANAQUIT   *Coereba flaveola*   10−12.5 cm (4−5″)
Black upperparts; white eye stripe and wing spot; gray throat; yellow breast, belly,
rump. **(p. 174)**

WORM-EATING WARBLER   *Helmitheros vermivorus*   13 cm (5.25″)
Buff-colored crown with black stripes, dull olive-colored upperparts, buff-colored
underparts. **(p. 160)**

LOUISIANA WATERTHRUSH   *Seiurus motacilla*   15−16 cm (6−6.25″)
White eye stripe, unflecked throat, streaked whitish underparts, bobs tail. **(p. 170)**

OVENBIRD   *Seiurus aurocapillus*   15 cm (6″)
Orange crown bordered by black stripes, heavily streaked underparts, white eye-ring.
(p. 169)

NORTHERN WATERTHRUSH   *Seiurus noveboracensis*   12.5−15 cm (5−6″)
Buff-colored eye stripe, streaked buff-colored underparts, flecks on throat, bobs tail.
(p. 170)

Blue background highlights endemic species.

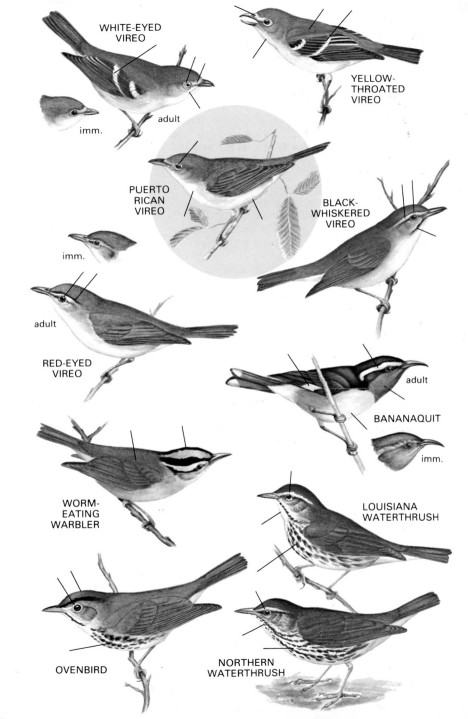

WHITE-EYED
VIREO

imm.

adult

YELLOW-
THROATED
VIREO

PUERTO
RICAN
VIREO

BLACK-
WHISKERED
VIREO

imm.

adult

RED-EYED
VIREO

adult

BANANAQUIT

imm.

WORM-
EATING
WARBLER

LOUISIANA
WATERTHRUSH

OVENBIRD

NORTHERN
WATERTHRUSH

Plate 34: Warblers I

PRAIRIE WARBLER *Dendroica discolor* 12 cm (4.75″)
Yellow underparts, blackish streaks on sides, bobs tail. (See Plate 36) **(p. 167)**

PALM WARBLER *Dendroica palmarum* 12.5–14 cm (5–5.5″)
Yellow undertail coverts, olive-colored rump, brownish back, chestnut cap (absent in winter), bobs tail. (See Plate 36) **(p. 167)**

YELLOW-THROATED WARBLER *Dendroica dominica* 13 cm (5.25″)
Yellow throat, white eye stripe, white neck patch. **(p. 165)**

CANADA WARBLER *Wilsonia canadensis* 13 cm (5.25″)
Adult: Black 'necklace', gray upperparts, yellow 'spectacles'. **Female:** 'Necklace' fainter. **Immature:** (See Plate 36) **(p. 173)**

ELFIN WOODS WARBLER *Dendroica angelae*
Adult: Black and white plumage, incomplete eye-ring, black crown, thin white stripe above eye, white patches on ear coverts and neck. **Immature:** Similar to adult, but greenish. **(p. 168)**

BLACKPOLL WARBLER *Dendroica striata* 12.5–14 cm (5–5.5″)
Male in Summer: Black cap, white cheek. **Female in Summer:** Grayish above, lighter below; lacks black cap; lightly streaked sides; white wing bars and undertail coverts; pale legs. **Winter:** (See Plate 36) **(p. 167)**

BLACK-AND-WHITE WARBLER *Mniotilta varia* 12.5–14 cm (5–5.5″)
Black and white striped, white striping on crown. **Female:** Lacks white eye-ring, whiter underparts. **(p. 159)**

YELLOW-RUMPED WARBLER *Dendroica coronata* 14 cm (5.5″)
Adult Male in Summer: Yellow rump, white throat, yellow patch on sides. **Adult Female and Winter Male:** Brownish with same pattern. **Immature:** (See Plate 36) **(p. 163)**

MAGNOLIA WARBLER *Dendroica magnolia* 11.5–12.5 cm (4.5–5″)
White tail markings distinguish it in all plumages. (See Plate 36) **(p. 162)**

CAPE MAY WARBLER *Dendroica tigrina* 12.5–14 cm (5–5.5″)
Adult: Heavy striping on yellow breast, yellowish rump, yellow patch behind ear. **Male in Summer:** Chestnut cheek patch. **Immature:** (See Plate 36) **(p. 162)**

BLACK-THROATED GREEN WARBLER *Dendroica virens* 12.5 cm (5″)
Yellow cheek, black throat. **Female and Immature:** Less black on throat. (See Plate 36) **(p. 164)**

BAY-BREASTED WARBLER *Dendroica castanea* 14 cm (5.5″)
Summer: Chestnut on head, throat and sides. **Female in Summer:** Duller than male. **Immature:** (See Plate 36) **(p. 166)**

CHESTNUT-SIDED WARBLER *Dendroica pensylvanica* 12.5 cm (5″)
Adult in Summer: Yellowish crown, chestnut sides. **Winter and Immature:** (See Plate 36) **(p. 166)**

Blue background highlights endemic species.

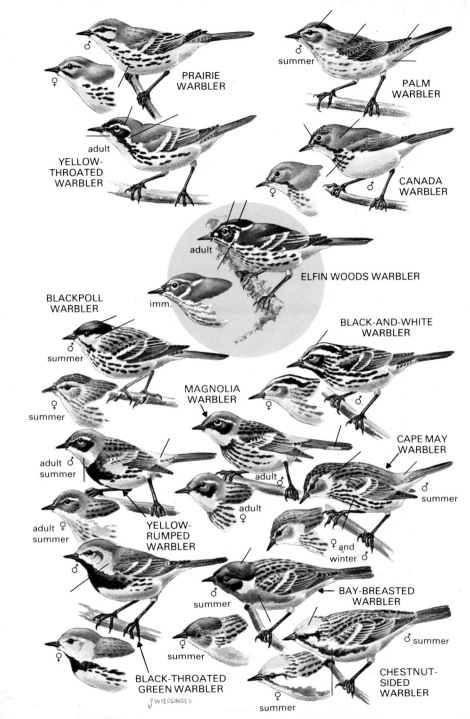

PRAIRIE
WARBLER

♂

♀

PALM
WARBLER

summer

YELLOW-
THROATED
WARBLER

adult

CANADA
WARBLER

♀

♂

ELFIN WOODS WARBLER

adult

imm.

BLACKPOLL
WARBLER

BLACK-AND-WHITE
WARBLER

♂

summer

♀

♀
summer

♂

MAGNOLIA
WARBLER

CAPE MAY
WARBLER

adult ♂

♂

adult
summer

adult
♀

summer

YELLOW-
RUMPED
WARBLER

♀ and
winter ♂

adult ♀
summer

♂

summer

BAY-BREASTED
WARBLER

♀

♀
summer

♂ summer

BLACK-THROATED
GREEN WARBLER

♀
summer

CHESTNUT-
SIDED
WARBLER

J WIESSINGER

Plate 35: Warblers II

MOURNING WARBLER *Oporornis philadelphia* 12.5 cm (5″)
Adult in Summer: Gray hood, *lacks* eye-ring. **Adult Male:** Black bib. **Winter Female and Immature:** (See Plate 36) **(p. 171)**

CONNECTICUT WARBLER *Oporornis agilis* 14–14.5 cm (5.5–5.75″)
Adult Male: Complete white eye-ring, gray hood. **Adult Female:** Duller. **Immature:** (See Plate 36) **(p. 171)**

COMMON YELLOWTHROAT *Geothlypis trichas* 12.5 cm (5″)
Male: Black mask, throat yellow. **Female:** Yellow throat and breast, dull white belly. **(p. 172)**

HOODED WARBLER *Wilsonia citrina* 14 cm (5.5″)
White outer tail spots. **Adult Male:** Black hood, yellow forehead. **Adult Female:** Yellow cheeks and often yellow forehead; *lacks* hood, but its outline may be present. **Immature:** (See Plate 36) **(p. 172)**

KENTUCKY WARBLER *Oporornis formosus* 14 cm (5.5″)
Adult: Black facial mark, yellow 'spectacles', olive green upperparts, yellow underparts. **Immature:** (See Plate 36) **(p. 171)**

YELLOW WARBLER *Dendroica petechia* 12.5–14 cm (5–5.5″)
Yellow coloration; yellow tail spots; rust-colored streaks on breast, faint or lacking in female. (See Plate 36) **(p. 161)**

GOLDEN-WINGED WARBLER *Vermivora chrysoptera* 12.5 cm (5″)
Yellow wing patch, black throat and cheek, gray upperparts, white underparts. **Female:** Gray throat and cheek. **(p. 160)**

NORTHERN PARULA *Parula americana* 10.5–12 cm (4.25–4.75″)
Bluish-gray upperparts, yellow wash on back, white wing bars, yellow breast and throat. **Male:** Breast band. **(p. 161)**

PROTHONOTARY WARBLER *Protonotaria citrea* 14 cm (5.5″)
Golden head, blue-gray wings. **Female:** Duller. (See Plate 36) **(p. 159)**

ADELAIDE'S WARBLER *Dendroica adelaidae* 12.5 cm (5″)
Bluish-gray upperparts, yellow markings above and yellow or white below eye, white on tail. **(p. 165)**

AMERICAN REDSTART *Setophaga ruticilla* 12.5 cm (5″)
Male: Black with large orange wing and tail patches. **Female:** Lighter with yellow patches. **(p. 173)**

BLACKBURNIAN WARBLER *Dendroica fusca* 13 cm (5.25″)
Adult Male: Orange throat and facial markings. **Adult Female:** Duller. **Immature:** (See Plate 36) **(p. 164)**

BLACK-THROATED BLUE WARBLER *Dendroica caerulescens* 13 cm (5.25″)
Adult Male: Blue back, black face. **Female:** Brownish with white wing spot. **Immature:** (See Plate 36) **(p. 163)**

MOURNING WARBLER

adult ♀

CONNECTICUT WARBLER

adult ♂

adult ♂ (summer)

adult ♂

♀

COMMON YELLOWTHROAT

KENTUCKY WARBLER

adult ♂

adult ♀

HOODED WARBLER

adult ♂

adult ♀

GOLDEN-WINGED WARBLER

♂

♀

♀

YELLOW WARBLER

♂

♀

PROTHONOTARY WARBLER

♂

♀

NORTHERN PARULA

♂

AMERICAN REDSTART

♀

♂

ADELAIDE'S WARBLER

BLACKBURNIAN WARBLER

adult ♂

adult ♀

BLACK-THROATED BLUE WARBLER

adult ♀

adult ♂

cjh 80

Plate 36: Fall Warblers

CANADA WARBLER *Wilsonia canadensis* 13 cm (5.25″)
Female and Immature: Yellow 'spectacles', faint 'necklace', gray upperparts, lacks white in wings and tail. **(p. 173)**

MOURNING WARBLER *Oporornis philadelphia* 12.5 cm (5″)
Immature and Winter Female: Incomplete eye-ring, buffy-gray band across breast, yellow belly. **(p. 171)**

CONNECTICUT WARBLER *Oporornis agilis* 14–14.5 cm (5.5–5.75″)
Immature: Complete white eye-ring, suggestion of hood, dull yellow belly. **(p. 171)**

HOODED WARBLER *Wilsonia citrina* 14 cm (5.5″)
White tail spots. **Female and Immature:** Yellow eye stripe. **(p. 172)**

KENTUCKY WARBLER *Oporornis formosus* 14 cm (5.5″)
Immature: Pale black facial markings, yellow underparts. **(p. 171)**

YELLOW WARBLER *Dendroica petechia* 12.5–14 cm (5–5.5″)
Yellow tail spots, yellow coloration. **(p. 161)**

PROTHONOTARY WARBLER *Protonotaria citrea* 14 cm (5.5″)
Female: Dull orange-yellow head, gray wings. **(p. 159)**

BLACK-THROATED BLUE WARBLER *Dendroica caerulescens* 13 cm (5.25″)
Female: White wing spot (sometimes absent), dark upperparts extending to cheek, light eye stripe. **(p. 163)**

PALM WARBLER *Dendroica palmarum* 12.5–14 cm (5–5.5″)
Winter: Yellowish undertail coverts, olive rump, faint eye stripe, brownish back, bobs tail. **(p. 167)**

PRAIRIE WARBLER *Dendroica discolor* 12 cm (4.75″)
Yellow underparts, streaks on sides, bobs tail. **(p. 167)**

CAPE MAY WARBLER *Dendroica tigrina* 12.5–14 cm (5–5.5″)
Winter: Striped breast, yellowish rump, yellow patch behind ear. **(p. 162)**

YELLOW-RUMPED WARBLER *Dendroica coronata* 14 cm (5.5″)
Winter: Yellow rump, white throat. **(p. 163)**

MAGNOLIA WARBLER *Dendroica magnolia* 11.5–12.5 cm (4.5–5″)
Immature: White tail markings. **(p. 162)**

BLACK-THROATED GREEN WARBLER *Dendroica virens* 12.5 cm (5″)
Immature: Cheek framed by yellow. **(p. 164)**

BLACKBURNIAN WARBLER *Dendroica fusca* 13 cm (5.25″)
Immature: Yellow throat and breast, whitish stripes on back. **(p. 164)**

CHESTNUT-SIDED WARBLER *Dendroica pensylvanica* 12.5 cm (5″)
Winter: Whitish underparts, wing bars, white eye-ring, yellowish-green upperparts. **(p. 166)**

BAY-BREASTED WARBLER *Dendroica castanea* 14 cm (5.5″)
Winter: Buff-colored undertail coverts, black legs and feet, may have bay wash on flanks (absent in immatures and some adults). **(p. 166)**

BLACKPOLL WARBLER *Dendroica striata* 12.5–14 cm (5–5.5″)
Winter: White wing bars, white undertail coverts, pale legs. **(p. 167)**

See also Plates 34 and 35.

CANADA WARBLER

MOURNING WARBLER

CONNECTICUT WARBLER

HOODED WARBLER

KENTUCKY WARBLER

YELLOW WARBLER

PROTHONOTARY WARBLER

BLACK-THROATED WARBLER

PALM WARBLER

PRAIRIE WARBLER

CAPE MAY WARBLER

YELLOW-RUMPED WARBLER

MAGNOLIA WARBLER

BLACK-THROATED GREEN WARBLER

BLACKBURNIAN WARBLER

CHESTNUT-SIDED WARBLER

BAY-BREASTED WARBLER

BLACKPOLL WARBLER

C Fisher

Plate 37: Orioles, Blackbirds and Allies

TROUPIAL *Icterus icterus* 25 cm (10″)
Large size, orange and black plumage, large white wing patch, black tail. **(p. 186)**

NORTHERN ORIOLE *Icterus galbula* 20 cm (8″)
Medium size. **Male:** Orange and black plumage, white wing bar, orange on tail.
Female and Immature: Orange-yellow underparts, white wing bars. **(p. 186)**

YELLOW-SHOULDERED BLACKBIRD *Agelaius xanthomus* 20–23 cm (8–9″)
Adult: Glossy black, yellow epaulets. **Immature** (not depicted): Duller with brown abdomen. **(p. 187)**

BLACK-COWLED ORIOLE *Icterus dominicensis* 20–22 cm (8–8.75″)
Adult: Black plumage; yellow on wings, rump and undertail coverts. **Immature:** Olive green, sometimes black or rust around the neck and head. **(p. 185)**

BOBOLINK *Dolichonyx oryzivorus* 18.5 cm (7.25″)
Breeding Male: Black underparts, white patches on upperparts. **Female and Nonbreeding Male:** Black and buff-colored stripes on crown, buff-colored underparts. **(p. 188)**

SHINY COWBIRD *Molothrus bonariensis* 18–20 cm (7–8″)
Medium size and tail length, conical bill. **Male:** Glossy black. **Female:** Grayish-brown, lighter below; light stripe above eye. **(p. 183)**

GREATER ANTILLEAN GRACKLE *Quiscalus niger* 25–30 cm (10–12″)
Glossy black coloration, V-shaped tail, light iris. **(p. 184)**

Blue background highlights endemic species.

NORTHERN ORIOLE

♂

♀

TROUPIAL

BLACK-
COWLED
ORIOLE

adult

imm.

YELLOW-
SHOULDERED
BLACKBIRD

♀ and
nonbreeding ♂

♂ breeding

BOBOLINK

SHINY
COWBIRD

♀

♂

GREATER
ANTILLEAN
GRACKLE

Plate 38: Tanagers and Finches

STRIPE-HEADED TANAGER *Spindalis zena* 16.5 cm (6.5″)
Male: White stripes on black head. **Female:** Olive-gray upperparts, underparts light with some streaking, faint head stripes. **(p. 175)**

ANTILLEAN EUPHONIA *Euphonia musica* 11.5 cm (4.5″)
Sky blue crown; rump and underpart yellow; forehead yellow. **(p. 174)**

SCARLET TANAGER *Piranga olivacea* 18 cm (7″)
Female, Immature and Winter Male: Yellowish-green plumage, notched tanage bill, dark wings (black in male). **Summer Male:** Scarlet with black wings. **(p. 175)**

PUERTO RICAN TANAGER *Nesospingus speculiferus* 18–20 cm (7–8″)
Adult: Olive brown upperparts, white underparts with dusky stripes on breast, white spot on wing. **Immature** (not depicted): Lacks wing spot, brownish underparts. **(p. 176)**

YELLOW-FRONTED CANARY *Serinus mozambicus* 11.5 cm (4.5″)
Yellow breast, rump and eye stripe; thick bill; dark moustache stripe. **(p. 189)**

SAFFRON FINCH *Sicalis flaveola* 14 cm (5.5″)
Adult: Medium size, yellow plumage, orange crown. **Immature:** Yellowish band across breast. **(p. 182)**

RED SISKIN *Carduelis cucullata* 10 cm (4″)
Small size. **Male:** Black hood, orange-red coloration. **Female:** Dark gray upperparts; light gray underparts; orange rump, wing bars and wash on breast. **(p. 189)**

Blue background highlights endemic species.

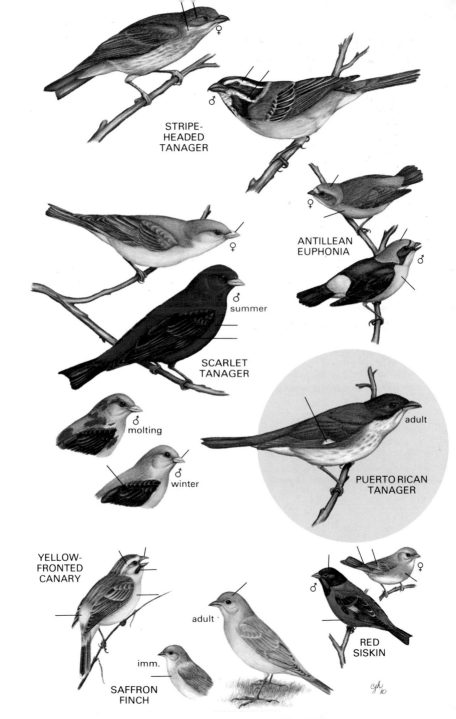

STRIPE-
HEADED
TANAGER

♀

♂

ANTILLEAN
EUPHONIA

♀

♂

SCARLET
TANAGER

♀

♂
summer

♂
molting

♂
winter

PUERTO RICAN
TANAGER

adult

YELLOW-
FRONTED
CANARY

adult

imm.

SAFFRON
FINCH

♂

♀

RED
SISKIN

Plate 39: Finch-like Emberizids

LESSER ANTILLEAN BULLFINCH *Loxigilla noctis* 14–15 cm (5.5–6″)
Male: Black with rufous forehead, throat and undertail coverts. **Female and Immature:** Drab olive with tawny undertail coverts. **(p. 180)**

PUERTO RICAN BULLFINCH *Loxigilla portoricensis* 16.5–19 cm (6.5–7.5″)
Adult: Black with rufous crown, throat and undertail coverts. **Immature:** Dark olive with rufous undertail coverts. **(p. 179)**

BLACK-FACED GRASSQUIT *Tiaris bicolor* 11.5 cm (4.5″)
Male: Black head and underparts, olive upperparts. **Female:** Drab olive plumage, lacks markings. **(p. 181)**

ROSE-BREASTED GROSBEAK *Pheucticus ludovicianus* 19–20 cm (7.5–8″)
Male: Black and white with rose-colored breast; large, pale bill. **Female:** Large size, white crown stripes, heavy bill. **(p. 177)**

YELLOW-FACED GRASSQUIT *Tiaris olivacea* 11.5 cm (4.5″)
Male: Yellow throat and eye stripe, black breast, olive back. **Female and Immature:** Yellowish facial markings. **(p. 181)**

INDIGO BUNTING *Passerina cyanea* 14 cm (5.5″)
Breeding Male: Blue plumage. **Nonbreeding Male:** Similar to female but with traces of blue on wings and tail. **Female:** Dull brown, light breast stripes and wing bars. **(p. 178)**

BLUE GROSBEAK *Guiraca caerulea* 16.5–19 cm (6.5–7.5″)
Male: Blue plumage, rust-colored wing bars. **Female:** Large size, heavy bill, rust-colored wing bars. **(p. 177)**

WHITE-THROATED SPARROW *Zonotrichia albicollis* 17 cm (6.75″)
White throat patch, yellow lores, and a white striped crown. **Winter:** Duller. **(p. 183)**

GRASSHOPPER SPARROW *Ammodramus savannarum* 12.5 cm (5″)
Adult: Yellowish lores, central whitish crown stripe, short tail, buff-colored breast. **Immature:** Lacks yellow lores, small amount of streaking on breast and flanks. **(p. 182)**

DICKCISSEL *Spiza americana* 15–18 cm (6–7″)
Yellowish eye stripe and breast, rust-colored patch at base of wing. **Male:** Black throat patch (reduced or absent in winter). **(p. 178)**

Blue background highlights endemic species.

LESSER
ANTILLEAN
BULLFINCH

♀
♂

PUERTO RICAN
BULLFINCH

adult

imm.

BLACK-FACED
GRASSQUIT

♀
♂
imm.

ROSE-BREASTED
GROSBEAK

♀

YELLOW-FACED
GRASSQUIT

♀
♂

♂

BLUE
GROSBEAK

♀

INDIGO
BUNTING

♂

♀

WHITE-
THROATED
SPARROW

GRASSHOPPER
SPARROW

imm.

adult

DICKCISSEL

♂
summer

♂ winter

Plate 40: Weavers and other Finches

PIN-TAILED WHYDAH *Vidua macroura* ♂ 30–33 cm (12–13″) ♀ 11.5 cm (4.5″)
Breeding Male: Long tail, black and white coloration, red bill. **Female and Nonbreeding Male:** Mottled rusty-brown above, red bill, black and white facial stripes. **Immature** (not depicted): Grayish-brown above, buff-colored eye stripe, bill black with pink base. **(p. 191)**

RED BISHOP *Euplectes orix* 12.5 cm (5″)
Breeding Male: Orangish-red and black plumage. **Female and Nonbreeding Male:** Sparrow-like, buff-colored eye stripe, buff-colored underparts finely striped, finely striped crown. **(p. 192)**

GRASSHOPPER SPARROW (For comparison)
Note central white crown stripe and ochre lores. (See Plate 39) **(p. 182)**

YELLOW-CROWNED BISHOP *Euplectes afer* 11.5–12.5 cm (4.5–5″)
Breeding Male: Yellow and black plumage. **Female and Nonbreeding Male:** Sparrow-like, yellowish eye stripe contrasts sharply with dark brown eye line, *lacks* central white crown stripe. **(p. 192)**

JAVA SPARROW *Padda oryzivora* 15–16.5 cm (6–6.5″)
Adult: Gray plumage, broad pinkish-red bill, white cheek, black crown. **Immature** (not depicted): Duller bill, buff-colored cheek, brownish body. **(p. 198)**

HOUSE SPARROW *Passer domesticus* 15 cm (6″)
Male: Black bib, light cheek. **Female:** Dull brown, streaked back, pale brown eye stripe and underparts. **(p. 190)**

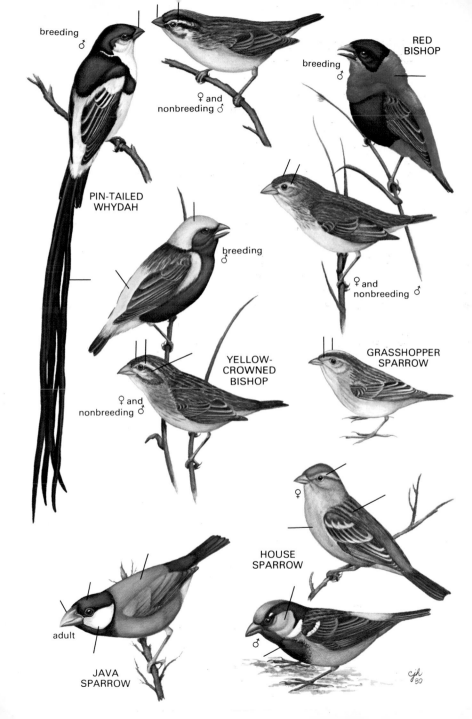

breeding
♂

♀ and
nonbreeding ♂

RED
BISHOP

breeding
♂

PIN-TAILED
WHYDAH

breeding
♂

♀ and
nonbreeding ♂

YELLOW-
CROWNED
BISHOP

♀ and
nonbreeding ♂

GRASSHOPPER
SPARROW

♀

HOUSE
SPARROW

adult

♂

JAVA
SPARROW

cjh
80

Plate 41: Waxbills and Allies

RED AVADAVAT *Amandava amandava*   10 cm (4″)
    Breeding Male: Deep red with white spots. **Female and Nonbreeding Male:**
    Brownish, red uppertail coverts, red bill, white spots on wings, black eye stripe.
    Immature (not depicted): Wing spots buff-colored, lacks red. **(p. 195)**

BLACK-RUMPED WAXBILL *Estrilda troglodytes*   10 cm (4″)
    Adult: Red bill, red line through eye, *lacks* red rump. **Immature:** Pale pinkish bill,
    lacks red eye line. **(p. 194)**

ORANGE-CHEEKED WAXBILL *Estrilda melpoda*   10 cm (4″)
    Adult: Reddish bill, reddish uppertail coverts, orange cheek patch. **Immature** (not
    depicted): Similar to immature Black-rumped Waxbill. **(p. 193)**

NUTMEG MANNIKIN *Lonchura punctulata*   11.5 cm (4.5″)
    Adult: Cinnamon hood, scaled underparts. **Immature:** Blackish bill, light cinnamon
    coloration, lacks adult markings. **(p. 197)**

CHESTNUT MANNIKIN *Lonchura malacca*   11.5 cm (4.5″)
    Adult: Black hood, large black patch on belly, bluish bill. **Immature:** Light brown,
    darker above; lacks adult markings. **(p. 197)**

WARBLING SILVERBILL *Lonchura malabarica*   11.5 cm (4.5″)
    Light brown upperparts, white underparts, white rump, dark tail. **(p. 195)**

BRONZE MANNIKIN *Lonchura cucullata*   10 cm (4″)
    Black hood, grayish-brown back, white belly, flanks with barring. **Immature:** Grayish-
    brown back, lacks other adult markings. **(p. 196)**

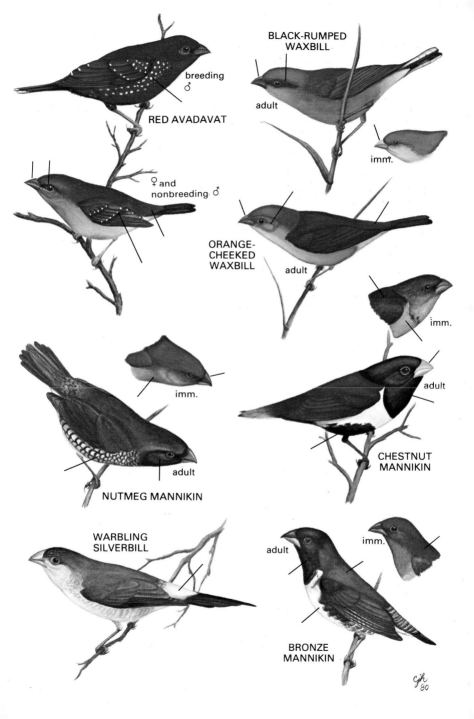

BLACK-RUMPED
WAXBILL
adult
imm.

breeding
♂

RED AVADAVAT

♀ and
nonbreeding ♂

ORANGE-
CHEEKED
WAXBILL
adult

imm.

imm.

adult

NUTMEG MANNIKIN

adult

CHESTNUT
MANNIKIN

WARBLING
SILVERBILL

imm.

adult

BRONZE
MANNIKIN

cjh
80

Species Accounts

Grebes
FAMILY: PODICIPEDIDAE

The grebes are an ancient family of highly aquatic birds. Unlike ducks, they have pointed bills, extremely short tails, and flattened lobes on each toe rather than webbing that connects the toes. Grebes are more adept swimmers than most ducks, being able to dive underwater in a flash, gradually sink out of sight, or submerge until only the head remains above the surface. Grebes in the region are very rarely seen to fly, which has led to the local belief that the birds are flightless. Though they can fly, they must run some distance over the water before taking off; on land they cannot walk, but must push themselves along on their breasts. The downy young are sometimes carried on a parent's back and may remain there during a dive.

LEAST GREBE   Plate 16
Tachybaptus dominicus

Identification: 23–26 cm (9–10.5″). The small size, blackish coloration, thin bill and yellow-orange iris are diagnostic. The white wing patch is a good field mark, but is not always visible.

Local Names: Diver, Helldiver, Diving Dapper, Tigua

Comments: A decidedly uncommon resident, it has been recorded from Puerto Rico, St Thomas, St John, Virgin Gorda, Water Island and St Croix. There are no recent records from the Virgin Islands. The species prefers freshwater cattail swamps where it stays among the vegetation and is extremely difficult to observe.

Voice: A rising, reed-like *week*.

Nesting: One to seven whitish eggs are laid in a floating nest. Breeding occurs through most of the year, but peaks in spring and fall.

Distribution: Throughout the Greater Antilles and Bahamas. Also from Texas through South America.

PIED-BILLED GREBE

Plate 16

Podilymbus podiceps

Identification: 30−38 cm (12−15″). The conical bill is diagnostic. In breeding plumage it has a black throat and a band across the bill.

Local Names: Diver, Helldiver, Diving Dapper, Zaramago

Comments: A common resident in Puerto Rico, but uncommon in the Virgin Islands. It prefers fresh water, but sometimes occurs in brackish lagoons.

Voice: A harsh cackle breaking into a distinctive *kowp, kowp, kowp*, slowing at the end.

Nesting: Two to six whitish eggs are laid in a floating nest. Breeding is concentrated in the spring, but occurs during all seasons.

Distribution: Throughout the Western Hemisphere.

Shearwaters
FAMILY: PROCELLARIIDAE

Shearwaters are highly pelagic species, rarely coming within sight of land except to breed. They have a typical pattern of flight, gliding on long, thin wings over the waves and in the troughs, only periodically issuing a short series of flaps. It is this stiff winged flight, low over the sea's surface, from which the family name is derived and which greatly aids in identification. These birds feed on small fish, squid, and other organisms on or near the surface of the ocean and are equipped with special salt glands which enable them to drink sea water. In fact, shearwaters and storm-petrels are so adapted to the sea that they are obligate salt water drinkers and apparently will die of thirst if only fresh water is available to them.

Even during the breeding season shearwaters are not readily observed, for they nest colonially on remote islets and mountain cliffs, usually in burrows, and are only active about the nest after dark. At night the wailing cries of these birds are conspicuous and the musty odor of the nesting areas often remains long after the birds have gone. Shearwaters in our region are burrow nesters and have legs incapable of supporting their bodies. On the ground they use their wings to help propel them forward on their breasts.

AUDUBON'S SHEARWATER   Plate 3
Puffinus lherminieri

Identification: 30 cm (12"). The rounded tail and distinctive method of flight distinguish it from the dark-backed pelagic terns. Young are dusky gray.

Local Names: Pimleco, Pampero

Comments: The breeding sites in the region include five islets around Culebra and in the Virgin Islands the cays of Saba, Cockroach, Sula and Frenchcap in addition to Round Rock and Tobago Island. It is usually found well out at sea from February to June, but it also occurs rarely in other seasons.

Voice: At night around the nests these birds utter mournful, catlike mews and plaintive, liquid, twittering notes (Pough).

Nesting: The breeding sites in the region are Cayos Matojo, Geniui and del Agua near Culebra and Saba, Cockroach, Sula and Frenchcap Cays, Tobago Island and Round Rock. A single white egg is laid in a burrow in the ground 60−90 cm (2−3') in length or in a cliff crevice. Breeding is from February to May.

Distribution: Throughout most of the West Indies and the warmer oceans of the world.

GREATER SHEARWATER   Plate 1
Puffinus gravis

Identification: 48 cm (19"). This is the largest shearwater in the region. It is generally similar in appearance to the Black-capped Petrel, but in the Greater, the white of the upperparts is much reduced on the hindneck and rump and is absent on the forehead. Its wingbeats are much slower than those of the Audubon's Shearwater or the Black-capped Petrel.

Local Name: Pampero mayor

Comments: Accidental at sea in the region from May to July. There is a record off Puerto Rico (June), a specimen washed up on Culebra (May) and small numbers have been sighted east and west of Anegada (July (2)).

Distribution: This species nests only among the small Tristan de Cunha Islands from November to April and then migrates up the western Atlantic through our region in spring and down the eastern Atlantic in fall.

BLACK-CAPPED PETREL   Plate 3
Pterodroma hasitata

Identification: 35—40 cm (14—16"). The white patches on the
   rump, hindneck and forehead are diagnostic.

Local Name: Diablotín

Comments: An accidental visitor to the seas surrounding
   Puerto Rico and the Virgin Islands. There are only three
   records from Puerto Rico and two fiom the Virgin Islands
   (including fossil remains from St Thomas). The species is
   generally found well out at sea.

Distribution: Breeds in burrows on only a few Caribbean
   islands, though found at sea off many of them, as well as off
   the eastern coast of North America.

Storm-Petrels
FAMILY: HYDROBATIDAE

   Storm-Petrels generally occur far out at sea and are the smallest
of pelagic birds, being little larger than swallows. They characteristically swoop and flutter low over the water, sometimes
pattering the surface with their feet. This habit reputedly led to
their name 'Petrel' from St Peter who doubted whether he could
walk on water. Superstition has it that their presence around ships
portends a storm. They nest in burrows on remote islets and are
unable to walk on land; thus, they must push themselves along
with their wings. In many species one parent tends the nest for
days without food before being relieved by its mate. The Wilson's
Storm-Petrel is believed by some experts to be the most numerous
bird in the world.

LEACH'S STORM-PETREL   Plate 3
Oceanodroma leucorhoa

Identification: 20 cm (8"). This small, dark seabird is
   distinguished from the similar Wilson's Storm-Petrel by its
   longer, more pointed wings, with more sharply angled wrists,
   pale brown wing band, white rump patch and notched tail
   which its feet do not extend beyond. The Leach's Storm-Petrel

is not a follower of boats as is the Wilson's and its flight is more bounding and erratic.

Local Names: Pamperito rabo horquillado, Golondrina de mar

Comments: A rare visitor to Puerto Rico and the Virgin Islands where it is found well offshore, primarily in the spring.

Distribution: Throughout the northern oceans, sometimes wintering well south of the equator.

WILSON'S STORM-PETREL
Plate 3
Oceanites oceanicus

Identification: 18—19 cm (7—7.5"). This small seabird is distinguished from the similar Leach's Storm-Petrel by being blacker, having more rounded wrist joints, and more fluttery but more direct flight with briefer glides. The rump patch is undivided, the tail square, and the feet extend beyond the tail, which is not the case in the Leach's.

Local Names: Mother Carey's Chicken, Pamperito rabo cuadrado, Golondrina de mar

Comments: A rare visitor to both Puerto Rico and the Virgin Islands where it is found well out at sea from April to June (there is one Feb. record). The species is regularly observed following boats, swooping like a swallow over the wake.

Distribution: Breeds in the Antarctic and adjacent islands December to February, migrating far north through most of the oceans of the world in other seasons.

Tropicbirds
FAMILY: PHAETHONTIDAE

As their name implies, the tropicbirds are confined to the tropical and subtropical oceans of the world. Two of the three living species occur in this region and all are characterized by long, streaming central tail feathers in adult birds. Even the tails of young birds appear pointed and aid in distinguishing them from terns. When near shore, their habit of making numerous approaches to the nesting cliffs before landing is distinctive.

Tropicbirds feed primarily on squid and fish out at sea where they dive on them from substantial heights. As their nasal openings are almost entirely blocked (as is the case with all the pelecaniformes), excess salt filtered from the sea water they drink passes through the mouth to the tip of the bill where the droplets are shaken off. Tropicbirds only infrequently alight on the water, and on land they shuffle around on their breasts.

RED-BILLED TROPICBIRD   Plate 2
Phaethon aethereus

Identification: 91−107 cm (36−42″) (including tail plumes), 46−51 cm (18−20″) (without plumes). The red bill, black barring on the back and the long tail plumes are characteristic. Care must be taken not to confuse this species with immature, White-tailed Tropicbirds which also have barring on the back, but do not yet possess elongated tail feathers.

Local Names: Truphit, Trophic, White Bird, Boatswain Bird, Marlinspike, Rabijunco piquicolorado

Comments: A common breeding resident in the Virgin Islands, but uncommon in Puerto Rico. It outnumbers the White-tailed Tropicbird in the cays around Culebra and the northern Virgin Islands. The species is absent outside of the breeding season.

Voice: A shrill, tern-like, *careek* or *kek* (Bond).

Nesting: Rock crevices on small remote cays are typical breeding sites. Nesting begins as early as November and continues through April. A single, heavily spotted egg is laid. Known breeding areas include Culebra's cays, Cockroach Cay, Water Island, and no doubt other small cays in the Virgin Islands.

Distribution: In the Caribbean it is found through the Lesser Antilles northwest to Culebra. The species occurs throughout a great portion of the world's tropical and subtropical oceanic belt.

WHITE-TAILED TROPICBIRD   Plate 2
Phaethon lepturus

Identification: 81 cm (32″) (including tail plumes), 37− 40 cm (15−16″) (without plumes). The long tail feathers and black markings on the mantle are distinctive. The immature has a barred back and short tail.

Local Names: Yellow-billed Tropicbird, Trophic, Truphit, White Bird, Boatswain Bird, Marlinspike, Long-tail, Rabijunco coliblanco, Chirre de cola blanca, Gaviota caracolera

Comments: A common breeding resident around sea cliffs and rocky cays in Puerto Rico and the Virgin Islands from March to July. However, a few birds have been seen as early as December and as late as August. After the breeding season they move out to sea. The species is easily seen among the Virgin Islands, but in Puerto Rico it is only common at the Guajataca cliffs on the north coast and at Mona Island. It is less common around Culebra and also can be seen infrequently at Fort San Cristobal in San Juan, Punta Salinas, Las Croabas, the Cabo Rojo Lighthouse, and east of Tallaboa.

Voice: A raspy *crick-et*.

Nesting: A cavity in a rocky crevice on a cliff by the sea is the typical nest site. A single pinkish egg, heavily splotched with brown, is laid. March through June is the principal breeding season.

Distribution: Throughout the West Indies and the warmer oceans of the world.

Boobies
FAMILY: SULIDAE

Boobies are long-billed, sleek plumaged birds that wander well out to sea from their colonial roosting and nesting areas. Their leisurely flapping and gliding flight, low over the water, is characteristic, as are their spectacular dives into the sea in pursuit of fish and squid.

MASKED BOOBY   Plate 2
Sula dactylatra

Identification: 81−91 cm (32−36″). Very similar to the Red-footed Booby but distinguished at a distance by its dark tail. Immatures have brownish-gray plumage.

Local Names: Blue-faced Booby, White Booby, Whistling Booby, Boba enmascarada

Comments: An extremely local resident in Puerto Rico and the Virgin Islands where the species is generally seen only on its breeding grounds and the adjacent seas. Though resident on Monito, it has yet to be observed from Puerto Rico proper. In the Virgin Islands it is found off St Thomas, at Cockroach Cay, Sula Cay, and near the Tobagos.

Nesting: One to two white eggs are laid in a scrape near a cliff face. Egg laying appears to have two peaks annually; one from January to June and the second from September to November. The only breeding areas in the region are Alcarraza off Culebra, Monito (PR), and Cockroach and Sula Cays (VI).

Distribution: Puerto Rico, the Virgin Islands and only a few other localities in the Caribbean. The species occurs widely through the tropical and subtropical oceans of the world.

BROWN BOOBY   Plate 2
Sula leucogaster

Identification: 71−76 cm (28−30″). The entirely brown head and upperparts sharply demarcated from the white belly and abdomen are certain field marks. Young birds are light brown on the belly and abdomen.

Local Names: Booby, White-bellied Booby, Boba prieta

Comments: A common permanent resident in Puerto Rico and the Virgin Islands and locally abundant near its nesting grounds. It is the most common of the three boobies in our region and the most likely to be seen from shore; it often rests on buoys or rocky cliffs. Brown Boobies are seen virtually everywhere in the Virgin Islands, but in Puerto Rico the best places to look for the bird are at Cabo Rojo Lighthouse and Las Croabas.

Voice: A hoarse *kak*.

Nesting: One to two white eggs are laid in a scrape on the ground. The birds usually nest in groups on remote islands. The breeding season is prolonged and varies as to period of occurrence from year to year, but generally peaks in winter.

Distribution: Throughout the West Indies and the warmer oceans of the world.

RED-FOOTED BOOBY   Plate 2
Sula sula

Identification: 66—76 cm (26—30″). The white hindparts of the brown color phase are diagnostic. The white-phased bird is distinguished from the Masked Booby at a distance by its white tail. Immatures are sooty brown, paler below, sometimes with a slightly darker band across the breast.

Local Names: White Booby, Red-faced Booby, Tree Booby, Boba patirroja

Comments: A locally abundant permanent resident near its nesting grounds in Puerto Rico and the Virgin Islands, but rare elsewhere. In Puerto Rican territory the species is abundant on the islands of Desecheo, Mona and Monito. In the Virgin Islands the Redfoot presently nests on Dutchcap and Frenchcap Cays.

Voice: A guttural *ga-ga-ga-ga*, of variable length, which trails off. Also a distinctive squawk.

Nesting: One to two white eggs are laid in a stick nest in a tree or bush. Egg laying peaks in March and April and again from August to December. Red-footed Boobies nest in colonies on the remote islands mentioned above (the Desecheo Island colony has been drastically reduced by predation from introduced monkeys). A few pairs have recently begun to nest on Cayo Geniqui off Culebra.

Distribution: Throughout the West Indies and the tropical and subtropical oceans of the world.

Pelicans
FAMILY: PELECANIDAE

Pelicans are large water birds, the resident species preferring coastal waters, but others inhabiting large, inland lakes. The Brown Pelican, with its 2 m (6½ ft) wingspread, is actually the smallest of living forms. These birds are often seen in small flocks flying just above the wave crests with wingbeats in perfect unison. It is locally believed that Brown Pelicans have a suicidal tendency and hang themselves intentionally in the forks of tree branches. Actually, this mortality is no doubt the result of the clumsiness of these large creatures, particularly young birds, among the slender branches of the mangroves rather than an intentional act on their part.

AMERICAN WHITE PELICAN   Plate 2
Pelecanus erythrorhynchos

Identification: 125–165 cm (50–65″). The distinctive yellow bill of this huge, white bird makes it unmistakable.

Local Name: Pelícano blanco

Comments: Accidental. Known from a specimen and sight record from Puerto Rico (Nov., Mar.) and a sight record from Vieques (Feb.).

Distribution: Western North America wintering into Central America and Cuba.

BROWN PELICAN   Plate 2
Pelecanus occidentalis

Identification: 107–137 cm (42–54″). The unusual bill and dark coloration of this large bird make it unmistakable. The back of the head and nape of the neck are reddish-brown in adults in breeding plumage. Immatures are an overall grayish-brown.

Local Names: Pelícano pardo, Alcatraz

Comments: A common resident along protected shorelines in Puerto Rico and the Virgin Islands most of the year, particularly in winter when North American migrants augment local numbers. Some local pelicans, in addition to the North American subspecies, appear to leave the region to nest elsewhere.

Voice: Adults are silent.

Nesting: Brown Pelicans nest colonially and generally construct stick nests in trees in which two to four white eggs are laid. Breeding dates vary from year to year and may occur during any season. Only one regularly used breeding colony is known in Puerto Rican waters and that is at Cayo Conejo near

Vieques. However, nesting periodically occurs at La Parguera, Montalva Bay and Añasco Bay. In the Virgin Islands, pelican nesting has been recorded from St Croix, Green Cay, Buck Island, St John, Lovango Cay, Congo Cay, Whistling Cay, Dutchcap Cay, and Little Tobago.

Distribution: Throughout the West Indies and most of the coasts of North, Central, and South America where water temperatures are warm.

Cormorants
FAMILY: PHALACROCORACIDAE

Cormorants are large, long-necked birds with hooked bills. They inhabit coastal waters or inland lakes. Those of the Northern Hemisphere are primarily black, each species having distinctive coloration and form to its gular pouch. Cormorants swim with their heads cocked up and their bodies low in the water, sometimes sinking so that only the head and neck are above the surface. They dive expertly in pursuit of fish, but must regularly perch in the sun with wings spread to dry their feathers which otherwise become waterlogged.

DOUBLE-CRESTED CORMORANT   Plate 16
Phalacrocorax auritus

Identification: 74—89 cm (29—35"). This cormorant's large size, totally black appearance, hooked bill, and habit of sitting with its wings spread, are important characteristics. It is a larger bodied bird than the Olivaceous Cormorant which is accidental in the region and differentiating these species should be left to experts. Immature cormorants are dark above and lighter below.

Local Name: Cormorán crestado

Comments: Unknown from the region prior to 1973, there have been dozens of observations of cormorants known to be either Double-cresteds (one photographed and three specimens), or not verified to species. Double-crested sightings are increasing rapidly, and the bird's status may soon warrant change from a rare visitor to an uncommon one.

Voice: Seldom heard off the breeding grounds. A variety of deep guttural grunts.

Distribution: Irregular in Puerto Rico and the Virgin Islands, but breeds in Cuba, the Bahamas, and occurs widely in North America through Mexico and Honduras.

OLIVACEOUS CORMORANT   Plate 16
Phalacrocorax olivaceus

Identification: 63–69 cm (25–27″). In the field it is nearly identical to the Double-crested Cormorant and due to the rarity of these birds, positive identification should be left to experts. The most noticeable field mark of the Olivaceous is its decidedly smaller bulk; it also has a thinner bill and a less orange gular area, which in breeding condition is edged with white.

Local Name: Cormorán oliváceo

Comments: There are three reports from Puerto Rico and two from Peter Island (Virgin Islands), all but one of these occurring since 1974. The bird is accidental in the region, though if the recent increase in sightings continues, it may soon become a rare or uncommon visitor.

Voice: A pig-like grunt.

Distribution: Breeds in the West Indies on Cuba and the Bahamas, straying elsewhere. Also from the extreme south central USA through Central and South America.

Frigatebirds
FAMILY: FREGATIDAE

The most accomplished of marine aerialists, frigatebirds have the largest wings relative to their weight of any birds (the skeleton weighs only about 250 g (8 oz)). Frigatebirds cannot dive or land on the ocean as do most other seabirds. They therefore rely on their speed and agility in the air to rob other seabirds of their prey, or snatch food items from the surface waters with their long bills. Frigatebirds are confined to tropical and subtropical seas.

MAGNIFICENT FRIGATEBIRD   Plate 2
Fregata magnificens

Identification: 94—104 cm (37—41″). The long, forked tail, slender wings (2.5 m (7½ ft)), and the bird's habit of floating motionless in the air make it easily identifiable. Males appear entirely black in the field, females have a white breast, and immatures have an entirely white head and breast.

Local Names: Man-o-war, Hurricane Bird, Weather Bird, Scissorstail, Cobbler, Tijereta, Tijerilla, Rabijunco

Comments: This seabird is a common permanent resident in Puerto Rico and the Virgin Islands. It occurs over bays and inshore waters, sometimes penetrating well inland.

Voice: Silent except for guttural noises during courtship.

Nesting: A single white egg is laid in a stick nest which is normally built in a low bush. Frigatebirds will not tolerate disturbances while incubating and thus are confined to the most remote cays and islets. The only nesting ground for this species in Puerto Rican territory is Monito Island. In the Virgin Islands colonies are known from Tobago Island, Anegada, and George Dog (Dutchcap's colony is defunct). Egg laying peaks from October to December, but developing young are on the nest for so long that colonies are virtually always active.

Distribution: Throughout the tropical and subtropical waters of the Western Hemisphere and around the Cape Verde Islands.

Herons, Egrets and Bitterns
FAMILY: ARDEIDAE

Most of the members of this large, cosmopolitan family of graceful birds wade in swamps and marshes in search of fish, frogs and other prey which they spear with their long, pointed bills. Undigested matter is regurgitated in the form of pellets. The white egrets are best distinguished in the field by differences in size and coloration of the bill and legs. Bitterns inhabit dense vegetation and often 'freeze' with their bills pointed upward using their camouflaged plumage to avoid detection. All birds in the heron family fly with the head drawn back and the neck in the form of an 'S', a valuable field characteristic.

GREAT BLUE HERON   Plate 7
Ardea herodias

Identification: 107—132 cm (42—52″). As the largest heron in the region, this primarily gray bird is hardly mistakable. The white color form (previously considered a separate species and called the Great White Heron) is distinguished from the Great Egret by its larger size and yellowish legs.

Local Names: Blue Gaulin, Gray Gaulin, Arsnicker, Morgan, Garzón azulado, Garzón cenizo, Garzón ceniciento, Garzón blanco (white form)

Comments: Decidedly uncommon in the summer in Puerto Rico and the Virgin Islands when it apparently retreats to remote areas to breed, but the rest of the year, when migrant and wintering birds augment the resident populations, it is fairly common. It can be encountered in almost any salt or freshwater pond or lagoon where it is usually found standing motionless waiting for a prospective meal to swim by. There are only five records of the white phase from Puerto Rico and one from the Virgin Islands.

Voice: A deep throaty croak like a large frog *guarr*.

Nesting: Known to nest on St Thomas, Green Cay, St Croix and Anegada, but no nest has yet been found in Puerto Rico. The nest is a platform of sticks located in a remote swamp. From two to four bluish eggs are laid. Breeding occurs in the spring and summer.

Distribution: Throughout the West Indies. Also through North and Central America to the northern coast of South America.

GREEN-BACKED HERON   Plate 8
Butorides striatus

Identification: 40—48 cm (16—19″). Distinguished from other herons by its small size, short neck, generally dark coloration and orangish legs.

Local Names: Green Heron, Least Pond Gaulin, Little Gaulin, Water Witch, Poor Joe, Bitlin, Gaulching, Martinete

Comments: A common year-round resident in Puerto Rico and the Virgin Islands at any body of water from a puddle to the border of a large lagoon. Its numbers are minimally augmented in winter by migrants from North America. This heron usually perches motionless on a snag low over the water waiting for unwary prey to approach. When surprised, the Green-backed Heron flies off, often emitting its characteristic call note.

Voice: Upon being flushed, it calls a distinctive, piercing *skow*. When undisturbed the bird issues a less irritating series of *kek*, *kak*, or *que* notes.

Nesting: Green-backed Herons usually nest singly, though sometimes in scattered colonies, often with other herons. Wooded swamps provide ideal habitat and even coconut palms are sometimes used. A platform of twigs of variable height in a tree or bush, makes up the nest and three greenish-blue eggs form a normal clutch. Breeding occurs primarily in the spring, but nests have been found during other seasons.

Distribution: Throughout the West Indies and much of temperate North America south to the northern tip of South America.

LITTLE BLUE HERON   Plate 7
Egretta caerulea

Identification: 56–71 cm (22–28″). Identified by its medium size and uniform dark gray appearance. Initially the plumage of the immature is entirely white and the bird strongly resembles the Snowy Egret, but it can be distinguished from the latter by the pale gray base of the bill, lack of yellow on the lores, and its greenish legs. Toward the end of its first year, the immature becomes mottled with the dark feathers of the adult plumage.

Local Names: Blue Gaulin, White Gaulin (immature), Garza azul, Garza blanca (immature), Garza pinta

Comments: A common resident in Puerto Rico and the Virgin Islands. It occurs in freshwater swamps, mangrove lagoons and virtually all other bodies of calm, shallow water.

Voice: A croaking, very throaty *gruuh*.

Nesting: Nesting is usually colonial in a wooded swamp. A platform is constructed high in a tree with two to four blue eggs forming a clutch. The breeding season runs from February to July.

Distribution: Throughout the West Indies. Also the eastern USA and southward through much of South America.

CATTLE EGRET   Plate 7
Bubulcus ibis

Identification: 48—64 cm (19—25 ″). Identified by its relatively small size and short, thick yellowish bill, it is the only heron of the uplands. The Great Egret, which is similar in appearance to the Cattle Egret, is an aquatic heron and is a much larger bird. Its bill is also yellower and longer. During the breeding season the Cattle Egret's feet turn from black to red, a tan wash appears on the crown, breast and upper back, the eyes turn red and the bill takes on a reddish tint.

Local Names: Cattle Gaulin, Garza del ganado, Garza africana

Comments: An abundant resident of Puerto Rico and common in the Virgin Islands. It occurs in pastures and fields wherever there is livestock or tractors plowing the soil. At dawn and dusk these herons fly in formation to and from their roosts which are usually in mangrove swamps or on mangrove islands. While other herons are almost never found away from water, the Cattle Egret is seldom found in it except to drink. This egret was first recorded in Puerto Rico in 1952 and in the Virgin Islands in 1953, the result of an unusual range expansion of the species through the Americas. Locally it is erroneously believed to have been specifically imported to alleviate an epidemic of ticks on cattle.

Voice: Much guttural squawking around the breeding colony.

Nesting: Nesting is colonial on mangrove cays or in other wooded areas near water. The nest is a platform of twigs and contains two to four bluish-white eggs. Breeding is primarily in spring and early summer, but also occurs in other seasons.

Distribution: Widespread in temperate and tropical portions of the world.

REDDISH EGRET   Plate 7
Egretta rufescens

Identification: 69—81 cm (27—32″). The black-tipped bill, flesh
colored at the base, is the most conspicuous field mark in either
the dark or white color phase. Other important field
characteristics are the ruffled appearance of the neck feathers
and the bird's habit of pursuing its prey so energetically at times
it appears to be dancing about in the water.

Local Names: Gaulin, Garza rojiza

Comments: Extremely rare in the region. Of the five records for
Puerto Rico, three are from Cartagena Lagoon. There is one
record for St Croix. The preferred habitat of this species is
shallow, protected coastal areas.

Voice: Squawks and croaks.

Distribution: A stray in Puerto Rico, the Virgin Islands and
Jamaica, but a breeding resident in Hispaniola, Cuba and the
Bahamas. Very local along portions of the southern USA and
Mexico. A migrant south to Venezuela.

GREAT EGRET   Plate 7
Casmerodius albus

Identification: 89—107 cm (35—42″). It is identified by its large
size, yellow bill and black legs. The white form of the Great
Blue Heron is somewhat larger and has yellow legs. The Cattle
Egret vaguely resembles the Great Egret in coloration, but it
is a much smaller, chunkier bird and prefers drier habitat.

Local Names: White Gaulin, White Morgan, Common Egret,
American Egret, Garza real, Garzón blanco

Comments: A fairly common resident in Puerto Rico, but
generally uncommon among the larger Virgin Islands and rare
or absent from the smaller ones. It is most abundant in the
swamps and lagoons of southwestern Puerto Rico, but occasionally can be found in most of the larger fresh and saltwater
swamp areas (excluding reservoirs).

Voice: A hoarse, throaty croak sounding like the winding of a
large clock.

Nesting: The Great Egret nests in wooded swamps among other
species of herons. St Croix is the only one of the Virgin Islands

where this species is known to have bred. The nest is a platform of sticks with two to five blue eggs. Breeding occurs principally in the spring, but is not confined to that season.

Distribution: Widespread in the New and Old World.

SNOWY EGRET   Plate 7
Egretta thula

Identification: 51—71 cm (20—28 ″). Distinguished by its black legs and golden toes, as well as its thin, pure black bill and yellow lores. Immature Snowies have a greenish-yellow band down the back of the legs.

Local Names: White Gaulin, Garza blanca

Comments: A fairly common resident in Puerto Rico and St Croix and generally uncommon among the remainder of the larger Virgin Islands. It prefers freshwater swamps, but can also be found around saltwater lagoons. Though uncommon or rare at most water bodies, this species often congregates in a few preferred localities.

Voice: A guttural *garr*, higher pitched and more raspy than the Great Egret.

Nesting: Breeds in Puerto Rico and the larger Virgin Islands. Nests are generally placed in mangrove trees that are in open, wet areas, usually on islets. Snowies breed primarily in spring in colonies with other heron species and lay two to five greenish-blue eggs in a flat nest of sticks.

Distribution: Throughout the West Indies and most of the New World.

TRICOLORED HERON   Plate 7
Egretta tricolor

Identification: 61—71 cm (24—28 ″). This heron is gray in overall appearance and is distinguished by its white belly and undertail coverts.

Local Names: Louisiana Heron, Gaulin, Switching-neck, Garza pechiblanca

Comments: A common resident of mangrove swamps and saltwater lagoons in Puerto Rico, rare in similar habitat on the larger of the Virgin Islands. It occurs infrequently in freshwater swamps.

Voice: A throaty *guarr* similar to that of the Snowy Egret.

Nesting: Nests in Puerto Rico and the larger Virgin Islands, often in colonies with other heron species. The nest is a platform of sticks and usually contains three to four bluish eggs. Breeding peaks in the spring as is the case with other herons.

Distribution: Throughout the Greater Antilles, Bahamas and a few other West Indian islands. Also much of temperate coastal North America south to northern South America.

BLACK-CROWNED NIGHT-HERON   Plate 8
Nycticorax nycticorax

Identification: 58—71 cm (23—28″). Adults are identified by their black crown and back, and their white face, underparts and head plumes. Immatures are entirely brown and can be distinguished from the very similar young Yellow-crowned Night-Heron by their browner appearance, larger white flecks and thinner bill. In flight only the feet of Black-crowned Night-Herons extend beyond the tail.

Local Names: Night Gaulin, Crabcatcher, Yaboa real

Comments: An uncommon and local resident on Puerto Rico and St Croix, it is rare on the other larger Virgin Islands. This species is, however, locally common at Cartagena Lagoon and Boquerón Refuge in southwestern Puerto Rico. Wintering migrants occur from North America. Freshwater swamps are the preferred habitat of this nocturnal heron though it is found at times in brackish water lagoons and salt ponds.

Voice: A distinctive *quark*, heard before sunup and after sundown.

Nesting: A bulky nest of twigs is built well up in a tree in a swamp or on a cay. Two to five pale greenish-blue eggs are laid. These herons nest colonially, from December to June.

Distribution: Widespread in the New and Old World.

YELLOW-CROWNED NIGHT-HERON   Plate 8
Nycticorax violaceus

Identification: 56–71 cm (22–28″). The gray underparts and
black and whitish head markings clearly identify the adult.
Immatures are very similar to young Black-crowned Night-
Herons, but can be distinguished by their heavier bill, grayer
plumage with smaller white flecks, and longer legs which extend
further beyond the tail in flight.

Local Names: Night Gaulin, Gray Gaulin, Crabcatcher,
Crabeater, Yaboa común

Comments: A common permanent resident in Puerto Rico and
fairly common in the Virgin Islands. Local birds are joined in
the winter by a few migrants from North America. The Yellow-
crowned Night-Heron is primarily nocturnal, but at times is
fairly active during the day. In the Virgin Islands this heron
is almost exclusively a denizen of mangrove swamps, though
it is sometimes found in dry thickets away from water. In Puerto
Rico it also occurs in freshwater habitats.

Voice: A distinctive *quark* very similar to that of the Black-crown.
It is regularly heard before sunup and after sundown.

Nesting: A bulky platform of twigs is constructed in a tree,
sometimes a good distance from water. Two to four pale
greenish-blue eggs are laid. Breeding occurs principally from
January through the spring.

Distribution: Throughout the West Indies. Also the eastern and
central USA south into coastal portions of South America.

LEAST BITTERN   Plate 8
Ixobrychus exilis

Identification: 28–35 cm (11–14″). Distinguished by its small
size, generally rusty coloration and the cream-colored patch
on the upper wing which is a good field mark in both perching
and flying birds.

Local Names: Bitlin, Gaulin, Martinetito

Comments: A fairly common resident in Puerto Rico, but now
very rare in the Virgin Islands, occurring only on the larger
islands. It is so well camouflaged that unless flushed, it often

goes unnoticed. Freshwater swamps with cattails are the prime habitat of the Least Bittern; however, it is occasionally seen along mangrove channels.

Voice: *Koo-koo-koo-koo*, almost a coo, the first syllable often higher than the others and the call accelerating slightly. Also a loud, harsh *kack*.

Nesting: The nest is of twigs or swamp plants above standing water and two to five bluish-white eggs are laid. Breeding occurs from April to July.

Distribution: Throughout the Greater Antilles and northern Bahamas and much of North, Central, and South America.

AMERICAN BITTERN   Plate 8
Botaurus lentiginosus

Identification: 58—61 cm (23—24″). The black neck mark and the habit of pointing the bill upward are good characteristics. In flight, the black wing tips are distinctive. Immature night herons are similar in appearance to this bittern, but are grayer and lack black on the neck and wing tips.

Local Names: Stake-driver, Shide-poke, Yaboa americana

Comments: An extremely rare winter visitor in Puerto Rico from September to April; there are single records from St Croix, and Virgin Gorda and two from St John. The species is known only from swampy freshwater habitats.

Voice: A peculiar pumping sound; *oong-ká-chunk*!

Distribution: Throughout the Bahamas and Greater Antilles and throughout North and Central America.

Ibises and Spoonbills
FAMILY: THRESKIORNITHIDAE

Ibises and spoonbills are medium-sized gregarious waterbirds of shallow coastal lagoons. Ibises have distinctive decurved bills while bills of spoonbills are spatulate. Both ibises and spoonbills fly with their necks outstretched.

GLOSSY IBIS   Plate 9
Plegadis falcinellus

Identification: 56—64 cm (22—25 "). The entirely dark coloration and long, decurved bill characterize this ibis.

Local Names: Ibis lustroso, Cigüeña, Coco prieto

Comments: Extremely local and irregular in Puerto Rico where it may breed, and extremely rare on St Croix and St Thomas. Some years it is common the year round in southwest Puerto Rico, particularly Cartagena Lagoon, though it is rare in the east, while other years it may not be observed at all.

Voice: A grunting sound followed by four bleating notes (Pough).

Distribution: Throughout the West Indies, though rare in the Lesser Antilles. Widespread in the New and Old World.

WHITE IBIS   Plate 9
Eudocimus albus

Identification: 56—71 cm (22—28 "). The long, decurved bill of this fairly large white bird makes it unmistakable. In flight the outstretched neck and the black wing tips aid in identification. Young are a uniform brown with a white belly and rump.

Local Names: Ibis blanco, Coco blanco

Comments: Accidental in Puerto Rico where it is known from four records including a specimen from 1900; it is unknown in the Virgin Islands.

Distribution: Throughout the Greater Antilles and Bahamas and the southeastern USA to northern South America.

ROSEATE SPOONBILL   Plate 9
Ajaia ajaja

Identification: 66—81 cm (26—32 "). The pink coloration and extraordinary spatulate bill are diagnostic. Immatures are almost entirely white, but display some pink.

Local Name: Espátula rosada

Comments: Accidental in the region; there are four records from Puerto Rico and one from Anegada.

Distribution: Cuba, Hispaniola and Great Inagua (accidental elsewhere in the West Indies). Also the extreme southern USA south through most of South America.

Flamingos
FAMILY: PHOENICOPTERIDAE

The flamingos form a unique family. Feeding with their heads upside down they filter small mollusks, crustaceans and other organisms from shallow lagoons, swallowing them with their heads still inverted, the water being strained out by the bird's specifically adapted tongue and bill. They are very gregarious and wary. In flight the neck is extended.

GREATER FLAMINGO   Plate 9
Phoenicopterus ruber

Identification: 107—122 cm (42—48 "). The rosy coloration, long legs and neck, and the strangely curved bill are unmistakable.

Local Names: American Flamingo, Fillymingo, Roseate Flamingo, Flamenco americano

Comments: Today flamingos are only accidental visitors to this region though formerly they were apparent residents, having been reported from Boquerón and Loíza River in Puerto Rico proper, the islands of Vieques and Culebra and in the Virgin Islands from St Thomas, St Croix, and Anegada. Indeed, certain localities in Culebra, St Thomas, and Anegada bear the name of this bird. Four juveniles and one adult bird visited the Cabo Rojo salt flats for approximately six months during 1986—87. These were believed to be strays from the Dominican Republic. Two died from colliding with power lines. There are also recent records of single, reputedly wild birds from St Thomas and Vieques. Care must be taken in distinguishing wild from escaped individuals. These recent sightings suggest the species may be on the verge of recolonizing this portion of its former range. The species frequents shallow lagoons and coastal estuaries.

Distribution: Throughout the Bahamas, Cuba, Hispaniola, the north coast of South America and its offshore islands. Also Florida, Yucatán, and the Galapagos Islands.

Ducks, Geese and Swans
FAMILY: ANATIDAE

The birds of this large, aquatic family are best treated by discussing the seven subfamilies that occur in the region.

Swans — In this region these very large birds, with entirely white plumage, dip for food with their long necks. They occur accidentally.

Geese — Are intermediate between ducks and swans in size and the length of their necks. They are the most terrestrial subfamily, often feeding on grains in meadows and uplands. They occur accidentally.

Whistling-Ducks — The largest of the ducks, they are nocturnal, often grazing in wet, grassy meadows, or dipping for food in shallow ponds. In flight their long feet trail beyond the tail, and the head is drooped making them easily recognizable.

Dabbling Ducks — This is the best represented subfamily in the region. Dabblers only feed in shallow waters as they cannot dive, and only tip their heads beneath the surface leaving their tails pointed upwards. On the other hand, dabblers can instantly take to the air when disturbed. Most have colorful iridescent patches on the secondaries referred to as the speculum. These patches are excellent aids in identification.

Diving Ducks — These ducks frequent areas of deep open water often diving and swimming to cover rather than taking flight when molested. Their feet are set far back on the body forcing them to run over the water's surface in order to take flight.

Stiff-tailed Ducks — These are small, but chunky ducks with short necks and stiff tails that are frequently held erect and are valuable aids in identification. They dive expertly and can rarely be forced to fly.

Mergansers — Accidental in the region, these ducks have modified bills with serrate edges and a hook at the tip, adapted for catching fish. Both species that occur here are crested.

TUNDRA SWAN
Cygnus columbianus

Plate 16

Identification: 122—140 cm (48—55″). This huge, white bird cannot be confused with any other in the region.

Local Name: Cisne silbador

Comments: Accidental. Single specimens from Puerto Rico (16 Dec. 1944) and St Thomas (31 Dec. 1983) represent the only records for the region.

Distribution: Northern North America wintering into the southern USA.

SNOW GOOSE
Chen caerulescens

Plate 16

Identification: 58—71 cm (23—28″). There are two distinct color phases. One is entirely white with black primaries. The dark phase is bluish-gray with a white head.

Local Names: Blue Goose (dark form), Gee, Ganso blanco, Ganso prieto (dark form)

Comments: Accidental in Puerto Rico and St Croix. Known from the latter locality only by a bone fragment and the former by a few reports of hunters. Goose sightings by hunters occur fairly regularly, but few have enough detail for species identification.

Distribution: Accidental in the West Indies. Widespread in North America.

FULVOUS WHISTLING-DUCK
Dendrocygna bicolor

Plates 17, 18

Identification: 46—51 cm (18—20″). The tawny coloration, thin white stripe along the side when sitting, and the white rump are diagnostic.

Local Names: Fulvous Tree Duck, Chiriría amarillenta, Pato silvón, Chiriría dominicana, Yaguaza dominicana

Comments: Uncommon in Puerto Rico, accidental in the Virgin Islands. The Fulvous Whistling-Duck has recently extended its range to Puerto Rico and is probably now a breeding resident. It is more of a swamp bird than the other whistling-ducks and like them is most active at night.

Voice: A squealing whistle *puteów* ⌐.

Nesting: Nest not yet recorded in Puerto Rico. Elsewhere 12 to 15 buff-white eggs are laid in a shallow bowl of grass or reeds in a marsh.

Distribution: The species occurs in five distinct populations: 1. southern USA to Mexico and the West Indies; 2. northern South America; 3. south-central South America; 4. East Africa; 5. India.

BLACK-BELLIED WHISTLING-DUCK   Plate 19
Dendrocygna autumnalis

Identification: 46—53 cm (18—21″). The large white wing patch and black belly are excellent field marks. In flight the upper sides of the wings are principally white. The female is duller.

Local Names: Black-bellied Tree Duck, Chiriría pinta

Comments: Accidental in Puerto Rico and St Croix though apparently once more common on the former island where it reportedly bred.

Voice: A characteristic shrill, chattering whistle (Pough).

Nesting: There is a single report from Puerto Rico of a nest with two eggs and two young in a hollow tree in February, 1922.

Distribution: Accidental through the Lesser Antilles to Puerto Rico. Also the southern USA south to central South America.

WEST INDIAN WHISTLING-DUCK   Plates 17, 18
Dendrocygna arborea

Identification: 48—56 cm (19—22″). The deep brown coloration and the white abdomen with black markings are diagnostic.

Local Names: Whistler, West Indian Tree Duck, Mangrove Duck, Night Duck, Chiriría antillana, Yaguaza, Pato nocturno

Comments: Once a common breeding resident in the region, now very rare in Puerto Rico and the Virgin Islands, though recently it has been reported regularly around Humacao (Puerto Rico).

The species is primarily nocturnal and is most regularly observed in early evening. It visits both fresh and saline water bodies, but is said to roost, feed and nest in trees in the hills.

Voice: It is from this duck's shrilly whistled *chiriria* that its common name in Spanish is derived.

Nesting: A cluster of palm fronds or a cavity in a tree are typical nest sites. Four to fourteen white eggs are laid. Apparently the nesting season is variable.

Distribution: Practically confined to the Greater Antilles and the Bahamas.

MALLARD   Plate 19
Anas platyrhynchos

Identification: 51−71 cm (20−28″). The green head and white neck ring of the male are characteristic. Mergansers have green heads like the male Mallard, but their bills are distinctly hooked at the tip. Female Mallards are a mottled brown and most easily distinguished by their blue speculum with white borders.

Local Name: Pato inglés

Comments: An extremely rare winter visitor to Puerto Rico and St Croix. On both islands it is often difficult to determine whether recent sightings are not of Mallards released locally.

Distribution: Rare in Cuba and accidental elsewhere in the West Indies. Widespread in North and Central America, Eurasia and parts of Africa (introduced elsewhere).

AMERICAN BLACK DUCK   Plate 19
Anas rubripes

Identification: 53−64 cm (21−25″). The dark brown coloration and purple speculum are important field marks. Female Mallards are similar to American Black Ducks but are a lighter brown and have white bands on either side of a blue speculum. In flight the underwings are white.

Local Name: Pato oscuro

Comments: Accidental. Known by three specimens taken in winter in Puerto Rico.

Distribution: Accidental in the West Indies. Throughout eastern North America.

NORTHERN PINTAIL   Plates 17, 18
Anas acuta

Identification: ♂ 69−74 cm (27−29″), ♀ 54−56 cm (21.5−22″). The male's brown head pattern and long pointed tail are distinctive. The female is mottled brown and can be identified by its noticeably pointed tail and long, slender neck. The speculum is rust colored.

Local Name: Pato pescuecilargo

Comments: An uncommon, but regular winter visitor to Puerto Rico and rare on St Thomas, St John, and St Croix. Pintails are one of the first ducks to arrive in the region, occurring as early as September and usually leaving by April. These birds prefer fresh water, but are sometimes found in salt ponds.

Distribution: Throughout the West Indies and through North America to northern South America. Also Eurasia and northern Africa.

WHITE-CHEEKED PINTAIL   Plates 17, 18
Anas bahamensis

Identification: 38−48 cm (15−19″). The red bill mark and white cheek are diagnostic. The speculum is green.

Local Names: Brass Wing, Brass Wing Teal, Summer Duck, Whitehead, Whitethroat, White-jaw, Bahama Duck, Bahama Pintail, Pato quijada colorada

Comments: A common resident in the Virgin Islands and fairly common very locally in Puerto Rico. It has greatly declined on the latter island and is now virtually confined to salt ponds on Culebra and Vieques and the swamps east of Ceiba, Naguabo and Humacao.

Nesting: A scrape is made on dry land and concealed under a clump of vegetation, sometimes a great distance from water, and five to twelve light tan eggs are laid. Breeding has been recorded during all months of the year and is variable on an annual basis. However, it appears to be heaviest from November to April.

Distribution: Throughout the West Indies with the exception of the southern Lesser Antilles. Also much of South America.

GREEN-WINGED TEAL Plates 17, 18
Anas crecca

Identification: 33−39 cm (13−15.5″). The male's green eye patch and speculum and the white vertical bar in front of the wing are diagnostic. Females and eclipse males are brown and very similar to female Bluewings. However, they can be distinguished by the absence of blue in the forewing.

Local Name: Pato aliverde

Comments: A rare winter visitor to Puerto Rico, St Thomas, St John, St Croix and Anegada from October to April. The species prefers fresh water.

Distribution: A rare visitor to the West Indies. Occurs throughout North and Central America and is widespread in Eurasia.

BLUE-WINGED TEAL Plates 17, 18
Anas discors

Identification: 38−40 cm (15−16″). The blue forewing and the duck's small size are important field marks for both sexes in any plumage. Males are in eclipse plumage during much of the winter and look like the females which are a mottled brown. In breeding plumage the males have a distinct white crescent on the face.

Local Names: Pato zarcel, Pato de la Florida

Comments: This is the common wintering duck of Puerto Rico and the Virgin Islands. It can be found on all types of water bodies from freshwater lakes to hypersaline salt ponds. Some of these teal arrive so early and others leave so late that the species can actually be observed the year round, but it is certainly most common from October to April.

Distribution: Throughout the West Indies and North America to northern South America.

CINNAMON TEAL   Plate 1
Anas cyanoptera

Identification: 38—40 cm (15—16″). The male's cinnamon-colored head and underparts easily identify him. The female cannot be distinguished in the field from a female Blue-winged Teal.

Local Name: Pato canela

Comments: Accidental. Known from four recent St Croix records (Sept., Oct. (2) and Nov.), each record from a different year and all since 1982. The species is apparently occurring with increasing frequency in the region.

Distribution: Accidental in the Bahamas, Cuba, Jamaica and St Croix. Occurs through much of western North America south to northern South America.

AMERICAN WIGEON   Plates 17, 18
Anas americana

Identification: 46—56 cm (18—22″). The male's white crown, light blue bill, white patch on the forewing and green speculum are diagnostic. Females lack the white crown, but can be identified by the other characteristics.

Local Names: Baldpate, Pato cabeciblanco

Comments: Locally a fairly common winter visitor to the Virgin Islands, but now uncommon in Puerto Rico. The species occurs from October to April.

Distribution: Throughout the West Indies and North America south to northern South America.

NORTHERN SHOVELER   Plates 17, 18
Anas clypeata

Identification: 43—53 cm (17—21″). The unusually large bill is diagnostic. The green head, white breast and rust-colored sides help identify the male. Females are mottled brown. The blue forewings are distinctive in flight and the speculum is green.

Local Names: Spoonbill, Shovel-mouth, Pato cuchareta

Comments: An uncommon winter visitor to Puerto Rico and extremely rare on St Croix, St Thomas and St John. Shovelers occur from October to May on both fresh and brackish bodies of water.

Distribution: Throughout the West Indies and North America south to Colombia. Also Eurasia to northern Africa.

WOOD DUCK Plate 19
Aix sponsa

Identification: 43−51 cm (17−20″). The crest and iridescent coloration distinguish the male. The female is identified by her crest and the form of her eye-ring.

Local Name: Huyuyo

Comments: Accidental. Known from only one collected specimen in Puerto Rico (Dec. 1974).

Distribution: Breeds in Cuba, but is a vagrant elsewhere in the West Indies. Occurs through most of eastern North America and along the west coast.

RING-NECKED DUCK Plates 17, 18
Aythya collaris

Identification: 40−46 cm (16−18″). In the male the bill coloration, black back and white vertical bar in front of the wing are important field marks. Females are distinguished by their bill pattern and unusual eye-ring.

Local Names: Black Duck, Pato del medio

Comments: An uncommon and local winter visitor to Puerto Rico generally from October to April. It is rare on St Croix and extremely rare on St John and St Thomas. However, this duck appears to be occurring more regularly in the region. The species prefers inland freshwater ponds and is regularly found at the large lake of the Dorado Beach Hotel (Puerto Rico).

Distribution: Throughout the West Indies and North America into Central America.

CANVASBACK   Plate 19
Aythya valisineria

Identification: 51—61 cm (20—24"). The sloping forehead profile is distinctive in both sexes. The male has a rust-colored head and neck.

Local Name: Pato piquisesgado

Comments: An accidental winter visitor to Puerto Rico known from only five sight records, four of them recent. The limited recovery of this species in North America may account for these occurrences.

Distribution: Rare in Cuba and accidental elsewhere in the West Indies. Occurs throughout North America irregularly to Guatemala.

LESSER SCAUP   Plates 17, 18
Aythya affinis

Identification: 38—46 cm (15—18"). In the male the dark head, breast and tail, and the whitish back and flanks are good field marks. Females are brown with a large white mark behind the bill. The very similar Greater Scaup is a vagrant in the region.

Local Names: Black Duck, Black-head, Pato pechiblanco, Pato turco

Comments: The Lesser Scaup has declined in the region and is now an uncommon winter visitor in Puerto Rico and is uncommon to rare in the Virgin Islands. It is almost always found in flocks on bodies of open water primarily from November to March, but has been recorded as early as September and as late as April.

Distribution: Throughout the Greater Antilles and Bahamas, but rare in the Lesser Antilles. Also North America south to northern South America.

BUFFLEHEAD   Plate 19
Bucephala albeola

Identification: 33—38 cm (13—15"). The white head patch of the male is diagnostic. The female is much browner than the male and is distinguished by the distinctive facial stripe.

Local Name: Pato pinto

Comments: Accidental. Known only from a single specimen collected by Stahl in the late 1800s in Puerto Rico.

Distribution: Accidental in the West Indies. Occurs throughout most of North America.

RUDDY DUCK
Oxyura jamaicensis

Plates 17, 18

Identification: 35—43 cm (14—17″). In the male the overall ruddy coloration, white cheek patch, blue bill and erect tail are characteristic. Females and young are predominantly brown. They are identified by the single brown stripe below the eye.

Local Names: Rubber Duck, Diving Teal, Red Diver, Pato chorizo

Comments: A fairly common, but very local resident in Puerto Rico. It is very uncommon in the Virgin Islands. Its numbers have significantly declined in recent decades. Though generally a year-round resident, primarily on freshwater ponds, this duck apparently moves among the islands when water conditions are unfavorable.

Nesting: The nest is built over water in swamp vegetation and four to twelve large white eggs are laid. The breeding season extends from October to June with the peak varying within these dates from year to year.

Distribution: Throughout the West Indies and North America to Central America.

MASKED DUCK
Oxyura dominica

Plates 17, 18

Identification: 30—36 cm (12—14″). The black face, white wing patch and erect tail identify the male. The female is brown and much like the female Ruddy Duck, but can be distinguished by the white wing patch and the presence of two brown stripes on the face rather than one.

Local Names: Quail Duck, Squat Duck, Pato enmascarado

Comments: A very rare permanent resident in Puerto Rico though recently reported regularly around Humacao. It is accidental on St Croix. The species prefers freshwater areas with much floating vegetation, but it has been observed on saltwater ponds such as at Flamenco Lagoon on Culebra, apparently while in transit between islands.

Nesting: The nest is built among swamp vegetation over or near the water. Eight to eighteen (the latter presumably by two females) whitish eggs form a clutch.

Distribution: Throughout the West Indies and Mexico south through South America.

HOODED MERGANSER   Plate 19
Lophodytes cucullatus

Identification: 40−48 cm (16−19″). The crest of the male with its large, white patch is distinctive. The female is distinguished from other mergansers by her darker face, bill and back, and smaller size.

Local Name: Mergansa de caperuza

Comments: Accidental. Known by a specimen (Dec.) and sight record (Nov.) from Puerto Rico, a specimen from St Croix (Dec.) and a sight record from St John (Dec.).

Distribution: Rare in the West Indies, but occurs throughout much of North America.

RED-BREASTED MERGANSER   Plate 19
Mergus serrator

Identification: 51−64 cm (20−25″). The male's crest, white collar and dark breast are distinctive. The female is distinguished from the very similar Common Merganser female (which has not been recorded here) by the blending of the head coloration into the gray of the neck.

Local Name: Mergansa pechirroja

Comments: Accidental. Known only from one collected specimen in Puerto Rico (Nov.) and single sight records from Mona (Nov.) and Vieques (Dec.).

Distribution: Rare in the West Indies, but occurs throughout most of North America and Eurasia.

American Vultures
FAMILY: CATHARTIDAE

This small New World family contains only seven species, all of which are large birds with unfeathered heads and necks. They are excellent soarers and all feed primarily on carrion.

TURKEY VULTURE   Plate 20
Cathartes aura

Identification: 69—76 cm (27—30"). Distinguished by its very large size, totally dark coloration, and its soaring flight with the wings held well above the horizontal. The red head of adults is only noticeable at close range. Immatures have dark gray heads.

Local Names: Buzzard, Aura tiñosa

Comments: Formerly speculated to have been introduced to Puerto Rico, it is more likely that this species spread to the island subsequent to deforestation and the shift to cattle production which created new habitat for the species to occupy. The Turkey Vulture is now a well established resident in the southwest. It is common from Ponce to Cabo Rojo but has been recorded as far east as Salinas and Coamo Springs and as far north as Añasco. There is one record for St Croix. The species is most regularly observed over arid scrublands.

Voice: A hiss.

Nesting: No nest is constructed. The one to three white eggs marked with brown are laid on the ground on a cliff ledge or under protective cover.

Distribution: Throughout the Greater Antilles and the northwest Bahamas. Widespread in the Western Hemisphere.

Hawks and Harriers
FAMILY: ACCIPITRIDAE

These predatory birds glide more frequently than the falcons and are further distinguished by their rounded rather than pointed wings.

SHARP-SHINNED HAWK   Plate 20
Accipiter striatus

Identification: 28—33 cm (11—13″). The dark slate gray upperparts and heavily barred rufous underparts of the adults are distinctive. Immatures are brown above and heavily streaked below. In flight, the short, rounded wings and long, narrow tail are characteristic. Sharp-shins fly through the forest alternately flapping and gliding.

Local Name: Gavilán de sierra, Falcón de sierra

Comments: Uncommon and very local in Puerto Rico. It inhabits heavily forested montane areas principally in the Luquillo Mountains and around Toro Negro and Maricao. There is one record from St John.

Voice: A high-pitched, slowly repeated *kew-kew-kew*, etc.

Nesting: A stick nest is built high in a tree and three white, speckled eggs form a normal clutch. Breeding is from spring to early summer.

Distribution: Throughout the Bahamas and Greater Antilles except Jamaica. Also North, Central, and South America.

RED-TAILED HAWK   Plate 20
Buteo jamaicensis

Identification: 48—64 cm (19—25″). The large size, red tail, white breast and streaked belly are good field marks. Immatures have finely barred grayish-brown tails.

Local Names: Chicken Hawk, Guaraguao colirrojo, Lechuza

Comments: A common permanent resident in all woodland areas in Puerto Rico and the Virgin Islands, where it is often seen soaring overhead.

Voice: A very distinctive hoarse, raspy scream *ke-aaar*, that fades away.

Nesting: A large, bulky nest is made of sticks. It is placed high in a tree and contains two to three dull white eggs which are sometimes spotted. The breeding season is from January to July.

Distribution: Through the West Indies to the northern Lesser Antilles and throughout North and Central America.

BROAD-WINGED HAWK   Plate 20
Buteo platypterus

Identification: 39 cm (15.5″). In adults, the tail, broadly banded with black and white, and the rufous breast are characteristic. This is the darkest subspecies of the Broad-winged Hawk. Immatures have dark bars on the breast and lack the distinctive tail bands of the adult. Broadwings flap more than the larger Redtails.

Local Name: Guaraguao de bosque

Comments: An uncommon and extremely local resident in Puerto Rico. It is confined to forested areas on El Yunque and around Río Abajo State Forest, though it may occur in unexplored portions of the haystack hills. There are infrequent reports from other forested mountain areas.

Voice: A high-pitched whistle, much more melodious than the call of a Redtail.

Nesting: A well concealed but bulky nest of sticks is built in a tree and two to three eggs are laid. Breeding occurs in the spring.

Distribution: Of scattered distribution in the West Indies and through eastern North America to northern South America.

NORTHERN HARRIER   Plate 20
Circus cyaneus

Identification: 46−61 cm (18−24″). The long wings and tail, and particularly the white rump identify this hawk which characteristically flies low over the ground with a series of heavy flaps and distinctive tilting glides, the wings held well above the horizontal. Males are a grayish-blue and females are brown.

Local Names: Harrier, Aguilucho pálido, Gavilán de ciénaga

Comments: An uncommon to rare winter visitor in Puerto Rico and the Virgin Islands, having been recorded in the latter only from St Croix and St John. It occurs over marshes and swamps primarily from October to March, but may arrive as early as September and stay as late as July.

Distribution: Throughout the West Indies and North America south to northern South America. Widespread in Eurasia.

OSPREY   Plate 20
Pandion haliaetus

Identification: 53–61 cm (21–24"). The white head with the black line through the eye is distinctive. In flight it appears almost totally white below.

Local Names: Fish Hawk, Eagle, Sea Eagle, Aguila pescadora, Aguila de mar

Comments: A fairly common winter visitor to the region, some birds even occurring in July and August. There is a record of a pair remaining through the summer and another building a nest on St Croix, a bird carrying sticks for a nest in Puerto Rico, a complete nest actually being constructed on Anegada, and a dubious March record of young being taken from a cliff nest on a cay near Tortola. It remains questionable whether the birds have ever nested successfully. The Osprey hunts over both fresh and salt water.

Voice: A series of abbreviated piercing whistles.

Distribution: Cosmopolitan.

Falcons
FAMILY: FALCONIDAE

The swift flying falcons do not characteristically soar or glide as do the other hawks and vultures. They can further be distinguished in flight by their pointed wings and long, narrow tails.

PEREGRINE FALCON   Plate 20
Falco peregrinus

Identification: 38–51 cm (15–20"). Its large size, pointed wings, long, narrow tail and rapid pigeon-like flight identify it on the wing. When perched its mask-like head pattern is distinctive. Adults are dark slate above and cream with dark bars below. Immatures are primarily brown and are heavily streaked below.

Local Names: Duck Hawk, Falcón peregrino

Comments: A regular, but uncommon to rare winter visitor in

Puerto Rico and the Virgin Islands where it frequents offshore cays and rocks, and water bodies containing an abundance of shorebirds or waterfowl. It sometimes is found inland. Peregrines occur primarily from October to April, probably being a little more common during migration. The earliest fall record is from August.

Distribution: Cosmopolitan.

MERLIN   Plate 20
Falco columbarius

Identification: 25—34 cm (10—13.5 ″). This medium-sized falcon is distinguished by its upperparts — slate gray in the male and dark brown in the female; heavily barred underparts and banded tail. Its great speed and agility in flight aid in identification.

Local Names: Pigeon Hawk, Esmerejón, Falcón migratorio

Comments: An uncommon winter visitor to Puerto Rico and the Virgin Islands from October to May. It rarely occurs in September and April. This species frequents coastal lakes and lagoons where shorebirds abound, but also occurs in forested areas.

Distribution: Throughout the West Indies and North America to northern South America. Also Eurasia.

AMERICAN KESTREL   Plate 20
Falco sparverius

Identification: 23—30 cm (9—12 ″). The small size, light brown back (with blue wings in the male), the red tail with a broad black terminal band, and the unusual facial pattern are distinctive.

Local Names: Sparrow Hawk, Killy-killy, Killy Hawk, Bastard Hawk, Falcón común

Comments: A fairly common permanent resident in the Virgin Islands, but only locally so in Puerto Rico. It prefers arid coastal areas where large trees are available for nesting. However, it also occurs in open localities in the mountains. This species is often seen on an exposed perch from which it hunts.

Voice: A high-pitched *killi-killi-killi* from which one of its common names is derived.

Nesting: Two to four tan eggs flecked with brown are laid in a cavity in a tree or on a cliff ledge. Breeding occurs primarily from February to June.

Distribution: Throughout most of the West Indies and the rest of the Western Hemisphere.

Junglefowl and Quail
FAMILY: PHASIANIDAE

This family includes a variety of primarily gregarious, terrestrial birds that fly strongly for short distances when pressed. The quails are characterized by their small size and short tails. Junglefowl are much larger birds, the males possessing very long tails.

NORTHERN BOBWHITE   Plate 23
Colinus virginianus

Identification: 25 cm (10 ″). These chunky, brown birds resemble small chickens quickly scampering about in the underbrush. They often do not flush until nearly underfoot when they burst from cover. The face of the male is primarily white and that of the female buff.

Local Names: Quail, Quail-dle, Codorniz

Comments: Rare on Puerto Rico and St Croix, islands to which it was first introduced as a game species about 1860 and 1810 respectively. Though the bird initially thrived on St Croix and was known to have bred and spread in Puerto Rico, the introduction of the mongoose nearly caused the extirpation of the bird on both islands. However, small covies of Northern Bobwhite continue to survive in southwestern St Croix, and on Puerto Rico where more recent releases have been made (1958, 1971). The species is holding on in scattered localities, most notably in the vicinity of Tortuguero Lagoon, Puerto Rico.

Voice: A clear whistled rendition of its name *bob-white* __/ or *bob, bob-white*.

Nesting: The nest is on the ground in a clump of grass and contains ten to fifteen dull white eggs. Breeding is from April to July.

Distribution: Introduced in Puerto Rico (including Mona Island, Culebra and Vieques), St Croix, Hispaniola, the Bahamas, Hawaii, and portions of western North America. Native through much of temperate North America south to Guatemala.

RED JUNGLEFOWL   Plate 23
Gallus gallus

Identification: ♂ 71 cm (28"), ♀ 43 cm (17"). The resplendent plumage of the male and more subdued plumage of the female are well known. The comb on the head is distinctive.

Local Names: Domestic Fowl, Chicken (♀), Rooster (♂), Gallina (♀), Gallo (♂)

Comments: These introduced birds are found in an entirely wild state on Mona Island and possibly also on Culebra and among Puerto Rico's haystack hills. They are not known to be feral in the Virgin Islands.

Voice: A universally recognized *cockadoodledoo*. Also a variety of clucks and other notes. Chicks give a soft, characteristic call note *pee-o*.

Nesting: A scrape is made on the ground, sometimes lined with twigs. Several white or light brown eggs are laid.

Distribution: Indigenous to southeast Asia. Introduced throughout the world.

Guineafowl
FAMILY: NUMIDIDAE

Native to Africa, guineafowl were introduced throughout the West Indies in the early sixteenth century. These large, chicken-like birds, with their bare heads and necks, are commonly maintained in a semidomesticated state on the farms of the islands.

They are highly gregarious and primarily terrestrial although they are powerful fliers for short distances.

HELMETED GUINEAFOWL   Plate 23
Numida meleagris

Identification: 53 cm (21″). Distinguished by the slate gray feathering with white spots and the nearly naked head and neck.

Local Names: Common Guineafowl, Guinea Bird, Guinea Hen, Guinea torcaz

Comments: This introduced bird is wild in small numbers in parts of St Croix, north central Puerto Rico and possibly elsewhere on the island. It is semiferal throughout much of Puerto Rico and St Croix preferring areas of arid scrub.

Voice: A wild, maniacal, cackling call.

Nesting: The nest is a scrape on the ground in which many light buff-colored eggs are laid.

Distribution: Introduced in the West Indies centuries ago. Native to central East Africa.

Rails, Gallinules and Coots
FAMILY: RALLIDAE

Rails are chicken-like marsh dwelling birds. They are secretive, primarily nocturnal, and are much more frequently heard than seen. Playing tapes of their calls from the edge of a marsh is an excellent way to discover their presence. They rarely flush, preferring to run for cover, but when they fly, they soon settle among dense vegetation in which they cannot be found. Their flight is labored, with legs dangling conspicuously. Rails have long toes and either long or short bills. Those with short, thick bills are often called crakes. Gallinules and coots are larger than rails and are more aquatic (the coots being most at home in the water). They resemble ducks, but have a distinctive bill with a frontal shield and when swimming, characteristically jerk their heads.

CLAPPER RAIL   Plate 15
Rallus longirostris

Identification: 35.5 cm (14″). This gray chicken-like bird is easily recognized by its long bill and habit of stalking among the mangrove roots. The Common Gallinule, which is also chicken-like and found in the mangroves, has a much shorter bill than the Clapper Rail.

Local Names: Marsh Hen, Mangrove Hen, Pollo de mangle

Comments: A common permanent resident in Puerto Rico, less so in the Virgin Islands. It is virtually confined to mangrove tracts where it is far more often heard than seen.

Voice: The call is a loud, grating series of *kek* notes slowing at the end. The cackle of one rail often sets off a chorus of others.

Nesting: The nest is a platform of sticks among the mangrove roots in which five to nine spotted, creamy-white eggs are laid. Breeding occurs the year round with peaks in spring (April to June) and fall (October to November).

Distribution: In the West Indies east to Guadeloupe. Also coastal USA south through South America.

SORA   Plate 15
Porzana carolina

Identification: 22 cm (8.75″). The stubby, yellow bill is distinctive. Adults have black on the face extending to the breast.

Local Names: Sora Rail, Sora Crake, Gallito

Comments: Generally an uncommon visitor to Puerto Rico and the Virgin Islands from October to April. However, it is common at least locally on St Croix and at Boquerón Refuge and Cartagena Lagoon in Puerto Rico. The Sora is probably more common than believed, as suggested by the large numbers heard at the latter two sites in early spring. It prefers freshwater swamps with thick vegetation, but also occurs in mangroves.

Voice: A clear, descending whinny and a plaintive, rising whistle *ker-wee*.

Distribution: Throughout the West Indies and North, Central and northern South America.

YELLOW-BREASTED CRAKE
Plate 15
Porzana flaviventer

Identification: 14 cm (5.5″). Very rarely seen well, it is distinguished by its tiny size and tawny yellow appearance. In flight the feet dangle and the head droops.

Local Names: Yellow-bellied Rail, Gallito amarillo

Comments: Uncommon in Puerto Rico and unknown from the Virgin Islands. A bird of freshwater swamps with short grass borders, it will not normally be observed unless one wades in the shallow water of the swamp edge. The bird will flush only a short distance before dropping into the vegetation again.

Voice: A *tuck* of medium pitch and strength, and a high-pitched, softly whistled *peep*.

Nesting: Five lightly spotted, pale cream eggs are laid in a woven nest atop a floating plant. The only known nest was found in March.

Distribution: The Greater Antilles and southern Mexico south through South America.

BLACK RAIL
Plate 15
Laterallus jamaicensis

Identification: 14 cm (5.5″). Distinguished by its tiny size, black bill and the white spots on its back. The downy young of gallinules, coots and other rails are black, but lack these field marks.

Local Name: Gallito negro

Comments: Now an extremely rare winter visitor to Puerto Rico. Once apparently a breeding resident, it was likely extirpated by the introduced mongoose. The species inhabits wet grassy areas, both saline and fresh. It can best be located by playing a tape of its call.

Voice: A *ki-ki-kurr* ⁻⁻____ the first two syllables being high-pitched whistles. The defense call is an emphatic and irregularly pulsing cackle.

Nesting: Elsewhere approximately seven buff-white eggs, finely spotted, are laid in a cup-shaped nest which is often hidden amidst, and supported by, a mat of dead marsh grass.

Distribution: East in the West Indies to Puerto Rico. Also the eastern and central USA to western South America.

PURPLE GALLINULE   Plate 15
Porphyrula martinica

Identification: 33 cm (13″). In adults the blue body coloration, yellow legs and bluish-white frontal shield are diagnostic. Immatures are a golden brown with yellow legs. They lack the flank stripe of the Common Moorhen.

Local Names: Gallareta azul, Gallareta inglesa

Comments: An uncommon to rare permanent resident over most of Puerto Rico's coast, but observed regularly at Cartagena Lagoon. There are two records from St Croix and one from St Thomas. The species primarily inhabits freshwater swamps with thick, emergent vegetation.

Voice: A high-pitched, melodious *klee-klee*, and many cackling and guttural notes.

Nesting: From three to twelve spotted, pinkish buff-colored eggs are laid in a low nest of vegetation among the cattails. Breeding appears to occur the year round with peaks in late August to October and April to May.

Distribution: The West Indies and the southeastern USA through Central and South America.

COMMON MOORHEN   Plate 15
Gallinula chloropus

Identification: 34 cm (13.5″). The red bill and frontal shield and the white line down the flank are distinctive. Immatures are gray and brown and lack the red bill, but they display the white flank stripe.

Local Names: Common Gallinule, Water Fowl, Florida Gallinule, Antillean Gallinule, Gallareta común

Comments: A common permanent resident in Puerto Rico, less so in the Virgin Islands. It occurs in all swamps and canals with emergent vegetation and in mangroves.

Voice: A variety of clucks and cackles, the most common being a piercing laugh-like cackle slowing at the end, *ki-ki-ki-ki-ka, kaa, kaaa*.

Nesting: Three to nine grayish-tan eggs, lightly spotted, are laid in a nest which is usually suspended over water. Breeding occurs the year round, but peaks in the spring.

Distribution: Cosmopolitan.

AMERICAN COOT   Plate 15
Fulica americana

Identification: 38—40 cm (15—16"). This bird appears black with a white bill and undertail coverts. In the field the lack of the white frontal shield on the forehead distinguishes it from the Caribbean Coot. In the fall gray immatures occur.

Local Names: Water Fowl, Mud Hen, Gallinazo americano

Comments: A fairly common visitor to Puerto Rico and uncommon in the Virgin Islands during most months except those of summer. When in the region it significantly outnumbers the Caribbean Coot. Open freshwater areas with much submergent vegetation are its preferred habitat.

Voice: A variety of croaks and cackles.

Nesting: Mixed pairs of American and Caribbean Coots have been observed breeding on St John.

Distribution: Widespread in the Western Hemisphere.

CARIBBEAN COOT   Plate 15
Fulica caribaea

Identification: 38—40 cm (15—16"). Identified by its black coloration and particularly the white frontal shield extending well up onto the crown. The American Coot does not have the white frontal shield extending as high on the forehead. Immatures are gray.

Local Names: Water Fowl, Gallinazo antillano

Comments: A decidedly uncommon year-round resident in Puerto Rico and rare in the Virgin Islands. Once abundant, it has been diminished greatly by overhunting and habitat destruction. It prefers freshwater areas.

Voice: A variety of croaking and cackling sounds.

Nesting: Breeding occurs the year round with peaks in spring and fall. Four to eight spotted, white eggs are laid in a floating nest. Recently cross-breeding with American Coots has been observed on St John.

Distribution: Confined to the West Indies, Florida, Venezuela, Trinidad, and Curaçao.

Limpkin
FAMILY: ARAMIDAE

The Limpkin is the sole member of this New World family. It dwells primarily in swamps, wading among the vegetation in search of snails. Limpkins are solitary, largely nocturnal, and often roost in trees.

LIMPKIN   Plate 9
Aramus guarauna

Identification: 69 cm (27 ″). This large, long-legged and long-necked wading bird is entirely brown with white streaks in its plumage. The long, slightly decurved bill is distinctive. The Limpkin is easily confused with young night-herons, but it is distinguished by its bill and longer legs.

Local Name: Carrao

Comments: The Limpkin is extremely rare in, if not already extirpated from, Puerto Rico. It is unknown from the Virgin Islands. A prized game species in the past, old hunters tell of having chased these primarily nocturnal birds through the dew laden underbrush in the early dawn hours until their feathers were so saturated with moisture they could not fly and were easily captured. Earlier investigators suggested that this story might pertain to the extinct, flightless Debooy's Rail (*Nesotrochis debooyi*), known only from fossil bones, but recent inquiries suggest that this is not the case. The species was last recorded in 1959 from Lake Loíza near Caguas. The most likely area for the continued survival of the bird is in the scattered swampy valleys of the haystack hills in and near the Río Abajo State Forest where people still report the bird.

Voice: A loud, piercing *carrao* which gives rise to its local Spanish name.

Nesting: The nest has not been found in Puerto Rico. Elsewhere four to eight spotted eggs are laid in a loose platform nest low above the ground in a thick tangle of vegetation, usually near water.

Distribution: The Greater Antilles, the extreme southeastern USA, and from southern Mexico through most of South America.

Plovers
FAMILY: CHARADRIIDAE

Plovers are chunky birds of which all species in the region, with the exception of the Killdeer, frequent the water's edge. They have relatively shorter bills, necks and legs than the similar appearing sandpipers. These surface feeding birds also have a distinctive broadening at the bill tip which the sandpipers lack. Five of the eight species here have neck markings.

NORTHERN LAPWING   Plate 10
Vanellus vanellus

Identification: 30 cm (12"). Easily distinguished by the crest which is present in all plumages. The conspicuous black and white color pattern is reduced in immatures as is the crest. The wing tips are rounded in flight.

Local Name: Avefría

Comments: Accidental. Known from a bird photographed at Roosevelt Roads Naval Base, Puerto Rico (1978−1979).

Distribution: Accidental in the West Indies and elsewhere in the Western Hemisphere. Native to Eurasia.

SEMIPALMATED PLOVER   Plate 10
Charadrius semipalmatus

Identification: 18.5 cm (7.25"). Identified by the brown upperparts, and light orange legs and base of the small bill.

Sometimes the breast band is incomplete and shows only as bars on either side of the breast. The bill is dark in winter.

Local Name: Playero acollarado

Comments: A common winter visitor to Puerto Rico and the Virgin Islands, a few individuals even occurring during the summer. It is typically found on tidal flats in flocks with other shorebirds.

Voice: The call note is a plaintive *weet*. There is also a questioning whistle *tee-weet* _ ⟋.

Distribution: Throughout the Western Hemisphere.

PIPING PLOVER   Plate 10
Charadrius melodus

Identification: 18 cm (7″). In summer plumage the pale gray upperparts and the light orange legs and base of the bill are distinctive. Sometimes the breast band is incomplete. In winter plumage the breast band may be absent, the bill turns blackish, and the legs become darker. It is then distinguished from the similar Snowy Plover by its relatively shorter, heavier bill, lighter legs and white rump. The similar Semipalmated Plover is decidedly browner above.

Local Name: Playero melódico

Comments: A rare winter visitor in Puerto Rico, occurring as early as August and as late as April. There are several records from St Croix and one from Anegada. This plover likes areas of recently dredged spoils.

Voice: A thin, whistled *peep* and *peé-lo* ⟍ .

Distribution: Throughout the West Indies but accidental in the Virgin Islands and the Lesser Antilles. Widespread in North America.

SNOWY PLOVER   Plate 10
Charadrius alexandrinus

Identification: 14—15 cm (5.5—6″). This plover is distinguished by its tiny size, pale coloration, slender black bill and particularly its dark legs. Summer plumaged adults have a black patch behind the eye which aids in identification. The similar Piping Plover has a relatively shorter, thicker bill and its legs do not get as dark as those of the Snowy.

Local Name: Playero blanco

Comments: An uncommon and extremely local resident in Puerto Rico and Anegada. There is one record from Culebra and a recent sighting from St John. It was a rare breeding resident on St Croix, apparently dispersing to other islands after nesting, but the species appears to have recently been extirpated from that island. In Puerto Rico the Snowy Plover is practically confined to the saline flats near the Cabo Rojo Lighthouse. It seems to favor only flats where crystalized salt lines the water's edge.

Voice: A whistle like a weak version of that used to call someone's attention ✓ .

Nesting: Three sand-colored eggs with scrawled markings are laid in a depression which is sometimes lined. Breeding occurs from January to August.

Distribution: Cosmopolitan.

WILSON'S PLOVER   Plate 10
Charadrius wilsonia

Identification: 18—20 cm (7—8″). The broad breast band and thick, black bill are good field marks.

Local Names: Sand Bird, Little Ploward, Nit, Thick-billed Plover, Playero marítimo

Comments: A common permanent resident in Puerto Rico and the Virgin Islands. It primarily inhabits the borders of salt ponds.

Voice: The call note is an emphatic raspy whistle *pete*. There is also a quick two to three syllable *ki-ki-ki*.

Nesting: The nest is a depression in the sand sometimes lined with bits of shell. Three splotched, light buff-colored eggs are laid in the spring.

Distribution: All warmer coastal areas of the Western Hemisphere.

KILLDEER   Plate 10
Charadrius vociferus

Identification: 25 cm (10″). The two black bands on the breast immediately distinguish this bird.

Local Names: Soldier Bird, Ploward, Playero sabanero

Comments: A common permanent resident in Puerto Rico but uncommon in the Virgin Islands. Numbers are augmented in fall, winter and spring by North American migrants. Killdeer prefer wet fields, short grass, mudholes, and the edges of freshwater ponds.

Voice: A plaintive, high-pitched *kee* and *dee-de* reminiscent of its name.

Nesting: The nest is a slightly lined depression on the ground and contains three to four heavily marked pale buff-colored eggs. Breeding occurs the year round, but peaks in spring.

Distribution: Throughout the West Indies and widespread in North America south to western South America.

LESSER GOLDEN PLOVER   Plate 10
Pluvialis dominica

Identification: 26 cm (10.5"). In winter plumage it is browner and generally darker than the very similar Black-bellied Plover. Its rump and tail are dark and it has no black in the axillars. In the rarely seen breeding plumage, the black of the underparts extends to the undertail coverts.

Local Names: American Golden Plover, Playero dorado

Comments: A rare fall migrant in the region occurring as early as August and as late as mid-December. It is extremely rare in the spring. The species occurs in upland fields or golf courses more regularly than it does on tidal flats.

Voice: A variety of calls including a single, loud whistle and a soft, warbled *cheedle-wur* ____ , sometimes given as a loud whistle. ___

Distribution: Widespread in the New and Old World.

BLACK-BELLIED PLOVER   Plate 10
Pluvialis squatarola

Identification: 26–34 cm (10.5–13.5"). The stocky build, short bill and light gray coloration help identify winter plumaged birds. In flight the white rump and black axillars distinguish the species in all plumages.

Local Names: Gray Plover, Playero cabezón

Comments: A common visitor to Puerto Rico and the Virgin
Islands from August to May. A few birds occur during the
summer along tidal mudflats and other water edges.

Voice: A single, plaintive *klee* and also a *klee-a-lee* ⁻ _ ⁻ .

Distribution: Cosmopolitan.

Oystercatchers
FAMILY: HAEMATOPODIDAE

The oystercatchers form a small family of stout, coastal birds
with large, brightly colored bills. Their bills are unusual in that
they are laterally compressed, an adaptation for opening bi-
valves, their chief food. These mollusks are sometimes immersed
in water before being swallowed.

AMERICAN OYSTERCATCHER   Plate 13
Haematopus palliatus

Identification: 48 cm (19″). The black hood and long orange-
red bill easily distinguish this species.

Local Names: Whelkcracker, Common Oystercatcher, Ostrero,
Caracolero

Comments: Oystercatchers are uncommon permanent residents
in coastal areas. They are rare in Puerto Rico, but are regularly
seen on rocky offshore islands such as Desecheo and Culebra
and the cays of the Virgin Islands. This species is typical of
stony beaches and rocky headlands.

Voice: A loud, emphatic, coarsely whistled *wheep*.

Nesting: One to three spotted buff-colored eggs are laid on bare
rock or sand. Breeding is in May and June.

Distribution: Cosmopolitan.

Stilts and Avocets
FAMILY: RECURVIROSTRIDAE

These are noisy, gregarious wading birds with very long legs. They occur in open, shallow wetlands.

BLACK-NECKED STILT   Plate 14
Himantopus mexicanus

Identification: 34−39 cm (13.5−15.5 "). The large size, long red legs, black upperparts and white underparts make this bird very distinctive.

Local Names: Redshank, Soldier, Crackpot Soldier, Telltale, Ally-moor, Civil, Viuda

Comments: Stilts are common nesting residents in the region from March to October. They are fairly common some winters and rare others. They frequent the borders of salt ponds and mangrove swamps where their loud calls and distinctive coloration make them highly conspicuous.

Voice: A loud raucous series of notes *wit, wit, wit, wit, wit.*

Nesting: The nest, built near water, is a platform of grass and twigs in which three to seven olive-green eggs with large splotches are laid. Breeding occurs from late April to August.

Distribution: Widespread in the New World.

AMERICAN AVOCET   Plate 14
Recurvirostra americana

Identification: 40−51 cm (16−20 "). The large size, sharply upturned bill, and black and white coloration are distinctive. In summer plumage the head and neck are cinnamon colored.

Local Name: Avoceta

Comments: Accidental. There are two records from Puerto Rico (Aug., Dec.), one from St Croix (Aug.), and one from the British Virgin Islands. It should be looked for along water edges, particularly after heavy storms.

Distribution: Accidental in the West Indies. Also through western North America to Guatemala.

Turnstones, Snipes and Sandpipers
FAMILY: SCOLOPACIDAE

The sandpipers are the second most abundant family in the region and the second most difficult group to identify at the species level. Of the 26 species that occur here, all but the Willet are transients from their breeding grounds, primarily in the far north. The sandpipers are characterized by their long legs and necks and thin, pointed bills. Most wade in shallow water, or on wet flats where they probe in the mud for invertebrates. They are highly gregarious and often occur in mixed feeding assemblages that aids in their identification. Several species remain in the region late enough so that they can be seen in their fine breeding plumage. In all species that occur here, with the notable exceptions of the Ruff and Wilson's Phalarope, both sexes have similar plumages.

RUDDY TURNSTONE   Plate 11
Arenaria interpres

Identification: 20.5—23 cm (8—9″). In winter plumage the dark breast markings and orange legs are diagnostic. Summer plumaged birds are distinguished by their unusual black and white facial markings and ruddy backs.

Local Name: Playero turco

Comments: A common visitor to Puerto Rico and the Virgin Islands in all months except June and July when it is uncommon. It is found on mudflats, pond edges and sandy coasts and normally forms looser flocks than other sandpipers.

Voice: A variety of calls including a loud, nasal *cuck-cuck-cuck*, getting louder to the end.

Distribution: Cosmopolitan.

COMMON SNIPE   Plate 14
Gallinago gallinago

Identification: 27−29 cm (10.5−11.5″). The long bill and striped head and back are good field marks.

Local Names: Wilson's Snipe, Becasina

Comments: A fairly uncommon visitor to Puerto Rico from October to April (sometimes occurring as early as August), though periodically found abundantly. It is uncommon in the Virgin Islands. The species prefers grassy freshwater edges and usually bursts from underfoot in a zig-zag flight.

Voice: A somewhat variable guttural squawk when flushed.

Distribution: Throughout the New World and Eurasia.

WHIMBREL   Plate 13
Numenius phaeopus

Identification: 38−46 cm (15−18″). Its large size and long, decurved bill are distinctive.

Local Names: Hudsonian Curlew, Playero pico corvo

Comments: A rare visitor to Puerto Rico, though it is fairly common in certain swamps on Roosevelt Roads Naval Base. Also rare but regular on St Croix, the species is extremely rare among the other Virgin Islands where it has been recorded from St Thomas, Anegada, Beef Island, and Necker Island. This sandpiper occurs the year round, though less so in June and July.

Voice: A hard, rapidly whistled *whip-whip-whip-whip*, or *kee-kee-kee-kee*, not as raspy as the call of a Yellowlegs. It also has other calls.

Distribution: Cosmopolitan.

ESKIMO CURLEW   Plate 13
Numenius borealis

Identification: 30−35 cm (12−14″). Much smaller and with a shorter and straighter bill than the very similar Whimbrel. It is identified by cinnamon underwings and unbarred primaries.

Local Name: Playero ártico

Comments: Known from the region by a single specimen taken near San Juan, Puerto Rico during the nineteenth century. It apparently was once a rare migrant. The species is now near extinction.

Distribution: Nested in northwestern Canada and Alaska and wintered in southern South America. A migrant in intervening areas.

UPLAND SANDPIPER   Plate 14
Bartramia longicauda

Identification: 28−32 cm (11−12.5″). Its short bill and preference for meadows rather than mudflats are important characteristics. Also, the wingbeats are distinctive, being very shallow like those of the Spotted Sandpiper.

Local Names: Upland Plover, Ganga

Comments: A rare spring (April to May) and fall (August to October) transient in Puerto Rico, accidental in winter. There are two records each from Anegada, St Thomas, and St Croix.

Distribution: Throughout most of the New World.

SPOTTED SANDPIPER   Plate 12
Actitis macularia

Identification: 18−20 cm (7−8″). In winter plumage important field marks are the entirely white underparts and orangish base of the bill. Breeding plumaged birds have distinct dark spots on the underparts. The teetering walk and the very shallow, rapid wingbeats in flight aid greatly in identification.

Local Name: Playero coleador

Comments: A common visitor to Puerto Rico and the Virgin Islands from August to May, and rarely in June and July. It prefers mangrove edges and the borders of streams, but is not generally found on mudflats with other shorebirds and does not typically flock.

Voice: A whistled *we-weet*.

Distribution: Throughout the Western Hemisphere.

SOLITARY SANDPIPER   Plate 12
Tringa solitaria

Identification: 19—23 cm (7.5—9″). The white eye-ring, dark upperparts and the black barring of the outer tail feathers are good field marks. In flight the wingbeats are deep and distinctive.

Local Name: Playero solitario

Comments: A common fall migrant and uncommon in winter and spring in Puerto Rico. In the Virgin Islands it is uncommon in fall and rare in winter and spring. The earliest record is July. Freshwater edges are its preferred habitat.

Voice: A hard, emphatic series of whistles when alarmed *weet-weet-weet*. Also a soft *pip* or *weet* when undisturbed.

Distribution: Throughout the Western Hemisphere.

LESSER YELLOWLEGS   Plate 14
Tringa flavipes

Identification: 25—28 cm (10—11″). The size, distinctive orangish-yellow legs and thin, straight bill identify this sandpiper. The thinner, shorter bill and the bird's call are probably the best characteristics for distinguishing it from the Greater Yellowlegs when the species are not together.

Local Names: Snipe, Playero guineilla pequeña

Comments: A common visitor to Puerto Rico and the Virgin Islands in all months except June and July when it becomes uncommon. It frequents both freshwater and saltwater habitats.

Voice: A one to two note call *cu-cu*, softer and more nasal than that of the Greater.

Distribution: Throughout the Western Hemisphere.

GREATER YELLOWLEGS   Plate 14
Tringa melanoleuca

Identification: 33—38 cm (13—15″). The large size, orangish-yellow legs and long, straight bill are good characteristics. These birds often occur with the more common Lesser Yellowlegs, allowing size comparisons. The Greater has a relatively longer, thicker bill that sometimes appears slightly upturned.

Local Names: Snipe, Playero guineilla grande

Comments: Common in the region in the fall and only fairly so in winter and spring. It is far less common in the Virgin Islands than the Lesser Yellowlegs. A few birds are found during the summer, but they do not nest. It frequents both freshwater ponds and tidal flats.

Voice: A loud, irritating whistle of three to four notes *cu-cu-cu*, or *klee-klee-cu* ⁻ ⁻ _ .

Distribution: Throughout the Western Hemisphere.

WILLET   Plate 13
Catoptrophorus semipalmatus

Identification: 38—40 cm (15—16 ″). Distinguished by its large size, light gray coloration, dark legs and thick bill. In flight the black and white wing pattern is unmistakable.

Local Names: Tell-bill-willy, Pilly-willick, Longlegs, Pond Bird, Duck Snipe, Laughing Jackass, Playero aliblanco

Comments: Fairly common from August to November, uncommon December to April and rare May to July in Puerto Rico and St Croix. During all seasons it is very uncommon on St Thomas and rare among the other Virgin Islands. Most birds recorded in the region are apparently migrants.

Voice: A sharp *chip-chip-chip*, a loud, piercing whistle, and other sharp, whistled calls.

Nesting: Four buff-colored eggs, heavily splotched, are laid in a slightly lined depression in the sand. This species is known to nest on St Croix and Anegada and apparently does so in Puerto Rico from May to July.

Distribution: Widespread in the New World.

RED KNOT   Plate 11
Calidris canutus

Identification: 25—28 cm (10—11 ″). The medium size, chunky
  build, greenish legs and relatively short bill distinguish this
  sandpiper. Some fall individuals may still have a pale rust-red
  breast.

Local Names: Knot, Playero gordo

Comments: An uncommon migrant in Puerto Rico in September
  and October occurring rarely as early as July and as late as
  January; it is rare during spring migration in March and April.
  The species is also rare but regular on St Croix where it has
  been recorded during every month of the year. It is extremely
  rare among the other Virgin Islands where it is known from
  St John, Anegada, and Necker Island. This species is generally
  found on sandy tidal flats with other shorebirds.

Voice: A very low-pitched, hoarse *knut*. Also a low whistled
  wah-quoit, ending in a slight roll (Pough).

Distribution: Cosmopolitan.

DUNLIN   Plate 13
Calidris alpina

Identification: 20—23 cm (8—9 ″). The heavy bill, distinctively
  downcurved at the tip, the chunky build, and the dark gray
  wash on the breast, head and upperparts identify this bird in
  winter plumage. Birds in breeding dress have a characteristic
  black belly. The hypothetically occurring Curlew Sandpiper
  strongly resembles the Dunlin when both species are in winter
  garb. The former can only be differentiated with certainty by
  its white rump.

Local Names: Red-backed Sandpiper, Playero espaldi- colorado

Comments: Extremely rare. Known from two sight records in
  Puerto Rico, four from St Croix, one each from St Thomas
  and St John, and a questionable one from Virgin Gorda. It
  favors mudflats and open beaches where it feeds with slow,
  deliberate movements.

Distribution: Accidental in the West Indies. Widespread in North
  America and the Old World.

LEAST SANDPIPER   Plate 12
Calidris minutilla

Identification: 12.5—16.5 cm (5—6.5″). Its tiny size and yellowish legs are the best field marks. Its brown coloration, streaked breast and slightly decurved bill at the tip aid in identification.

Local Names: Peep, Playerito menudo

Comments: A fairly common visitor to Puerto Rico and the Virgin Islands from August to May, occurring rarely in June and July. It is often found on mudflats with the Semipalmated Sandpiper.

Voice: A thin, soft whistle *wi-wi-wit*. Also an almost whinny-like trill that drops a bit in pitch and volume *tr-tr-tr-tr-tr-tr*.

Distribution: Widespread in the New World.

BAIRD'S SANDPIPER   Plate 1
Calidris bairdii

Identification: 18—19 cm (7—7.5″). The similarity of this accidentally occurring sandpiper to many other species require that it be identified with extreme caution. Baird's Sandpiper is distinguished from the Semipalmated, Western and Least by its larger size and its wings extending noticeably beyond the tail. The wings of the White-rumped Sandpiper also extend beyond its tail and the bird is the same size as a Baird's, consequently these two species can only be safely separated by observing them in flight. The white on the rump of Baird's Sandpiper is divided into lateral patches by a dark central stripe. In the White-rumped the white patch is continuous. Baird's has a buffier breast than most similar sandpipers. It also picks for its food rather than probes.

Local Name: Playero de Baird

Comments: Extremely rare. Known from ten sightings on St Croix since 1982. Not yet recorded elsewhere in the region. It should primarily be expected during spring and fall migrations. This species is easily overlooked due to its similarity to other more common sandpipers.

Distribution: Widespread in the New World.

WHITE-RUMPED SANDPIPER
Calidris fuscicollis

Plate 12

Identification: 18−20 cm (7−8″). The white uppertail coverts distinguish this from other small sandpipers in flight. It is distinctly larger than the similar Semipalmated and Western and is a darker gray in winter plumage and darker brown in summer. The breast is also more heavily streaked.

Local Names: Peep, Playero rabadilla blanca

Comments: An uncommon migrant in Puerto Rico and the Virgin Islands from August to October and rare during the spring in March and April. There are several December records. The species is regularly found on flats with other shorebirds.

Voice: A distinctive squeak, *peet*, or *jeet*. Also a thin, high-pitched trill.

Distribution: Widespread in the New World.

PECTORAL SANDPIPER
Calidris melanotos

Plate 11

Identification: 20−24 cm (8−9.5″). The medium size, yellowish-green bill and legs, and sharp demarcation between the heavily streaked breast and white belly are good field marks.

Local Names: Grassbird, Playero manchado

Comments: A fairly common fall migrant in Puerto Rico and the Virgin Islands from August to early November. Sometimes great flocks of as many as 5000 occur. The species is rare in the region in spring, rarer in winter and accidental in summer. This bird prefers wet meadows and is not frequently found in association with other sandpipers. Golf courses after heavy rains are a favorite haunt.

Distribution: Widespread in the New World.

SEMIPALMATED SANDPIPER
Calidris pusilla

Plate 12

Identification: 14−16.5 cm (5.5−6.5″). Identified by its small size, black legs and medium-length black bill. This is the principal small sandpiper one should know well and against which all others should be compared.

Local Names: Peep, Playerito gracioso

Comments: An abundant visitor to Puerto Rico throughout the year though present in reduced numbers in May and June. It is generally uncommon in the Virgin Islands. This species often occurs in large flocks and can be found along virtually all water edges from puddles to salt ponds.

Voice: In flight a hoarse, shrill *cherk* and when flushed an abrupt *ki-i-ip* (Pough).

Distribution: Widespread in the New World.

WESTERN SANDPIPER   Plate 12
Calidris mauri

Identification: 15—18 cm (6—7″). The relatively long bill, heavy at the base and decurved at the tip, is the best field mark for distinguishing the Western from the very similar Semipalmated Sandpiper which overlaps it in size. The scapulars may remain rusty into the fall.

Local Names: Peep, Playerito occidental

Comments: A fairly common visitor to Puerto Rico, but rare in the Virgin Islands. It occurs primarily from September to March but has been found in all other months. This species frequents mudflats, usually occurring in mixed flocks with the very similar Semipalmated Sandpiper. Westerns should be looked for in slightly deeper water than the Semipalmated.

Voice: In flight a *kreep*, coarser and more querulous than that of the Semipalmated (Pough).

Distribution: Throughout much of the New World but reaching only northern South America.

SANDERLING   Plate 12
Calidris alba

Identification: 18—21.5 cm (7—8.5″). In winter plumage this is the lightest of sandpipers, with white underparts and light gray upperparts. In flight a conspicuous wing stripe aids in identification. Breeding plumaged birds have distinctly rust-colored heads and breasts.

Local Name: Playero arenero

Comments: A fairly common visitor to Puerto Rico from September to April and rarely through the summer. In the Virgin Islands it is rare in all seasons. This sandpiper has a particular preference for sandy beaches where flocks advance and retreat with each wave.

Voice: A distinctive *whit*.

Distribution: Cosmopolitan.

SHORT-BILLED DOWITCHER   Plate 11
Limnodromus griseus

Identification: 26—30 cm (10.5—12″). The very long, straight bill is distinctive. In flight the white patch extending well up the back is diagnostic (see Long-billed Dowitcher).

Local Names: American Dowitcher, Chorlo pico corto

Comments: A locally common migrant and fairly common winter visitor to Puerto Rico but rather uncommon in the Virgin Islands. The species occurs in all months of the year, but is rare from May to July. Dowitchers associate in flocks and prefer tidal mudflats where they feed with vertical thrusts of the bill, a habit which helps identify the birds.

Voice: A soft, rapid whistle *wee-wee-weet*.

Distribution: Widespread in the New World.

LONG-BILLED DOWITCHER   Plate 11
Limnodromus scolopaceus

Identification: 28—32 cm (11—12.5″). This dowitcher is very difficult to distinguish from the Shortbilled. In winter it can be safely identified only by voice or by bill length when 7.5 cm (3″) or more. In breeding plumage the underparts are rusty colored to the lower belly, and the flanks are barred, whereas the Shortbill's are spotted.

Local Names: American Dowitcher, Chorlo pico largo

Comments: The status of this species in the region is uncertain.

One specimen has been collected on Anegada and on several occasions on St Croix these birds have been identified by their calls. There are several reports of long-billed birds occurring among dowitchers with shorter bills. As both dowitchers were until recently considered a single species, they have received limited attention.

Voice: A thin, peeping note singly or in series.

Distribution: Throughout the Western Hemisphere.

STILT SANDPIPER   Plate 11
Calidris himantopus

Identification: 20−21.5 cm (8.5″). The Stilt Sandpiper is difficult to identify. The best field marks are its white rump, dull greenish legs and its long bill, thick at the base with a slight droop at the tip. In breeding plumage the bird has rust-colored cheeks and crown. The bill is shorter than that of dowitchers.

Local Name: Playero patilargo

Comments: A fairly common visitor to Puerto Rico and the Virgin Islands in fall and winter, but becoming rare in the spring. There are few June and July records.

Voice: A very soft, unmusical and unabrasive *cue*.

Distribution: Throughout most of the Western Hemisphere.

MARBLED GODWIT   Plate 13
Limosa fedoa

Identification: 40−51 cm (16−20″). The large size, long, slightly upturned bill and absence of white on the rump identify this species.

Local Name: Barga jaspeada

Comments: An extremely rare migrant and possible winter visitor in the region (one January record). There are three records each from Puerto Rico and St Croix and one from Anegada. The species should be looked for on mudflats and in marshy areas.

Distribution: Rare in the West Indies, but occurs throughout much of the Western Hemisphere.

HUDSONIAN GODWIT   Plate 13
Limosa haemastica

Identification: 33—40 cm (13—16"). The slightly upturned bill and black tail with a white base are diagnostic.

Local Name: Barga aliblanca

Comments: An extremely rare fall migrant in Puerto Rico (four records) and St Croix (two records). The species occurs at grassy freshwater pond edges and mudflats.

Distribution: Rare in the West Indies, but occurs throughout the Western Hemisphere.

RUFF (female: REEVE)   Plate 11
Philomachus pugnax

Identification: ♂ 30 cm (12"), ♀ 23—28 cm (9—11"). In winter plumage it is best distinguished by its fairly chunky build, erect posture, the yellow (sometimes orange) base of the bill and the buffy breast which is somewhat scaled in appearance. The legs are often light, varying from dull yellow to orange, green or brown. In flight this species displays characteristic long, oval white patches at the base of the tail. Breeding plumaged males exhibit extreme variability in coloration, but all are easily distinguished by the elaborate breast and head feathers.

Local Name: Combatiente

Comments: Very rare from August to May. Known from four sightings in Puerto Rico, three from Anegada, two from St Croix and one from St Thomas. It generally occurs in the company of Yellowlegs, preferring to feed along the muddy shoreline where its movements are rather sluggish.

Distribution: Accidental in the West Indies and elsewhere in the Western Hemisphere. Widespread in the Old World.

WILSON'S PHALAROPE   Plate 14
Phalaropus tricolor

Identification: 23 cm (9"). Distinguished in winter plumage by its thin, straight bill, totally white breast and a faint dark mark through the eye. Breeding plumaged males have a tan wash on the neck while females have a chestnut band starting at the shoulder and blending into black behind the eye. The conspicuous habit of spinning in the water to stir up food is a certain field mark of phalaropes.

Local Name: Falaropo de Wilson

Comments: A very rare visitor to the region between August and March, being seen with increasing frequency. There are four records from Puerto Rico and regular records from St Croix during the 1980s. It swims more than other shorebirds.

Distribution: Accidental in the West Indies. Through much of North America to South America.

Gulls, Terns and Allies
FAMILY: LARIDAE

This family consists of several distinctive subgroups:

Gulls and Terns − The gulls and terns form a cosmopolitan subfamily that primarily frequents coastal waters, rivers and large lakes. Gulls are more robust than terns with broader wings and fan-shaped tails. Adults are usually a combination of white, gray and black, while immatures, which may take several years to develop adult plumage, are principally brown. Terns are slim birds of graceful flight, often with long, notched tails, black about the head, and thin, pointed bills. Unlike gulls, which feed off the surface, many terns hover and dive into the water after fish. Both terns and gulls are quite gregarious and generally nest in colonies.

Jaegers and Skuas − In this region jaegers and skuas are found over the open ocean and are rarely seen from land. They are predatory birds with hooked bills, often harassing gulls and terns and forcing them to drop their catches. The name jaeger is derived from the German word *Jager* meaning hunter. Their flight is very swift and direct like that of a falcon and there is a sharp bend at the angle of the wing. The bases of the primaries form a distinctive white patch. Several species have dark color phases, but these are very rare in the region. The long central tail feathers in adult jaegers are diagnostic in each species; skuas lack these.

Skimmers − This very distinctive subgroup contains only three species with widely separated ranges. They are characterized by having the lower mandible significantly longer than the upper one. Both the upper and lower mandibles form two blades with the sharp edges facing one another. The birds feed by plowing the surface of calm waters with the lower bill and snapping up fish and other organisms.

LESSER BLACK-BACKED GULL   Plate 1
Larus fuscus

Identification: 53—63 cm (21—25″). Adults are distinguished by their large size, dark mantle and yellow legs. Immatures are nearly identical to Great Black-backed and Herring Gulls of the same age, thus identifying the young of these accidentally occurring species in the field should only be attempted by experts with assistance from more comprehensive guides to these birds.

Local Name: Gaviota menor espaldinegra

Comments: Accidental. Known from two Puerto Rico records (Feb., Mar.) and one from St Croix (Mar.) all in different years.

Distribution: Accidental in the West Indies, this gull is native to Europe, western Asia, and portions of Africa.

GREAT BLACK-BACKED GULL   Plate 4
Larus marinus

Identification: 69—79 cm (27—31″). The large size, black mantle and flesh-colored legs distinguish adults. The immature is easily confused with young Herring Gulls, but the former has a whiter head, rump, tail and underparts.

Local Name: Gaviota mayor espaldinegra

Comments: Accidental. Known from one bird photographed (Oct. to Jan.), two observed in Puerto Rico (Feb. (2)) and a sight record from Mona Island (Dec.).

Distribution: A vagrant to the West Indies, the gull's normal range includes the more northerly shores of the Atlantic Ocean east to northern Russia.

HERRING GULL   Plate 4
Larus argentatus

Identification: 56—66 cm (22—26″). Its large size helps to identify this gull. Young birds in their first winter have a

characteristically dark head and tail. During the second winter
the broad, poorly defined tail band is diagnostic. Adults have
a distinctive red mark on the bill.

Local Name: Gaviota argentea

Comments: A rare visitor to Puerto Rico and the Virgin Islands
from fall through the spring. There is one summer record. It
is a harbor gull only seen with regularity in San Juan bay. A
new species to the region, it is on the increase, but its numbers
are still low.

Distribution: Throughout the Northern Hemisphere.

RING-BILLED GULL   Plate 4
Larus delawarensis

Identification: 46–51 cm (18–20″). The ring on the bill of the
adult is distinctive. Young birds can be distinguished by the
narrow black band on the tail.

Local Name: Gaviota piquianillada

Comments: A common, but extremely local year-round visitor
to Puerto Rico where it is known almost exclusively from San
Juan harbor. Here a few can regularly be seen, though more
sparingly in summer, on the mudflats by Constitution Bridge.
One to two birds have been seen between July and March on
St Croix and there are several records from St Thomas and
one from St John. Not known from the region prior to 1960,
the species is increasing and will no doubt soon be recorded
from other localities.

Voice: A high-pitched *kee-ow, kee-ow, kee-ow*.

Distribution: Throughout the Bahamas and Greater Antilles and
throughout North America south to Panama.

COMMON BLACK-HEADED GULL   Plate 4
Larus ridibundus

Identification: 39–43 cm (15.5–17″). The immature in winter
plumage is identified by the black band on the tail, black spot
behind the eye and thin black bill, ochre at the base. Adults in
winter are similar, but have a dark red bill and lack the black
tail band. Adults in breeding plumage have not yet been
recorded. In all plumages this gull can only be distinguished

from the very similar Bonaparte's Gull, a vagrant to the region, by the dusky undersides of the primaries. The Gull-billed Tern is also similar in winter to the Common Black-headed Gull, but has a heavier bill and a lighter and larger spot behind the eye.

Local Name: Gaviota cabecinegra

Comments: A rare fall and winter visitor to Puerto Rico where it is observed with regularity only in San Juan harbor. There is one summer record. In the Virgin Islands there is a record of two immatures from Mangrove Lagoon, St Thomas and single records for St Croix and Tortola.

Distribution: Rare in the West Indies and eastern North America. Widespread throughout much of Eurasia occurring to northern Africa and the Philippines.

LAUGHING GULL   Plate 4
Larus atricilla

Identification: 38—43 cm (15—17"). The black head easily distinguishes the adult in summer. In winter the adult's head is white with dark markings. Young birds have a black tail band and a dark head and breast. This is the only common gull of the region.

Local Names: Sea Gull, Booby, Gullie, Gaviota gallega

Comments: A common spring and summer breeding resident in the region, rare in winter except in San Juan harbor where it remains common. The species frequents coastal waters.

Voice: A squawky, somewhat variable *caw* and *caw-aw*. Also what sounds like a laugh *ka-ka-ka-ka-ka-ka-ka-kaa-kaa-kaaa-kaaa*.

Nesting: Three to four grayish-brown eggs with large splotches are laid in a well woven nest on the ground. Rocky offshore cays are generally used for nesting which occurs in late spring and early summer.

Distribution: Throughout the New World.

GULL-BILLED TERN   Plate 6
Sterna nilotica

Identification: 33—38 cm (13—15"). The thick, black bill is distinctive. In winter plumage the large gray spot behind the eye helps identify this tern.

Local Names: Gullie, Egg Bird, Gaviota piquigorda

Comments: Uncommon in Puerto Rico, St Thomas, St Croix and Anegada from May to September. It is very rare outside of these months except in San Juan harbor where it is locally common in fall, winter and spring. This tern is typically found over freshwater lakes and brackish lagoons.

Voice: A raspy, insect-like *kay-ti-did, za-za-za* and *cha-chi*.

Nesting: In the region this tern was only known to nest on Cockroach Cay but does so no longer. Presently it probably nests on Anegada. Breeding is colonial in late spring and early summer. Two to three buff-colored eggs with spots are laid on the ground in a scant nest.

Distribution: Cosmopolitan.

FORSTER'S TERN   Plate 5
Sterna forsteri

Identification: 35−38 cm (14−15″). In winter plumage the distinct black mark behind the eye, which does not continue across the nape, is the surest field mark. Only winter-plumaged birds occur in the region.

Local Name: Gaviota de Forster

Comments: Extremely rare from January to early April. There are five records from Puerto Rico and three from the Virgin Islands. The species is apparently increasing in the region as all sightings have been since 1970. This tern can be found on mudflats resting with other terns, most regularly in San Juan harbor.

Distribution: The Greater Antilles, Bahamas, and North and Central America.

COMMON TERN   Plate 5
Sterna hirundo

Identification: 33−40 cm (13−16″). The deeply forked tail and dark outer primaries are important field marks. It is distinguished from the very similar Roseate Tern by its shorter tail which does not extend beyond the wing tips when the bird is perched.

Local Names: Gullie, Egg Bird, Gaviota común

Comments: Common in Puerto Rico and uncommon in the Virgin Islands during all seasons except winter when it is rare in both localities. During spring and fall, migrants augment local numbers. The species prefers shallow coastal waters.

Voice: A high-pitched *kik*, and when disturbed a sharp *kee-ar-r-r* with downward inflection.

Nesting: The only nesting colonies in the region are in the Virgin Islands on Little Flat Cay, Saba Cay, Dog Island and Shark Island. Generally three light brown eggs with dark splotches are laid in a scrape in the sand or among rocks in late spring.

Distribution: Cosmopolitan.

ROSEATE TERN

Plate 5

Sterna dougallii

Identification: 35−39 cm (14−15.5″). The longer, more deeply forked tail and paler mantle and primaries distinguish the Roseate from similar terns. When sitting, its tail feathers extend beyond the wing tips. The tail of the very similar Common Tern does not reach the wing tips. Common and Roseate Terns in this region often have similar bill coloration, thus this is a poor field mark.

Local Names: Sea Gull, David, Davie, Gullie, Palometa

Comments: A common breeding resident in the Virgin Islands, less common in Puerto Rico. It occurs primarily from April to September, but can be seen rarely in other months. Roseates prefer inshore areas and bays.

Voice: A squeaky, high-pitched *che-wít* and *kree-wít*, sometimes with the accent on the first syllable. When agitated it also calls a nasal *knaa*.

Nesting: Three to four eggs are laid in a rock crevice or a scrape in the soil on an offshore cay. These have a bluish tint and are covered with large brown splotches. Nesting is colonial and takes place in May and June.

Distribution: Nearly worldwide.

ARCTIC TERN Plate 1
Sterna paradisaea

Identification: 35−39 cm (14−15.5″). Very similar to the much more frequent Roseate and Common Terns. In breeding plumage the Arctic is distinguished from the Common Tern by its longer tail extending to the wing tips when perched, its entirely red bill, short legs, and less black in the primaries both on the upperside and underside of the wing (the black is nearly confined to the tips of the primaries). It differs from the Roseate Tern by its entirely red bill, gray rather than white mantle, darker and shorter tail (that of the Roseate extends beyond the wing tips when the bird is perched), and slightly darker wing tips. In nonbreeding plumage the bill of the adult Arctic Tern is black.

Local Name: Gaviota del árctico

Comments: Accidental. There are two records from around St John (Sept., Oct.) and three near St Croix (July, Aug., Sept.). There are no records from Puerto Rico. The Arctic Tern typically occurs further out to sea than the Common or Roseate Terns.

Distribution: A circumpolar breeder of the northern latitudes, it migrates to winter in southern oceans, sometimes as far south as the Antarctic.

BRIDLED TERN Plate 6
Sterna anaethetus

Identification: 35−38 cm (14−15″). The deep brownish-gray back, white line extending above and behind the eye and the white nape distinguish this tern. The very similar Sooty Tern appears to have solid black upperparts and a distinctive call.

Local Names: Egg Bird, Booby, Gaviota monja

Comments: A common nesting resident in the region from May to August and seen on rare occasions in other months. The Bridled Tern occurs offshore, particularly around rocky cays which the more common Sooty Tern also frequents.

Voice: A *wah* like a baby crying.

Nesting: One spotted egg of whitish ground color is usually laid in a rock crevice on an offshore cay. Breeding is generally between May and August.

Distribution: Virtually throughout the West Indies and tropical and subtropical seas of the world.

SOOTY TERN   Plate 6
Sterna fuscata

Identification: 38—43 cm (15—17 "). The appearance of having entirely black upperparts and white underparts distinguishes this tern. The similar Bridled Tern, which is also pelagic, has a brownish-gray back and a white nape.

Local Names: Egg Bird, Booby, Hurricane Bird, Gaviota oscura.

Comments: A common nesting resident in the region from May to August, it is rare in other months. It frequents offshore waters primarily around the cays where it breeds.

Voice: A sharp turkey-like gobble *tek-a-lik,*   . Also a raspy *kreck.*

Nesting: Thousands breed on islets around Culebra and smaller colonies occur elsewhere. The immense colony formerly on Punta Flamenco, Culebra has been greatly reduced, possibly due to habitat modification as a result of grazing. Nesting is from May to August. A single egg, extremely variable in coloration, is laid in a scrape under protective vegetation.

Distribution: Virtually throughout the West Indies and the tropical and subtropical seas of the world.

LEAST TERN   Plate 6
Sterna antillarum

Identification: 21.5—24 cm (8.5—9.5 "). Identified by its small size, yellow bill and feet and white forehead. Immatures and fall adults have a dark bill, lack the black cap and have a black line behind the eye. Immatures have darker wings. Least Terns can best be distinguished from winter plumaged Black and Forster's Terns by their smaller size and dull yellow feet.

Local Names: Sea Swallow, Peterman, Egg Bird, Kill-em-polly, Gaviota pequeña

Comments: An uncommon and very local breeding resident in the region. It has been recorded in every month except January, but is only found regularly from May to August. It generally occurs in calm waters, often not far from the flats where it breeds.

Voice: A variety of calls including a squeaky, high-pitched *o-ik* like a rusty pump, a common *chick* and a raspy, harsh and drawn out *waack*.

Nesting: Two to four heavily marked grayish-white eggs are laid in a scrape in the sand or on coral rubble. The birds nest in colonies on remote flats from May to August.

Distribution: Cosmopolitan.

ROYAL TERN   Plate 5
Sterna maxima

Identification: 46—53 cm (18—21 ″). The large size and brilliant fire-orange bill identify this tern.

Local Names: Gaby, Sprat Bird, Gullie, Egg Bird, Gaviota real

Comments: A common breeding resident in Puerto Rico and the Virgin Islands. However, it is uncommonly seen in summer when it is local around the several islets where it nests.

Voice: A harsh, high-pitched *kri-i-ik*, very similar to a parakeet.

Nesting: Breeding is loosely colonial in May and June when one, rarely two, white to pale buff-colored eggs spotted with brown are laid in the sand or a scrape on a remote cay. Six nesting colonies are known in the region.

Distribution: In coastal areas throughout most of the Western Hemisphere and the west coast of Africa.

CAYENNE TERN   Plate 5
Sterna eurygnatha

Identification: 40 cm (16 ″). The fairly large size and entirely dull yellow bill identify this tern. Sometimes birds are observed with varying degrees of black in the bill. These may have resulted from interbreeding with Sandwich Terns.

Local Name: Gaviota de Cayena

Comments: A rare and irregular visitor to Puerto Rico in all seasons and a rare breeding resident in the Virgin Islands. In Puerto Rico this tern is typically found in harbors such as those of San Juan and Mayaguez. Some authorities consider the Cayenne Tern a morphological form of the Sandwich Tern.

Nesting: Nests in late spring on Pelican Cay off St Thomas and on Anegada. Breeds in mixed pairs with Sandwich Terns. The nest is a scrape in the sand.

Distribution: Puerto Rico and the north and east coasts of South America including Trinidad and Tobago and other coastal islands.

SANDWICH TERN   Plate 5
Sterna sandvicensis

Identification: 35–40 cm (14–16″). The slender, black bill with its yellow tip is diagnostic.

Local Names: Cabot's Tern, Gullie, Egg Bird, Gaviota piquiaguda

Comments: Uncommon in Puerto Rico though locally abundant in San Juan harbor the year round. The species is common on Anegada, but is uncommon among the rest of the Virgin Islands. The Sandwich Tern appears to be gradually increasing in abundance in the region.

Voice: A variety of somewhat similar raspy and raucous call notes, *ki-rrit*, *krrit*, or just *kit*.

Nesting: The only certain breeding colonies in the region are on Anegada, two cays off St Thomas and two off Culebra. Usually two variously colored eggs are laid in the sand in late spring.

Distribution: Of nearly worldwide distribution.

CASPIAN TERN   Plate 5
Sterna caspia

Identification: 48–58 cm (19–23″). The large size and blood-red bill are good field marks. In winter plumage this tern has black flecks on the forehead as compared to the white forehead of the Royal Tern.

Local Name: Gaviota de Caspia

Comments: An extremely local visitor to Puerto Rico. One or two individuals have occurred regularly during all seasons of the year in San Juan harbor since the 1960s. There are a few recent records from Vieques and St Croix.

Distribution: A visitor to the Bahamas and Greater Antilles. Of nearly worldwide distribution.

BLACK TERN   Plate 6
Chlidonias niger

Identification: 23−25 cm (9−10″). In winter plumage the generally dark upperparts and unusual head markings are distinctive. It is only infrequently seen in its all black breeding plumage.

Local Name: Gaviota ceniza

Comments: A fairly common transient in Puerto Rico from late August through early October; additionally, there are two spring and two winter records. In the Virgin Islands it has only been recorded off islets near Virgin Gorda and at St Croix and Anegada. This tern occurs at both fresh and brackish ponds where it often hovers and flits about erratically.

Voice: A sharp metallic *peek* (Danforth).

Distribution: Cosmopolitan.

BROWN NODDY   Plate 6
Anous stolidus

Identification: 38 cm (15″). This dark brown tern with its white cap is unmistakable. Immatures are whitish on the forehead only.

Local Names: Noddy Tern, Lark, Egg Bird, Booby Blackbird, Cervera

Comments: A common late spring and early summer nesting resident in Puerto Rico and the Virgin Islands. It is found rarely through the rest of the year. This tern generally occurs well offshore, often around rocky islets.

Voice: The common call note is a harsh *kar-r-rk* and a scolding note resembles *kwok, kwok* (Wetmore).

Nesting: A single buff-colored egg, lightly spotted, is usually laid upon a ledge on the steep edge of a small offshore cay. Nests are sometimes built upon vegetation or in crevices. Nesting occurs from April to August.

Distribution: Throughout the West Indies and most tropical and subtropical seas of the world.

POMARINE JAEGER   Plate 3
Stercorarius pomarinus

Identification: 53—56 cm (21—22″). The blunt, twisted central tail feathers are diagnostic. This is the largest of the three jaegers, all of which have been recorded in the West Indies. The Pomarine and Parasitic Jaegers each have a dark and a light color phase. Immature birds lack the long tail feathers of adults and appear grayish-brown. The white webbing in the primaries identify them as jaegers.

Local Name: Págalo pomarino

Comments: An irregular visitor to waters well off the shores of Puerto Rico and the Virgin Islands from October to March; however, after storms it may be found near shore.

Distribution: Irregular in the West Indies. Breeds in the Arctic and winters throughout nearly all the oceans of the world.

SKUA   Plate 3
Catharacta 'skua'

Identification: 51—61 cm (20—24″). Distinguished by its massive build for a seabird and the conspicuous white patch at the base of the primaries. The scientific species name 'skua' is in quotation marks above because records do not indicate which of several similar species of skuas occur in the region. They could either be the reddish-brown Great Skua (*C. skua*) which tends to show a dark cap, the very large Brown or Southern Skua (*C. lonnbergi*) considered by some authorities to be a distinct species and identified by being dark chocolate brown with white flecks on the back, or the South Polar Skua (*C. maccormicki*) of which the light phase has a tan head while the dark phase is similar to the Great Skua, but lacks the rusty colored feathers.

Local Name: Págalo grande

Comments: Accidental. There are two records from off Puerto

Rico and two from off the Virgin Islands. The species occurs from November to May generally well out at sea, and thus the frequency with which it actually occurs offshore cannot be determined with accuracy.

Distribution: Skuas breed at both poles and range widely over the oceans of the world.

BLACK SKIMMER   Plate 4
Rynchops niger

Identification: 43—51 cm (17—20″). The long, orange bill tipped with black makes this bird unmistakable. Immatures are brown above flecked with white.

Local Name: Pico de tijera

Comments: An extremely rare transient in Puerto Rico (seven records) and the Virgin Islands (three records). It has been encountered well offshore, apparently migrating, and resting on mudflats with terns and gulls. It may occur in any season.

Distribution: A transient in the West Indies, but a breeding bird along most of the eastern coasts of the Americas. Some birds winter on the west coast of Mexico and Central America.

Pigeons and Doves
FAMILY: COLUMBIDAE

The pigeons are a cosmopolitan family of plump, gregarious birds. A clapping or whirring sound of the wings is often conspicuous as they take flight and most species are strong flyers. There is no sharp line differentiating pigeons from doves, the latter generally being smaller and longer tailed. The native doves of the region, with the exception of the Whitewings, feed on the ground while indigenous pigeons are arboreal.

WHITE-CROWNED PIGEON   Plate 25
Columba leucocephala

Identification: 33—35.5 cm (13—14″). The body appears entirely slate gray with the exception of the distinct white crown. The crown of the female is a grayish-white and immatures have still grayer crowns.

Local Names: Blue Pigeon, White Head, Baldpate, Paloma cabeciblanca

Comments: Once an abundant breeding bird in Puerto Rico and the Virgin Islands, this species is now rare on Puerto Rico proper and decidedly uncommon on most of the larger and more heavily populated of the Virgin Islands. The species is still fairly common in some mangroves, particularly on smaller, undisturbed islands. White-crowns are most common in this region in spring and summer when visitants from other islands augment local numbers and breed. Where food is available year round these arboreal pigeons are resident, and most localities where the species breeds have a few birds throughout the year. Hunting is primarily responsible for the White-crown's demise and where it is not permitted the bird often recuperates well. An excellent example of this is the grounds of the Dorado Beach Hotel in Puerto Rico where a resident population of several hundred White-crowns prospers while the species is virtually absent from adjacent coastal areas.

Voice: *Cruu, crú, cu-cuu, crúuu* _/_ _ ‾\. Much faster and less deliberate than the Scaly-naped Pigeon, with the second syllable having a characteristic rising inflection.

Nesting: White-crowns are colonial nesters, making flimsy twig nests, typically in mangroves or areas of dry scrub. Two glossy white eggs are laid. Breeding is primarily from March to July, but occurs as late as September. During a given year nesting seasons differ from area to area depending on local conditions.

Distribution: Throughout the West Indies as far south as St Lucia. Also the Florida Keys and western Caribbean islands.

SCALY-NAPED PIGEON   Plate 25
Columba squamosa

Identification: 35.5—40 cm (14—16″). At a distance this pigeon appears entirely slate gray. At close range the head, neck and breast have a wine tint. Young birds are more ruddy than adults. Scaly-naped Pigeons are slightly larger than White-crowns and lack any white on the head. They are much larger and darker than doves.

Local Names: Red-necked Pigeon, Blue Pigeon, Red Head, Paloma turca, Paloma rubia

Comments: The common, resident, arboreal pigeon of the mountain forests of Puerto Rico and the Virgin Islands where it is frequently seen flying rapidly over the forest canopy. On occasion, particularly in the Virgin Islands and on Puerto Rico's larger offshore islands, the species ranges into well wooded areas of the lowlands and the White-crowned Pigeon ranges up into the hills so that both species are found together.

Voice: The distinctive common call heard frequently in the early morning is an emphatic *cruu, cruu-cru-cruuu* the heaviest accent being on the fourth syllable. The first syllable is separated by a pause and is very soft. A verbal rendition of the last three syllables would be *Who are you!* — ‾ _ ‵.

Nesting: A frail stick nest is made in a tree or bush. On uninhabited islands these pigeons have been reported even to nest on the ground. Two glossy white eggs are laid. Breeding is principally from March to August.

Distribution: Throughout the West Indies except for the Bahamas. Also islands off Venezuela.

PLAIN PIGEON   Plate 25
Columba inornata

Identification: 38—40 cm (15—16″). Paler than the other large pigeons, with more brown in the plumage. In flight a thin white line transversing the wing is diagnostic. Immature birds are darker than adults. When perched this species is difficult to distinguish from the Scaly-naped Pigeon, but can be identified by the wine color on the wing and belly, and white band on the leading edge of the wing.

Local Name: Paloma sabanera

Comments: The Plain Pigeon is extremely endangered and known to survive in numbers only in the forested ravines and bamboo clumps surrounding Lake Cidra. Continued development in the area threatens to extirpate the bird from the island. This species is unusually tame and can often be seen on telephone wires over residences in the area. Approximately 100 birds are known to survive. There are periodic reports of Plain Pigeons from scattered localities throughout Puerto Rico. It is questionable whether the bird on Puerto Rico is an endemic subspecies.

Voice: _A deep, deliberate *whóo, wo-oo,* ⁄ _ or *who, oo-óo,* _ _ and other variations.

Nesting: Plain Pigeons build fragile stick nests in bamboo clumps or clusters of vines. Only a single dull white egg is laid, but three clutches may be raised in a season. Nesting occurs primarily from February to August, though a few birds have been known to nest in the fall.

Distribution: Puerto Rico, Cuba, Hispaniola, and Jamaica.

ROCK DOVE   Plate 25
Columba livia

Identification: 33—35.5 cm (13—14 ″). Very variable in color. Wild birds normally have a black tail band and white rump. Their plumage is distinctly more colorful than that of the native wild pigeons.

Local Names: Domestic Pigeon, Paloma casera

Comments: The abundant, tame, resident species of city streets and populated rural areas of Puerto Rico and the Virgin Islands. Though very tame and always willing to take a hand-out, the species breeds in the wild and many birds are no doubt feral. Rock Doves rarely occur in the more remote habitats where the other large pigeons of the region are found.

Voice: A varied assortment of gentle cooing notes.

Nesting: Nests are constructed on buildings, bridges or other available ledges and in palms. Two white eggs are a normal clutch.

Distribution: Found throughout the West Indies, North, Central and South America, and temperate portions of the Old World. Introduced through much of its range.

MOURNING DOVE   Plate 25
Zenaida macroura

Identification: 28—33 cm (11—13 ″). Its long, wedge-shaped tail fringed with white is distinctive. There is no white in the wings as there is with the Zenaida and White-winged Doves.

Local Names: Tórtola rabilarga, Rabiche

Comments: An uncommon resident on Puerto Rico's coast, its numbers are increasing. It now occurs on Culebra and Vieques, but not the Virgin Islands. Unknown from Puerto Rico prior to 1935, flocks of as many as 200 birds recently have been seen. Open country near bodies of fresh water are the preferred habitat though it is found in the lower mountains where the proper conditions are available. The Mourning Dove is most common in southwestern Puerto Rico and on Vieques. It is a ground feeder and usually occurs in flocks except when adults pair to breed.

Voice: A mournful cooing almost identical to the Zenaida Dove, *coo-oo, coo, coo, coo*, the second syllable rising sharply ⌐ _ _ _ .

Nesting: A nest of twigs and grasses is constructed at a low to medium elevation in a bush or tree, though at times on the ground. Two white eggs make up a clutch. Breeding is from March to July.

Distribution: The Greater Antilles, Bahamas, and North and Central America.

ZENAIDA DOVE   Plate 25
Zenaida aurita

Identification: 25−28 cm (10−11″). The white band on the trailing edge of the secondaries, coupled with the rounded tail, is distinctive. The Mourning Dove has no white in the wings and the White-winged Dove has a large white wing patch.

Local Names: Mountain Dove, Tórtola cardosantera

Comments: A common resident in Puerto Rico and the Virgin Islands. It is a ground dweller of open areas primarily on the coast, but occurs into the mountains where suitable habitat is available. Where hunting is restricted this dove is surprisingly tame and may become abundant. The grounds of hotels, universities, public beaches and the like are ideal localities for this bird.

Voice: A gentle cooing, almost identical to the Mourning Dove, *coo-oo, coo, coo, coo*, the second syllable rising sharply ⌐ _ _ _ .

Nesting: A thin platform of twigs in a bush or tree, though sometimes on the ground, makes up the nest. Two white eggs are laid. Breeding peaks in the spring, but may occur at any time of year.

Distribution: Throughout the West Indies, infrequently occurring on the southern coast of Florida. Also the coast of the Yucatán Peninsula and its offshore islands.

WHITE-WINGED DOVE   Plate 25
Zenaida asiatica

Identification: 28—30 cm (11—12″). The large white wing patch, rather than a thin white band on the trailing edge of the secondaries, distinguishes the White-winged Dove from the very similar Zenaida Dove in flight. Perched, the former displays more white in the wing. The Plain Pigeon has a white band transversing its wing, but this bar is much narrower than that of the Whitewing, and the Plain Pigeon is a much larger and grayer bird.

Local Name: Tórtola aliblanca

Comments: An uncommon resident in Puerto Rico, a very rare visitor in spring to St Croix and a single record for St John. The species was first recorded in Puerto Rico in 1943 and is gradually becoming more common. The White-winged Dove is confined to coastal regions where it primarily frequents arid scrub, but also occurs in mangrove swamps and some well protected open woodland within San Juan (Isla Grande).

Voice: *Coo-co,co-coo* or *coó-co,co-co-coó* on a single pitch. Also a distinctive yodel-like cooing modulating between two notes ⌣ ⌒ ⌣ ⌒ ⌣ ⌒

Nesting: These doves nest colonially making frail nests of twigs and grasses at low to moderate heights above the ground. Two white eggs are laid. The breeding season is from April to August with a peak in May and June.

Distribution: Puerto Rico (including Mona Island and Vieques), St Croix, St John, the other Greater Antilles, the Bahamas, and small islands of the western Caribbean Sea. Also southern North America, Central America, and the central portion of South America's west coast.

RINGED TURTLE-DOVE   Plate 25
Streptopelia risoria

Identification: 28—30 cm (11—12 ″). The only light tan dove in
the region, excepting a few domestic pigeons, it has a distinct
black band around the nape of the neck.

Local Names: Barbary Dove, Tórtola collarina, Paloma collarina

Comments: Regularly seen in a semidomesticated state in rural
areas of Puerto Rico and St Croix. There is one sight record
for St John. It is possible that in some localities the species is
established in a feral state, but this is not yet verified. One nest
has been found in the wild.

Voice: A variety of calls including *whó-cru-ru-ru-ru-oo,who*. The first
syllable is loudest followed by a guttural trill. The last note fades
away‾ __ _ _ _ _ ‾ ₎ ·

Nesting: Successful nesting has been observed in upland forests
and mangroves of St Croix. The nest is a frail, shallow platform
of twigs in which two eggs are laid.

Distribution: Introduced in Puerto Rico and elsewhere. Native
to North Africa.

SPOTTED DOVE   Plate 25
Streptopelia chinensis

Identification: 30 cm (12 ″). The black band spotted with white
on the nape, the long tail broadly tipped with white, and the
light gray bend of the wing distinguish this dark dove.

Local Name: Tórtola moteada

Comments: Very local around the Estate Canaan on St Croix
resulting from releases. The Spotted Dove occurs in such small
numbers that it may not survive though it is currently breeding
in the wild. It has not been introduced to the other Virgin
Islands or Puerto Rico.

Voice: A variety of cooing calls.

Nesting: About 20 pairs breed in the spring around Estate
Canaan.

Distribution: Introduced in St Croix and many other parts of
the world. Native to Southeast Asia including India, China,
and Indonesia.

COMMON GROUND-DOVE   Plate 25
Columbina passerina

Identification: 15—18 cm (6—7″). The only tiny dove of this region. It flashes rufous in the wings in flight. The female is slightly paler above and duller below than the male.

Local Name: Rolita

Comments: An abundant resident in Puerto Rico and the Virgin Islands, it occurs primarily in coastal habitat from mangroves, palm groves and residential areas to cane fields and arid scrublands. It is probably most common in arid regions and is only absent from heavily wooded areas. As its name implies this dove is primarily terrestrial, but sometimes seeks refuge in the cover of trees.

Voice: A monotonous, often repeated call on a single note, *coo, coo, coo, coo,* etc.

Nesting: A nest of rootlets, grasses or twigs is placed in a bush, tree or on the ground. Generally two glossy white eggs are laid per clutch with breeding occurring from February to October with a peak from April to June.

Distribution: Virtually throughout the West Indies and also the southern USA, Central America, and northern South America.

RUDDY QUAIL-DOVE   Plate 25
Geotrygon montana

Identification: 25 cm (10″). This dove of the forest floor is distinguished by its predominantly rusty coloration. The female is less ruddy than the male. Other quail-doves in the region have a white rather than buff-colored stripe below the eye and whiter underparts.

Local Name: Paloma perdiz rojiza

Comments: A fairly common resident in Puerto Rico. There are several records from St John and St Croix and one from St Thomas. The Ruddy Quail-Dove inhabits heavily forested areas of the hills and mountains seasonally migrating to different elevations up to approximately 650 m (2000 ft). It dwells on the forest floor where it is much more often heard than seen. However, in the early morning numbers may be flushed from trails and road edges. The coffee plantations, where rotting oranges supply an abundance of food, and the lower slopes of the Luquillo Mountains are probably where this quail-dove is most common. With the gradual reforestation of the larger Virgin Islands, the Ruddy Quail-Dove may colonize these areas.

Voice: A mournful coo gradually fading in strength and sometimes in pitch, like blowing across the mouth of a bottle. Very ventriloquial.

Nesting: A loose nest of twigs and leaves is constructed near, and sometimes on, the ground. Two light buff-colored eggs are laid. Breeding occurs from February to August.

Distribution: Puerto Rico and most of the West Indies, Central America and South America except for the southern portion.

KEY WEST QUAIL-DOVE   Plate 25
Geotrygon chrysia

Identification: 28–30 cm (11–12″). The white line under the eye, ruddy back and wings and primarily white underparts distinguish this quail-dove. The Bridled Quail-Dove has browner upperparts and the Ruddy Quail-Dove has more rufous underparts and a duller streak below the eye.

Local Name: Paloma perdiz aúrea

Comments: A rare and local resident in Puerto Rico, not known from the Virgin Islands. The Key West Quail-Dove is generally found among well wooded scrubby thickets in arid areas, where it stays near the ground and is more often heard than seen. It is known on Puerto Rico's south coast primarily from Ponce west and on the north coast among the haystack hills from Arecibo to Isabela. Additionally, a small, isolated population inhabits a wooded area south of Tortuguero Lagoon. The Key West Quail-Dove also occurs very locally on Vieques.

Voice: A moan on one pitch, gradually increasing in volume and then fading rapidly. Very ventriloquial.

Nesting: Reported to nest in low undergrowth or on the ground. The nest is a loose platform of twigs. Ordinarily two buff-colored eggs are laid. Breeding is in the spring.

Distribution: Puerto Rico and Vieques west through the Greater Antilles, and some of the Bahamas, accidental in Florida.

BRIDLED QUAIL-DOVE   Plate 25
Geotrygon mystacea

Identification: 30 cm (12″). The white streak below the eye, brown upperparts (except for crown and neck) and rufous limited to a patch on the wing distinguish this from other quail-doves.

Local Names: Partridge, Wood Dove, Barbary Dove, Marmy Dove, Moustached Quail-Dove, Paloma perdiz bigoteada, Perdiz de Martinica, Gitana, Tornasól

Comments: A common resident on the larger, more heavily forested Virgin Islands but extremely rare and local in Puerto Rico. The history of the Bridled Quail-Dove in this region is rather strange. For many years the species was known from Puerto Rico only by a single specimen from Culebra. Recently, populations were discovered on Vieques, Roosevelt Roads Naval Reserve, and in the haystack hills south of Arecibo. In the Virgin Islands the Bridled Quail-Dove was very scarce in the early part of the century, but has made a strong comeback on most of the larger islands. This species is confined to dense forests with thick undergrowth where it spends most of its time on the ground. It is much more frequently heard than seen. Generally, the Bridled Quail-Dove inhabits forested hills while the Key West prefers arid scrub, but both species apparently occur together in the haystack hills south of Arecibo.

Voice: A mournful *who-whóoo*, on one note or descending towards the end, getting loudest in the middle of the second syllable and then trailing off. Sometimes the first syllable is omitted.

Nesting: A flimsy nest of twigs is usually built at a low elevation above the ground. Several nests are constructed before one is settled upon as a nest site. Generally, two salmon-buff eggs are laid. Breeding occurs from late spring to mid-summer and to a lesser extent from October to December.

Distribution: Puerto Rico (including Vieques and possibly Culebra), the larger of the Virgin Islands with the exception of Anegada, and south through most of the Lesser Antilles to St Lucia.

Parrots and Parakeets
FAMILY: PSITTACIDAE

The parrots form a distinctive family typical of warmer climates. They are easily recognized by their raucous calls, large heads and extremely heavy bills which are often used to assist them in their movements among the tree branches. All species regularly seen in the region are gregarious and primarily green and all the *Amazona* parrots, as well as many of the parakeets, have blue primaries. Those referred to as parakeets are distinguished by their long, pointed tails and smaller size. Flight is direct with rapid, shallow wingbeats. With the exception of the endemic Puerto Rican Parrot, the species occurring in the region have been introduced, primarily as a result of caged birds escaping. The Brown-throated Parakeet is long established, but the remaining introductions were apparently made during the late 1950s and the 1960s.

BUDGERIGAR   Plate 26
Melopsittacus undulatus

Identification: 18 cm (7″). The typical pet shop parakeet or 'budgie' is well known to everyone. Its natural coloration is green below with a yellow head and back heavily barred with black; however, varieties in a wide range of other colors have been bred.

Local Names: Parakeet, Budgie, Periquito de Australia

Comments: A regular escapee in the San Juan area, particularly around Río Piedras, it may have become established as a breeding bird. Budgies are generally found singly feeding with flocks of weavers in short grass.

Voice: A sharp screech.

Distribution: Introduced in Puerto Rico and elsewhere. Native to Australia.

ORANGE-FRONTED PARAKEET   Plate 26
Aratinga canicularis

Identification: 23−24 cm (9−9.5″). A medium-sized parakeet with an orange forehead and white eye-ring. The primaries are blue. Immatures have a smaller orange forehead patch than adults.

Local Names: Halfmoon Conure, Orange-fronted Conure, Petz Conure, Periquito frentianaranjado

Comments: A rare, recently introduced species in Puerto Rico, it occurs in small numbers in San Juan and wooded pastures near Las Croabas in Fajardo; it may possibly be established.

Voice: Raspy squawks, not as harsh as that of the Monk Parakeet.

Nesting: The nest has not yet been found in Puerto Rico.

Distribution: Puerto Rico (introduced). Native to Mexico and Central America.

BROWN-THROATED PARAKEET   Plate 26
Aratinga pertinax

Identification: 23−28 cm (9−11″). The face and forehead are yellowish-orange while the throat, breast and belly are duller. The primaries are blue.

Local Names: Parakeet, Caribbean Parakeet, Brown-throated Conure, Periquito gargantimoreno

Comments: This parakeet, apparently introduced to St Thomas from Curaçao many years ago, is fairly common on that island, particularly near the eastern end. In 1974 it was found on Puerto Rico's eastern tip and has bred there. In recent years it has also been recorded from Culebra, where it probably breeds, Tortola where it may be established, and St John where it apparently is not established. Unidentified flocks of parakeets that may be of this species occur on Tortola. In St Thomas the bird prefers wooded thickets in the hills.

Voice: A raucous squawk.

Nesting: It has the extraordinary habit of constructing its nest cavities in active termite nests. Breeding is from March to July and four to seven chalky white eggs normally form a clutch.

Distribution: Introduced in St Thomas and southern Florida. It has expanded its range to Puerto Rico and Culebra and possibly Tortola and St John. Native to Panama, northern South America, and its adjacent islands.

HISPANIOLAN PARAKEET   Plate 26
Aratinga chloroptera

Identification: 28—30 cm (11—12 ″). The white eye-ring and the red bend of the wing are important characters. In flight the red underwing coverts are diagnostic. The tail is long and pointed.

Local Names: Hispaniolan Conure, Periquito de La Española

Comments: Introduced recently, a flock of as many as 15 has been seen around Mayaguez and a few birds are known from San Germán and Lares. The Hispaniolan Parakeet is probably established in Puerto Rico, but no evidence of nesting has yet been found. Observations are primarily from forested areas among the hills and lower mountain slopes. At least one bird occurred for several months on Mona Island.

Voice: Raucous squawks.

Distribution: Introduced into Puerto Rico. Native to Hispaniola.

MONK PARAKEET   Plate 26
Myiopsitta monachus

Identification: 28 cm (11 ″). A fairly large parakeet with the crown, breast and belly gray. The hindneck and the rest of the upperparts are green. The flight feathers are blue.

Local Names: Quaker Parakeet, Quaker Conure, Gray-breasted Parakeet, Periquito monje

Comments: Recently introduced, it is common around El Morro in Old San Juan and the Isla Grande Reserve in Santurce. It is now also fairly common in the Luquillo Beach-Fajardo area and uncommon elsewhere on the coast. The species is expanding its range and should be looked for in palm groves. One individual bird has been observed on St Croix.

Voice: An unusually loud and raucous series of squawks.

Nesting: Unique among all psittacines in that it constructs a large, sometimes huge stick nest, often at the base of palm fronds. This nest is used communally and contains separate chambers for the various pairs of parakeets. Five to eight eggs form a clutch.

Distribution: Puerto Rico (introduced) and now established locally in the USA. Native to the central portion of South America.

CANARY-WINGED PARAKEET   Plate 26
Brotogeris versicolurus

Identification: 23 cm (9″). A small parakeet (though larger than a budgerigar), that when perched appears entirely green with the exception of its ivory colored bill and a yellow margin on the leading edge of the wing. In flight the wings flash a large whitish-yellow triangle that is unmistakable.

Local Names: Canary-winged Bee Bee, White-winged Parakeet, Bee Bee Parrot, Periquito aliamarillo

Comments: Locally common, though widely dispersed in Puerto Rico. It is the most successfully established of the introduced psittacines in Puerto Rico and can be seen in flocks of over 100 birds. This species frequents woodland areas along the coast, low hills, and the foothills of the higher mountains. Flocks move about feeding on seasonal fruits and sometimes cause damage to farmers' crops. This parakeet is most readily seen on the campus of Inter American University in San Germán where a flock resides the year round. Another large flock roosts near Punta Miquillo in Río Grande from which the parakeets can be seen dispersing at dawn.

Voice: High-pitched squawks.

Nesting: Three nests have been found, all excavated within termite nests.

Distribution: Introduced in Puerto Rico and elsewhere. Native throughout most of South America.

RED-CROWNED PARROT   Plate 26
Amazona viridigenalis

Identification: 30–33 cm (12–13″). Very similar to the Puerto Rican Parrot, but with more red on the crown. In flight the Red-crowned flashes an orange-red patch in the wing. The habitats of these two species are not known to overlap. At close range the lilac coloration on the crown of this parrot can be observed.

Local Names: Green-cheeked Amazon, Cotorra coronirroja

Comments: Recently introduced and established in Puerto Rico where it is known from Río Piedras, Vega Baja, Rincón and Salinas. Though still rare, it is most easily encountered in the parrot roost at Dr Julia Hospital in Hato Rey, the Agriculture Experimental Station in Río Piedras and at the entrance to the Salinas Training Area.

Voice: A distinct call, not nearly as raspy and raucous as most parrots, *keet, kau-kau-kau-kau*.

Nesting: A nest with young was in the cavity of a dead tree.

Distribution: Introduced in Puerto Rico and elsewhere. Native to Mexico south through Central America and northern South America.

YELLOW-CROWNED PARROT   Plate 26
Amazona ochrocephala

Identification: 35.5 cm (14″). The largest of the region's green parrots, it has yellow on the head which may cover from the neck up, or just occur in odd patches on the face, neck or crown. In flight a red patch is visible in the wing.

Local Names: Yellow-headed Parrot, Yellow-headed Amazon, Yellow-crowned Amazon, Cotorra cabeziamarilla

Comments: Introduced recently, it is rare in Puerto Rico where it is known to breed. There have been sightings of small numbers at various localities along the north coast. It is most readily observed at the Río Piedras Agriculture Experimental Station and the parrot roost at Dr Julia Hospital in Hato Rey.

Voice: Raucous squawks.

Nesting: Found nesting from February to June in a hollow Royal Palm on the golf course of the Dorado Beach Hotel.

Distribution: Introduced in Puerto Rico and southern California. Native from Mexico to central South America.

ORANGE-WINGED PARROT   Plate 26
Amazona amazonica

Identification: 32 cm (12.5″). This parrot has yellow on the cheeks and crown. The lores and eye stripe are blue. In flight an orange-red patch in the wing is conspicuous.

Local Names: Orange-winged Amazon, Cotorra alianaranjada

Comments: Recently introduced and probably breeds; it is fairly common in the San Juan area, particularly near Dr Julia Hospital in Hato Rey and at the Agriculture Experimental Station in Río Piedras. It has not been recorded elsewhere in Puerto Rico. Two or three birds have been reported together on St Croix for over a year.

Voice: The call is weaker, less raucous and is higher pitched than most other parrots, *kweet, kweet, kweet, kweet.*

Nesting: The nest has not yet been found in Puerto Rico.

Distribution: Introduced in Puerto Rico and elsewhere. Native to Trinidad, Tobago, and northern and central South America.

HISPANIOLAN PARROT   Plate 26
Amazona ventralis

Identification: 28—30 cm (11—12″). The white eye-ring and forehead, black mark behind the eye and maroon belly are characteristic of this parrot. In flight it flashes blue primaries and no red or orange wing patch.

Local Names: Hispaniolan Amazon, Dominican Parrot, Santo Domingo Parrot, Salle's Parrot, Cotorra de La Española, Cotorra dominicana

Comments: Recently introduced; an uncommon resident in the woodlands of Puerto Rico's coastal plain and low hills. A few birds have also survived on St Thomas and St Croix for several years, but are probably not established. Large numbers of these parrots are apparently illegally imported into the region from Hispaniola by persons wanting to bring them back as pets. It is a frequently related story, though unconfirmed, that a boat bringing a shipment of Hispaniolan Parrots to Puerto Rico in the early 1960s was not permitted to unload its cargo, where-upon the ship left the port of Mayaguez and released its cargo, letting the birds fly to the island.

Voice: While perched or in flight this parrot typically emits a series of three or more squawks among its wide repertoire of other harsh notes.

Nesting: Cavities in trees are the principal nest sites. Breeding is primarily in the spring with two to three white eggs forming a normal clutch.

Distribution: Introduced in Puerto Rico, St Thomas and St Croix. Native to Hispaniola.

PUERTO RICAN PARROT   Plate 27
Amazona vittata

Identification: 30 cm (12″). Identified by its white eye-ring, red forehead, and two-toned blue primaries. It may be confused with the very similar Red-crowned Parrot now established along the coast, but the latter has an orange-red patch in the wing.

Local Names: Puerto Rican Amazon, Cotorra de Puerto Rico

Comments: The endemic Puerto Rican Parrot is one of the rarest birds in the world. In 1975, only 13 wild parrots were known to survive in the rain forest of the Luquillo Mountains in addition to another eight birds in captivity. Fortunately, numbers have increased slightly since then and as of December 1988 there were between 30 and 36 birds in the wild and 46 in captivity. The few remaining wild birds might best be looked for in the vicinity of the recreation area along Route 191 in the Luquillo Forest.

It required six years of intensive studies on the parrot, sponsored by the US Fish and Wildlife Service and the US Forest Service, before the complicated factors responsible for the species' near demise were finally pinned down with some degree of accuracy. The cutting of the forests of the lowlands no doubt destroyed the large majority of the parrot's native habitat, particularly the huge old trees that contained rotten cavities essential for the nesting of the species. Along with the clearing of the land came the planting of crops, which in past centuries were frequently raided by the parrots.

Because of their threat to agriculture, these slow flying birds were routinely shot by farmers. They were also regularly collected to be sold as pets. This practice has continued right up until recent years and is particularly detrimental, because a technique sometimes used to harvest young birds from inaccessible nests is to cut the entire limb from the nest tree just before the nestlings fledge. This type of nest destruction, coupled with the devastating effect that the hurricanes San Felipe (1928) and San Ciprián (1932) had on the 'Palo Colorado' (*Cyrilla racemiflora*) trees that supply almost all the suitable parrot nesting cavities in the Luquillo Forest, has left few appropriate nest site for the parrots in the areas where they typically breed.

Other lesser factors, but important ones, that are having a negative influence on the remaining population of Puerto Rican Parrots are the arboreal Brown or Roof Rat, the predatory Pearly-eyed Thrasher which preys on untended eggs and chicks, a warble fly (family Muscidae), the larvae of which sometimes infest nestlings so badly that they do not survive, and the Red-tailed Hawk. Fortunately, management practices have improved to the point where many of these threats have been brought under control.

Voice: A wide variety of raucous squawks including a distinct bugling call which is issued only in flight.

Nesting: A large, deep tree cavity is used for nesting and three to four white eggs form the normal clutch. Breeding occurs from late February through early June.

Distribution: Confined to Puerto Rico proper. An endemic subspecies once known from the island of Culebra is now extinct.

BLACK-HOODED PARAKEET   Plate 26
Nandayus nenday

Identification: 35.5 cm (14″). A large parakeet, distinguished by its black head, red thighs and long tail.

Local Names: Nanday Conure, Black-hooded Conure, Periquito caperuzado

Comments: Recently introduced; rare and local in Puerto Rico in the northeast (Isla Verde, Fajardo and Palmer), northwest (Aguadilla) and the southwest (La Parguera). It has been recorded only in small numbers and possibly is not yet established, but appears to be increasing. This parakeet seems to prefer thicketed pastures and sparsely wooded areas and should be looked for around the entire coast. A single bird, apparently an escapee, has been observed for years on St Croix.

Voice: Raucous squawks.

Nesting: There are no nesting records from Puerto Rico.

Distribution: Introduced in Puerto Rico and elsewhere. Native to central South America.

Cuckoos and Anis
FAMILY: CUCULIDAE

Cuckoos are slender birds with long tails and long, thin bills that are somewhat decurved. They are very slow and deliberate in their movements among the tree branches and their flight is direct. Many species, though not those in this region, are brood parasites laying their eggs in the nests of other birds. The anis which are confined to the New World tropics and subtropics form an unusual assemblage of three species within the Cuculidae. All are black with a characteristic broad bill and have the unique communal nesting habit described for the Smooth-billed Ani.

MANGROVE CUCKOO   Plate 21
Coccyzus minor

Identification: 28—30 cm (11—12″). Distinguished by the black mark through the eye and its buff-colored underparts. Flight is direct with short glides with no rufous visible in the wings.

Local Names: Mani Coco, Cow Bird, Cat Bird, Dumb Bird, Rain Bird, Maybird, Four o'clock Bird, Coffin Bird, Gogo, Pájaro bobo menor

Comments: A fairly common permanent resident in Puerto Rico and the Virgin Islands where it is found in greatest numbers in dry scrub. This cuckoo also inhabits mangrove swamps, coffee plantations and most areas with significant forests or thickets except for high mountains. It tolerates a greater diversity of habitats than the Yellow-bill.

Voice: Similar to that of the Yellow-bill, but slower and more nasal.

Nesting: A flimsy stick nest is constructed and two to three blue eggs are laid. The limited data on its breeding season suggest it extends from February to June.

Distribution: Throughout most of the West Indies, southern Florida, Central America and northern South America.

YELLOW-BILLED CUCKOO   Plate 21
Coccyzus americanus

Identification: 28−32 cm (11−12.5″). Distinguished by its completely white underparts. The rufous patch in the wings in flight is diagnostic.

Local Names: Rain Bird, Rain Crow, Pájaro bobo piquiamarillo

Comments: An uncommon nesting resident in Puerto Rico, fairly common in the spring and fall when migrants occur. It is rare in winter in Puerto Rico and during all seasons in the Virgin Islands where it has been found to nest on St Croix. During April and October Yellow-bills sometimes pass through the region in very large concentrations. This species is most commonly found in arid scrubland though it also occurs in mangrove swamps and woodlands at low elevations. It is found more commonly than the Mangrove Cuckoo only in the dry forests near Guánica, Puerto Rico.

Voice: A throaty *ka-ka-ka-ka-ka-ka-ka-ka-ka-kow, kow, kow, kow* (or *kowp, kowp, kowp, kowp* at end). The volume increases initially, then remains constant. The call slows substantially during the final syllables.

Nesting: A flimsy stick nest is made in which two to five blue eggs are laid. Breeding occurs from May to July.

Distribution: The Greater Antilles, northern Lesser Antilles and Bahamas. Also from the USA to South America.

PUERTO RICAN LIZARD-CUCKOO   Plate 22
Saurothera vieilloti

Identification: 40−48 cm (16−19″). Distinguished from other cuckoos by its larger size, very long tail, and two toned underparts (gray on chin and breast, cinnamon on belly and undertail coverts). Immatures have a cinnamon wash rather than gray on the breast.

Local Name: Pájaro bobo mayor

Comments: A fairly common though inconspicuous permanent resident of forested areas in Puerto Rico. More often heard than seen. The Puerto Rican Lizard-Cuckoo is common in the haystack hills of the north coast, coffee plantations, and all mountainous areas with thick forests. It occurs in numbers in xeric forests in the vicinity of Guánica. This species is quite inactive, often sitting quietly among dense vegetation. Apparently oblivious of the threat of humans, this cuckoo shows little alarm at one's approach. The diet of this bird is entirely animal matter consisting primarily of small lizards though also including large spiders and insects. Locally it is often called the 'Pájaro de agua' ('Water Bird') because its call is believed to forecast rain.

Voice: An emphatic *ka-ka-ka-ka*, etc., of long duration gradually accelerating and becoming louder, sometimes with altered syllables at the end. It also gives soft *caws* and other call notes.

Nesting: The nest is a loose structure of sticks and leaves in which two to three white eggs are laid. Breeding appears to occur throughout the year based on the limited data that exist on the nesting of this species. The Puerto Rican Lizard-Cuckoo, unlike many other species in its family, is not known to lay its eggs in the nests of other birds.

Distribution: Virtually confined to Puerto Rico proper, though there are single specimens from the islands of Vieques and St Thomas.

SMOOTH-BILLED ANI   Plate 21
Crotophaga ani

Identification: 30−33 cm (12−13″). A large, entirely black bird with a very heavy, parrot-like bill. Its conspicuous long, flat tail distinguishes it from the only bird with which it might be confused, the grackle, whose tail is V-shaped. Flight is straight, performed by rapid but shallow wing strokes followed by short glides.

Local Names: Black Witch, Black Parrot, Black Daw, Long-tailed Crow, Tickbird, Savanna Blackbird, Old Arnold, Chapman Bird, Garrapatero, Judío

Comments: The ani is a common permanent resident in Puerto

Rico and the Virgin Islands, living in small flocks in open lowland habitats with scattered trees or bushes. These vary from large gardens and sugar cane fields to pastures and arid scrublands.

Voice: A very loud and conspicuous squawky whistle *a-leep*

Nesting: The Smooth-billed Ani, along with the other two members of its genus, is unique in the bird world in building a bulky nest which is sometimes used communally by several females. Twenty or more eggs are regularly found in a single nest with groups of four to five eggs being laid in layers separated by leaves. Only the top eggs ever hatch. The eggs are sky blue with a chalky white coating that is easily scratched off. Breeding apparently occurs the year round, but peaks in spring.

Distribution: The Greater Antilles, Bahamas, some of the Lesser Antilles, southern Florida, and southwest Costa Rica through most of South America.

Barn-Owls
FAMILY: TYTONIDAE

The barn-owls form a small family of widely distributed birds. They have a heart-shaped facial disk, long legs and exhibit habits very similar to the typical owls. Barn-owls are highly nocturnal and primarily depend on their acute sense of hearing to locate prey. More fossil than living species are known.

COMMON BARN-OWL   Plate 21
Tyto alba

Identification: 30−43 cm (12−17″). The very light face and underparts distinguish this owl.

Local Name: Lechuza

Comments: An accidental visitor to Puerto Rico from North America. There have been four records (December, January) of the bird since 1947, though none, as yet, from the Virgin

Islands. An endemic Puerto Rican Barn-Owl (*T. cavatica*) once occurred on Puerto Rico, but it is apparently extinct. Judging from a related form surviving on Hispaniola, it was probably darker than the North American bird.

Distribution: The Greater Antilles, Bahamas and some of the Lesser Antilles. The species is of cosmopolitan distribution.

Typical Owls
FAMILY: STRIGIDAE

The typical owls are nocturnal birds of prey (though some may be seen abroad during the day) that complement the hawks which are daytime predators. They are characterized by a distinctive facial disk, a large head with the eyes directed forward, and silent flight. Owls swallow their food whole and regurgitate bones, feathers, insect wings, etc., in a compact pellet.

PUERTO RICAN SCREECH-OWL   Plate 21
Otus nudipes

Identification: 23–25 cm (9–10″). The only small owl in Puerto Rico and the Virgin Islands. Grayish-brown above, white below marked with heavy brown streaks. Some birds are decidedly more rust-colored than others. This species has no ear tufts.

Local Names: Cuckoo Bird, Puerto Rican Bare-legged Owl, Múcaro de Puerto Rico

Comments: This is the common resident owl of Puerto Rico's wooded areas, from the forests and coffee plantations of the mountains to isolated dense tree stands on the coast. Its distribution is limited by the availability of trees with adequate cavities. The bird is completely nocturnal and is rarely seen during the day, unless flushed from the dense thicket or tree cavity in which it roosts. However, the species actively calls in the evening and early morning. Once having located a calling bird it can be brought in by imitating the squeaking of a mouse. With the aid of a flashlight one can get an excellent view of this raptor.

In Puerto Rico there is a widespread belief that the screech owl feeds on ripening coffee beans, causing substantial damage to the crop. This contention has been tested on several occasions by attempting to feed coffee beans to captive owls, and by examining the stomach contents of owls collected in the wild. The results indicate that, contrary to common folklore, this owl feeds entirely on animal matter including a host of injurious insects, and refuses to take coffee beans. The results of these experiments have been disseminated through local agricultural bulletins and even in an elementary school textbook on birds, but the tale that the owls eat the beans of coffee continues to be widely accepted.

Another widely accepted belief, at least in northwestern Puerto Rico, is that this owl can be used to cure asthma. In some sectors it is said an immature owl must be caught and fried with no seasoning. In other areas the contention is that only the heart serves as a cure; this is taken from a live bird, briefly placed in a flame to dry, and then eaten immediately. Fortunately, it appears the beliefs of humans have had a minimal impact on this little owl, as it continues to be common in coffee plantations and other wooded areas.

This owl may be extinct on Vieques, from which it has been reported only once. It may occur in small numbers on Culebra. The species is extremely rare among the Virgin Islands where it has been collected or reported from St Thomas, St John, St Croix, Virgin Gorda and Tortola. Strong circumstantial evidence suggests that this owl either nests or roosts on Guana Island. Pellets have been found in two caves in 1984 and 1985, and vocalizations have been reported by several people.

Voice: Usually a tremulous trill, though sometimes it chatters, whoops, or emits a maniacal laugh.

Nesting: Two white eggs are laid in a tree cavity. The breeding season is from April to June.

Distribution: Known only from Puerto Rico and the Virgin Islands.

SHORT-EARED OWL   Plate 21
Asio flammeus

Identification: 35−43 cm (14−17″). The large owl of Puerto Rico's open country. Light below with streaking on the breast, reduced on the belly. Most easily identified by its size and habits. The flight is characteristic, consisting of alternate flapping and gliding in a somewhat erratic pattern. It shows conspicuous black wrist patches on the light underwings and large buff patches on the upperwings in flight.

Local Names: Múcaro real, Múcaro de sabana, Buho

Comments: Uncommon in Puerto Rico, but apparently more abundant than it was previously. It is also known from Mona Island, Culebra and St Thomas. Occurring sparingly in open country around Puerto Rico's coastal plain, its preferred habitats include open pasture, short-grass marshland, and airport edges. Sugar cane fields apparently are not suitable for this owl.

The Short-eared Owl is a crepuscular species being seen most readily when it is active at dawn and dusk. It has the distinctive habit of flying low over open country in search of its prey. This species can also be found perched on fence posts, or in low bushes. During the day it takes cover under low shrubs and will only flush when approached within a few feet.

Voice: A short, emphatic *bow-wow*. Also a distinct noise produced by clapping its wings together beneath its body.

Nesting: Three to four white eggs are laid in a scrape under a bush or thick clump of grass. March appears to be the principal month for nesting; however, there is a record of a female with a nest in August.

Distribution: In the West Indies it breeds in Puerto Rico and Hispaniola and is a vagrant elsewhere. Of worldwide distribution.

Goatsuckers
FAMILY: CAPRIMULGIDAE

The name 'goatsuckers' derives from the ancient myth that at night these birds use their gaping mouths to rob goats of their milk, causing the udders to dry up and the animals to go blind. This was long ago shown to have no foundation, but rather the birds use their huge, bristled mouths to snare nocturnal insects on the wing. During the day most species are inactive and rest on the ground or lengthwise on a branch where their mottled plumage serves as perfect camouflage.

CHUCK-WILL'S-WIDOW   Plate 28
Caprimulgus carolinensis

Identification: 28–33 cm (11–13″). The species has a dark mottled plumage of black, brown and buff. It is significantly larger than the endemic Puerto Rican Nightjar and lacks the white wing bars of the West Indian Nighthawk. The inner vanes of the outer tail feathers of the male are mostly white. These are dark in the female.

Local Name: Guabairo mayor

Comments: A rare but regular migrant and winter visitor to Puerto Rico and the Virgin Islands from September to March. It is entirely nocturnal and very rarely seen during the day unless flushed from its hiding place among deep thickets. A woodland species, it sometimes is flushed at night from roads through that habitat. This occurs most regularly in winter and spring on Route 191 above the recreation area in the Luquillo Forest (Puerto Rico).

Voice: A clearly whistled rendition of its name with the first syllable weakest *chuck, will's-wid-ow.* It seldom calls in the region.

Distribution: The Greater Antilles, Bahamas and from eastern North America to northern South America.

PUERTO RICAN NIGHTJAR   Plate 28
Caprimulgus noctitherus

Identification: 21.5 cm (8.5″). A small cryptically plumaged goatsucker, it is distinguished from the migrant Chuck-will's-widow by its distinctly smaller size, less ruddy plumage and by the greater amount of white in the tail of the male. It is readily distinguished from the Antillean Nighthawk by the lack of a white bar in the wing.

Local Names: Puerto Rican Whip-poor-will, Guabairo pequeño de Puerto Rico

Comments: A rare resident endemic to Puerto Rico. It is known from a cluster of five localities, all mature, dry, semideciduous forests 7—10 m in height with open understory and dense leaf litter. All five sites are in the island's arid southwest. Locally common only in and around Guánica State Forest, the bird's distribution appears to be limited both by the availability of suitable habitat and the presence of nest and chick predators, specifically the feral cat and mongoose.

The Puerto Rican Nightjar becomes active after dark, sallying forth from a perch to pursue nocturnal flying insects beneath the forest canopy. It calls throughout the year, particularly at dusk and before dawn, enabling one to locate this elusive bird. Calling is most active from November to May, decreasing with egg-laying.

The known history of the Puerto Rican Nightjar is a fascinating story worth summarizing here. Until the past decade the only available information concerning the species was one skin collected in 1888, from which the species was described, and some subfossil bones taken from cave deposits. It was not until 1961 that George Reynard, who was travelling in Puerto Rico taping bird calls, went to Guánica Forest to tape a curious call discovered by Ricardo Cotté, then of the Fish and Wildlife Division of the Puerto Rico Department of Agriculture. Though the call was recorded, it was some time before the responsible bird was collected. Meanwhile, the mysterious nocturnal call left no small number of ornithologists baffled as to just what animal was emitting the strange vocalization. The issue was cleared when a specimen was taken later that same year (though discussion still rages as to whether the species should be considered truly distinct from the North American bird). It was not until 1973, however, that the species' range and numbers were actually determined; a total of 450 to 500 pairs of birds appeared to make up the entire population, the majority of them at Guánica Forest, with outlying populations in Susúa State Forest and east of Guayanilla. More recent studies carried out in 1984 and 1985 indicate that the Puerto Rican Nightjar has expanded its population to both the east and west and now numbers approximately from 670 to 800 breeding pairs.

However, all is not rosy for the Puerto Rican Nightjar. Rhesus Monkeys have recently invaded its habitat and could prove to be significant nest predators. Furthermore, major developments contemplated near Guánica Forest along the coast could augment the numbers of cats and other mammalian pests to the point where the nightjar is disastrously affected.

Considering the obscurity in which the Puerto Rican Nightjar remained until recent years, it is ironic that apparently a Civilian Conservation Corps camp located in Guánica Forest from 1935 to 1945 was so disturbed by the nocturnal calling of these birds that a request was made that they be chased away!

Voice: An emphatic, whistled *whip, whip, whip*, etc., normally two to fifteen in a sequence. Nights that are very bright or very dark are poor for calling.

Nesting: One to two eggs form a normal clutch and these are laid directly on the leaf litter of the forest floor beneath a bush. The eggs are buffy-brown splotched with darker markings, particularly around the broad end. The breeding season runs from late February to early July. The male primarily incubates the eggs.

Distribution: Known only from Puerto Rico where it is restricted to scattered localities on the southwest coast.

COMMON NIGHTHAWK
Plate 28

Chordeiles minor

Identification: 20—25 cm (8—10″). Its conspicuous, white wing patch and erratic flight are distinctive. It can only be differentiated in the field from the West Indian Nighthawk by its call.

Local Names: Mosquito Hawk, Piramidig, Killy-dadick, Gie-me-me-bit, Querequequé migratorio, Gaspayo, Capacho

Comments: Known from St Croix and St John, and no doubt a rare spring and fall transient in the other Virgin Islands and Puerto Rico based on the occurrence of the species elsewhere in the West Indies. It has habits nearly identical to those of the West Indian Nighthawk.

Voice: A distinctive, nasal *ñeet*.

Distribution: Throughout the Western Hemisphere.

ANTILLEAN NIGHTHAWK
Plate 28

Chordeiles gundlachii

Identification: 20—25 cm (8—10″). Identified by the thick, white bar crossing each wing, and its erratic flight. Its conspicuous call distinguishes it from the Common Nighthawk which is identical in appearance.

Local Names: West Indian Nighthawk, Mosquito Hawk, Piramidig, Killy-dadick, Gie-me-me-bit, Querequequé antillano, Gaspayo, Capacho

Comments: An uncommon summer resident and breeding bird in Puerto Rico and the Virgin Islands. It is regularly observed from May to August though recorded as early as April and as late as October. There is one December record. Unlike the other West Indian caprimulgids, nighthawks are somewhat crepuscular in habit, making them more observable. They may even be seen abroad during daylight hours when the weather is overcast. This species usually feeds on flying insects high over fields and pastures. Migrants from other Greater Antillean islands and the Bahamas pass through Puerto Rico and the Virgin Islands in the spring and fall swelling the species' numbers. The Common Nighthawk also occurs at this time.

Voice: A loud, raspy, distinct, *que-re-que-qué*, the Spanish name for the bird in Puerto Rico, or *pity-pit-pit*.

Nesting: Generally a single egg is laid directly on the ground in an open area in May or June. However, there are a few records of nests with two eggs. The eggs have a blue tint and are heavily marked with brown.

Distribution: Breeds in the Greater Antilles and the Bahamas. Winters in South America.

Swifts
FAMILY: APODIDAE

Three species of this unique, cosmopolitan family occur in the region. Swifts are the most aerial of land birds pursuing flying insects on the wing throughout the day without landing to rest. They are propelled extremely rapidly by shallow flaps of their stiff, bow-shaped wings. One species is reported to hold the speed record for all birds, an amazing 322 km per hour (200 miles/h). Swifts use saliva in the construction of their nests. Some species make nests purely of saliva and these nests are highly esteemed by the Chinese for soup and for medicinal purposes.

BLACK SWIFT   Plate 28
Cypseloides niger

Identification: 15—18 cm (6—7 ″). The only swift regularly seen in Puerto Rico. Swifts are easily distinguished by their long fluttering wings and 'flying cigar' appearance. This species appears entirely black.

Local Names: Black Swallow, Rain Bird, Vencejo negro

Comments: Occurs uncommonly in the mountains of Puerto Rico from April to August where it probably breeds, and is at times seen on the coast, particularly after inclement weather. It is rarely found during other months of the year. This swift is of accidental occurrence in the Virgin Islands.

Voice: When flying low a soft *tchip, tchip* can be heard (Danforth).

Nesting: The nest has not yet been found in Puerto Rico.

Distribution: Throughout the West Indies. Puerto Rican and Lesser Antillean birds probably winter in Guyana. Also occurs in western North America and Central America.

SHORT-TAILED SWIFT   Plate 28
Chaetura brachyura

Identification: 10 cm (4 ″). There are several small dark swifts of this genus that occur in the West Indies and all are hardly identifiable from one another in the field. The Shorttailed, under ideal field conditions, might be distinguished by its light gray rump, uppertail and undertail coverts.

Local Name: Vencejo colicorto

Comments: Accidental. There is one sight record (May) from Puerto Rico and a specimen and sight record (July) from St Croix.

Voice: All West Indian swifts of this genus utter a soft chippering on the wing (Bond).

Distribution: Native to St Vincent and northern South America.

CHIMNEY SWIFT   Plate 1
Chaetura pelagica

Identification: 12.5 cm (5″). Smaller than the Black Swift, not
as dark, and flies with more rapid wingbeats. Distinguished
under ideal conditions from the accidentally occurring Short-
tailed Swift by its slightly larger size, paler throat and its darker
rump, uppertail and undertail coverts.

Local Name: Vencejo de chimenea

Comments: Extremely rare in the Virgin Islands where there are
five recent records from St Croix and one from St John. Dates
range from October to May with one sighting in July. There
are no records for Puerto Rico.

Voice: A distinctive twittering while in flight.

Distribution: Through the Bahamas and Greater Antilles
(excluding Puerto Rico) east to St Croix and St John. Also
much of North, Central and South America.

Hummingbirds
FAMILY: TROCHILIDAE

The members of this large, New World family are particularly
abundant in the tropics. Most are brilliantly iridescent, but appear
black in poor light. They characteristically have long pointed bills
for probing into flower corollas from which they obtain insects,
and suck nectar with their long, tubular tongues. These diminutive
creatures feed by hovering before blossoms with wings beating
nearly 50 times per second. This gives them the appearance of
a large bee and, in fact, the smallest hummingbird in the world,
indeed the world's smallest bird, is called the Bee Hummingbird.
It is endemic to Cuba and 14 of these mites weigh but one ounce.
Hummingbirds are very aggressive, particularly around their
feeding territories.

PUERTO RICAN EMERALD   Plate 29
Chlorostilbon maugaeus

Identification: 9–10 cm (3.5–4″). One of Puerto Rico's two
small hummingbirds, it is readily identified by its small size,

forked tail, and lack of a crest. The male Puerto Rican Emerald is green above and below with a black tail and a flesh-colored lower mandible. The female is similar, but has white underparts, an entirely black bill and the outer tail feathers tipped with an off-white. The tiny Antillean Crested, confined primarily to the northeast coast, has a noticeable crest and a rounded tail. The other hummingbird of the mountains in Puerto Rico is the Green Mango, which can be distinguished from the Emerald by its larger size, decurved bill, and rounded tail.

Local Names: Fork-tailed Hummingbird, Zumbadorcito de Puerto Rico

Comments: Though the endemic Puerto Rican Emerald is most common in mountain forests, it is also found irregularly on the coast, particularly the drier south coast. This species has even been recorded within coastal mangroves. In the mountains females prefer the shade while males frequent more exposed, sunnier sites, usually at greater heights above the forest floor. These preferences are not so marked in dry areas where both sexes inhabit shaded localities. The two sexes of the Puerto Rican Emerald exhibit differential feeding preferences; the female feeds heavily on insects and spiders it gleans from the limbs and leaves of trees, while primarily the male forages for the nectar of blossoms. It is believed by country people in Puerto Rico that the nests of hummingbirds are effective in the treatment of asthma attacks. In some areas the nest is burned and the ashes used to brew a tea then served to the sufferer, in others the nest is simply hung from a string around the neck.

Voice: A series of *tic* notes given at various speeds and a thin, rapid trill with a high-pitched buzz at the end.

Nesting: A tiny cup-shaped nest of fine fibers is constructed and coated with lichens. Two white eggs are laid with breeding occurring primarily from February to May, but with irregular nesting through the rest of the year.

Distribution: Known only from Puerto Rico proper.

ANTILLEAN MANGO   Plate 29
Anthracothorax dominicus

Identification: 11−12.5 cm (4.5−5 ″). A large hummingbird distinguished by the light, yellowish-green upperparts. The male can also be recognized by the black on the breast. The female is the only large hummer in the area that is white below. It also has white tips on the outer tail feathers. Young males appear very much like females, but soon show traces of the male plumage on their underparts.

Local Names: Puerto Rican Golden Hummingbird, Doctorbird, Zumbador dorado, Zunzún dorado, Colibrí dorado

Comments: This is the common large hummingbird of Puerto Rico's coastal plain, with the exception of the east coast, which is dominated by the Green-throated Carib. The Antillean Mango is particularly common along the drier southern coast. It has become increasingly rare in the Virgin Islands and has been extirpated from most of them though it is still known from Virgin Gorda, Anegada and Beef Island and may occur on St Thomas. This hummer's decline in the Virgin Islands and on Puerto Rico's east coast apparently is the result of competition from the Green-throated Carib which has recently expanded its range into this area.

Voice: An unmusical, thin trill that is quite loud; also sharp chipping notes.

Nesting: Two white eggs are laid in a deep, downy cup-shaped nest often coated on the exterior with spider webs. Breeding occurs from March to August.

Distribution: Puerto Rico, the Virgin Islands and Hispaniola.

GREEN MANGO   Plate 29
Anthracothorax viridis

Identification: 11—14 cm (4.5—5.5 ″). Both sexes can be readily distinguished by their relatively large size and entirely emerald green underparts. The Puerto Rican Emerald, which occurs in the same habitat, is much smaller and has a notched tail.

Local Names: Puerto Rico Mango, Zumbador verde, Zunzún verde, Colibrí verde

Comments: The common large hummingbird of the coffee plantations and forests of Puerto Rico's central and western mountains to which it is endemic. The species is rare in the Luquillo Mountains of northeast Puerto Rico. The Green

Mango is irregularly seen on the coast, particularly in the western portion of the island where, in many localities, it appears to be seasonal, taking advantage of flowering seasons of certain plants, and where it may be found in association with the Antillean Mango. As is the case with all five resident hummingbirds in Puerto Rico, this species feeds to a large extent on animal matter, primarily insects and spiders. These are gleaned from among the tree limbs, leaves and bark as well as from flower corollas. Undigested animal remains are formed into minute pellets and regurgitated. The Green Mango also relies on nectar for sustenance and among its favorites are the yellow flowers of Mahoe (*Pariti tiliaceum*), Rangoon Creeper (*Quisqualis indica*) and various trumpet creepers (*Ipomoea*). Where tobacco is grown, this hummer has been blamed for eating tobacco seeds. As investigations indicate that animal matter accounts almost entirely for the solid portion of this bird's diet, it would appear that there is no basis to this allegation.

Voice: The call, a trill-like twitter, is infrequently heard. When angered this hummer issues loud, harsh rattling or chattering notes. The call note is a hard *tick*.

Nesting: Two white eggs are laid in a cup-shaped nest that is coated with lichens. The periods of breeding have not been well studied, but nesting birds have been recorded in October, December, February, and May. As is typical with hummingbirds, the male does not attend the nest or help feed the young.

Distribution: Endemic to Puerto Rico.

GREEN-THROATED CARIB   Plate 29
Eulampis holosericeus

Identification: 11–12.5 cm (4.5–5″). The large size, slightly decurved bill and green breast are good field marks. Though the green breast is an important field mark, it is not easily seen, thus this species can readily be confused with the Antillean Mango which is of similar size and frequents the same habitat. The range of the Green-throated Carib does not overlap with that of the Green Mango, which has a green belly as well as a green breast. The sapphire blue mark on the breast of the carib is a poor field mark as it is discernible only under ideal conditions.

Local Names: Doctorbird, Blue-breasted Hummingbird, Emerald-throated Hummingbird, Green Carib, Green Doctorbird, Zumbador pechiazul

Comments: A common permanent resident on Puerto Rico's northeast coast, particularly in the areas of Fajardo and Ceiba. However, it has been found as far west as Rincón which marks Puerto Rico's western tip. The Green-throated Carib is apparently extending its range in Puerto Rico. It is a common species on the islands off Puerto Rico's east coast and abounds in coastal areas throughout the Virgin Islands. It has basically the same range as the smaller Antillean Crested Hummingbird.

Voice: A sharp *chewp*, and a loud wing rattle (Wetmore).

Nesting: Two white eggs are laid in a downy nest with lichens lining the exterior. The breeding season generally extends from March to early June.

Distribution: Eastern Puerto Rico, the Virgin Islands and the Lesser Antilles.

ANTILLEAN CRESTED HUMMINGBIRD   Plate 29
Orthorhyncus cristatus

Identification: 8—9.5 cm (3.25—3.75″). A tiny hummer, the only crested one in Puerto Rico or the Virgin Islands. The female and young male have an inconspicuous crest and in Puerto Rico the female might be mistaken for a Puerto Rican Emerald, but the latter has a forked tail.

Local Names: Doctorbird, Little Doctorbird, Gilt-crested Hummingbird, Zumbadorcito crestado

Comments: Common on Puerto Rico's northeast coast from Fajardo to Ceiba. Along the south coast it has been reported as far west as Ponce. Its range appears to be gradually expanding in Puerto Rico. It has not been recorded in the mountains. The Antillean Crested Hummingbird abounds on the islands and islets of Puerto Rico's east coast and throughout the Virgin Islands. On the larger islands it prefers the coast, but also ranges inland.

Voice: A combination of emphatic notes usually including a *pit-chew* like a ricocheting bullet.

Nesting: Two white eggs are laid in a tiny, cup-shaped nest of cotton or fine fibers with lichens coating the exterior.

Distribution: Eastern Puerto Rico, the Virgin Islands, and the Lesser Antilles.

RUBY-THROATED HUMMINGBIRD   Plate 1
Archilochus colubris

Identification: 8—9.5 cm (3—3.75″). The male is easily distinguished from any other hummer in the region by its red throat. The breast and abdomen are dull white and the upperparts are green. Females are entirely green above and white below. They are best separated from other local white breasted female hummingbirds by the presence of a small white spot behind the eye.

Local Name: Zumbadorcito de garganta roja

Comments: Accidental. Known to occur in Puerto Rico from a drawing, a sight record, and a photograph. There are no records for the Virgin Islands.

Distribution: Through the Bahamas and Greater Antilles. Occurs through much of eastern North America and Central America.

Todies
FAMILY: TODIDAE

The todies are most closely related to the motmots and more distantly to kingfishers. Though the family is now confined to the Greater Antilles, it is believed to have originated from a Central American stock now extinct. Fossil evidence indicates that the family once extended northward well into North America. The tody has a voracious appetite; a captive specimen ate about 40% of its weight in insects daily. The average number of insects caught by a single bird in the Luquillo Mountains is 1.8 per minute from dawn to dusk. Todies have some of the highest rates of feeding young ever recorded for insectivorous birds.

PUERTO RICAN TODY   Plate 30
Todus mexicanus

Identification: 11 cm (4.5"). A diminutive, chunky forest bird,
it is the only small species in the region, other than
hummingbirds, that is primarily bright green. The ruby red
throat, long broad red bill, yellow flanks, and short, non-
hovering flights of one meter (on the average), readily distinguish this species. Young todies lack the red throat and possess
a shorter bill than adults.

Local Names: San Pedrito, Medio peso, Papagayo

Comments: The Puerto Rican Tody is a common resident species
endemic to Puerto Rico. It is found in almost all forested areas
of the island, being common in damp forests, coffee plantations
and dense growth of hills and mountains, where the bird is
difficult to see, but is often heard. It is less common near the
peaks of the highest mountains such as El Yunque, and is
generally rare in the lowlands, except in arid areas in the south
with dense thickets, where it is common, particularly in
Guánica Forest. When perched, the tody has the peculiar habit
of pointing its bill upward and, with rapid, jerky movements
of the head, scanning the undersurfaces of the leaves above it
for insects. On spying a prey item the tody sallies out, snaps
up the morsel, and proceeds to a new perch all in one short,
curved arc. In fact, the bird depends almost exclusively on this
method of procuring its food. Todies normally forage low to
the ground, averaging levels up to ¼ the height of the canopy.
They are most active on sunny mornings after rain, with high
peaks of activity in March and September. Knocking two stones
together will often attract them. The scientific name *mexicanus*
was obviously a misnomer, derived from the fact that the
original specimens were erroneously labeled as having been
obtained in Veracruz and Tampico, Mexico.

Voice: A loud nasal *beep* or *bee-beep* is characteristic. Also wing-
rattling is made in flight with the narrow-tipped primaries,
mostly during courtship, territorial defense, and nest defense.

Nesting: The tody excavates a curved burrow with a terminal nest
chamber into an earth bank, but twice as many burrows are
abandoned as are actually used. From one to four shiny white
eggs are laid (the average being 2.3) with breeding occurring
primarily from March to July. Interestingly, third and fourth

adults, probably previous offspring of the nesting pair, sometimes assist the parents in raising their nestlings. This increases the number of offspring which eventually fledge.

Distribution: Endemic to Puerto Rico.

Kingfishers
FAMILY: ALCEDINIDAE

The kingfishers are a cosmopolitan family with only one representative in the region. They are a distinctive group characterized by their large heads, long, pointed bills and often brilliant coloration. Many feed on fish and hover as does the Belted Kingfisher. Kingfishers excavate nesting burrows in clay banks.

BELTED KINGFISHER   Plate 23
Ceryle alcyon

Identification: 28—35.5 cm (11—14 "). Distinguished by its large bill and crest, its rattling call and habit of diving for fish. The female differs from the male in having a rusty-orange band across the lower breast.

Local Names: Kingfisherman, Martín pescador, Pájaro del rey

Comments: A fairly common visitor to Puerto Rico and the Virgin Islands from October to April though occurring in small numbers in August, September, and May. While among the islands it can be found along rivers, lake edges, lagoon fringes, and the shores of other bodies of water. It often issues its ratchety call from a conspicuous perch adjacent to calm water over which it sallies in search of fish. On encountering its prey the bird frequently hovers before plunging after it into the water.

Voice: A loud rattle.

Distribution: The West Indies and North, Central and northern South America.

Woodpeckers
FAMILY: PICIDAE

As the name of the family so aptly implies, woodpeckers use their chisel-like bills not only to bore into trees in search of insects, but also to excavate nest holes. These birds have unusually long tongues for extracting insects from deep cavities. Most species have two hind toes which help support them and the stiff tail serves as an additional prop while climbing. Males of most species have red markings about the head.

PUERTO RICAN WOODPECKER   Plate 24
Melanerpes portoricensis

Identification: 23—27 cm (9—10.5 "). Distinguished by its red throat and breast, white rump and its unbarred back and wings. Females and immatures have less red on the underparts than adult males. Flight is undulating as is the case with most woodpeckers.

Local Name: Carpintero de Puerto Rico

Comments: Endemic to Puerto Rico and Vieques, this is the only common woodpecker on the former island, but it is rare on the latter. The habitat of the Puerto Rican Woodpecker includes any wooded areas from mangrove swamps and coconut plantations on the coast to montane forests. However, it appears to be most common in the hills and lower mountains including areas where coffee is grown. The species is often found in small congregations of from two to five or more birds. Stomach analyses show that wood boring larvae, ants and earwigs are among its principal foods, although seeds and fruits are regular food items.

Voice: A wide variety of calls, the most common one being *wek, wek, wek-wek-wek-wek-wek*, etc., becoming louder and faster as it proceeds. Other vocalizations include *kuk* notes like a hen, and *mew* notes.

Nesting: The drilling of nest cavities generally begins in January with young hatching in March and April. Nest cavities are usually high in trees and contain four white eggs.

Distribution: Puerto Rico proper, rare on Vieques.

YELLOW-BELLIED SAPSUCKER   Plate 23
Sphyrapicus varius

Identification: 20—21.5 cm (8—8.5″). The large white patch on
the wing is diagnostic and is conspicuous both in birds that are
perched and in flight. The male has a red throat while that of
the female is white. Immatures are dull brown, but display the
white wing patch of adults. The species makes characteristic
lines of holes around trunks of trees.

Local Name: Carpintero pechiamarillo

Comments: A rare winter visitor to Puerto Rico and the Virgin
Islands from October to April. The species has generally been
recorded from sparsely wooded areas, though it may well occur
in mountain forests.

Voice: A plaintive *new*, but rarely known to call on its wintering
grounds.

Distribution: Throughout the West Indies and North and Central
America.

Tyrant Flycatchers
FAMILY: TYRANNIDAE

The tyrant flycatchers are a large New World family predominantly inhabiting South America. Most species are dull plumaged
with a colorful crown patch that is usually concealed. Many species
typically sit on exposed perches from which they sally forth to snare
flying insects. Their broad bills, with bristles at the base, are well
adapted for this habit. A few species feed heavily on berries. Flycatchers are poor songsters, even in the breeding season. Some
forms are extremely aggressive, particularly in the breeding season
when they attack all birds, even large hawks and herons, that
intrude in their territories.

GRAY KINGBIRD   Plate 31
Tyrannus dominicensis

Identification: 23—24 cm (9—9.5″). Gray above, pale gray-white
below with a distinct black mark extending just under the eye

to the ear. The yellow and orange-red crown patch is rarely
seen.

Local Names: Chichery, Chinchiry, Petchary, Pitirre

Comments: One of the most common and conspicuous resident
species in Puerto Rico and the Virgin Islands. It is regularly
seen on exposed perches such as telephone wires from which
it periodically sallies in pursuit of large insects. This flycatcher
is found well into the mountains where open habitat is available.

Voice: Like its local common names *chichery* (English), and *pitirre*
(Spanish). Also a sharp *peet*, *burr* and *tirré*.

Nesting: An open, loosely constructed nest contains two to four
reddish eggs heavily marked at one end with irregular splotches.
The breeding season runs primarily from April to July.

Distribution: The West Indies, Florida and northern South
America. Birds migrate from the westernmost islands and
Florida in winter.

LOGGERHEAD KINGBIRD   Plate 31
Tyrannus caudifasciatus

Identification: 23.5—26 cm (9.25—10.25″). Very dark above,
appearing black on the crown. The underparts are pure white.
The yellow crown patch is seldom seen. The somewhat similar
Puerto Rican Flycatcher is substantially smaller, has a relatively
smaller bill and its coloration is not so distinctively 'two-toned'.

Local Names: Puerto Rican Petchary, Clérigo

Comments: A fairly common permanent resident of lower
montane forests in Puerto Rico, not known from the Virgin
Islands. The Loggerhead Kingbird is found only in forested
areas, occurring most commonly among coffee plantations. It
also inhabits the haystack hills of the north coast and is fairly
common in certain mangrove swamps, though absent from
others. While the Loggerhead is very active at dawn, it seems
less active than other flycatchers later in the day. This species
is rare in the Luquillo Mountains.

Voice: A wide variety of calls including emphatic, mallet-like chattering notes in a series, or other vocalizations with a *bzze-beep* or *bee-beep* in them such as *joú-bee-beep* ⟋ _ ⏤. Also a melodious laugh like an unenthusiastic version of a Puerto Rican Woodpecker call.

Nesting: A cup-shaped nest is usually built high above the ground and contains two to three salmon-colored eggs with brown and violet markings at the broad end. Breeding is principally from February to June, but some nesting has been noted in the fall.

Distribution: Puerto Rico and Vieques (rare) through the rest of the Greater Antilles into the Bahamas.

PUERTO RICAN FLYCATCHER   Plate 31
Myiarchus antillarum

Identification: 18.5 − 20 cm (7.25 − 8 "). A medium-sized flycatcher with a dark back and head and light underparts. It is most readily distinguished from the similar Caribbean Elaenia by its darker upperparts, the absence of wing bars and the lack of a conspicuous yellow wash on the belly. The Loggerhead Kingbird is a larger flycatcher, more distinctly two-toned, with a much heavier bill. The call of the Puerto Rican Flycatcher is its best field mark.

Local Names: Stolid Flycatcher, Juí de Puerto Rico

Comments: Endemic to the region, it is common on Puerto Rico proper, fairly so on Vieques and rare on Culebra. Among the Virgin Islands it is uncommon but regularly observed in parts of St John and is rare on St Thomas, Virgin Gorda, and Tortola. It inhabits wooded areas including mangrove borders, arid scrub, coffee plantations, the haystack hills and montane forest except for the higher slopes. This inconspicuous and inactive bird would readily go unnoticed were it not for its distinctive call which heralds its presence. Previously lumped with similar birds from a number of other West Indian islands and called the Stolid Flycatcher, the Puerto Rican Flycatcher was determined to be a distinct species by Dr Wesley Lanyon in 1967, based on his study of the differences in vocalizations of these birds.

The Puerto Rican Flycatcher was near extinction in the early

1930s. It became so in the Virgin Islands, due to the destruction of forests, and in Puerto Rico it had nearly been extirpated as a result of the hurricane of 1928.

Voice: The most characteristic call is a plaintively whistled *whee* ⟍ from which the bird's Spanish name is derived. There is also a dawn song *whee-a-wit-whee*, the two middle syllables of which are unmusical and sometimes sung independently during the day. Lanyon describes other calls including an emphatic *huit, huit*, a rolling *pee-r-r-r* and a rasping note.

Nesting: Three to four yellowish-white eggs with spots concentrated at the broad end are laid in a tree hole nest which is lined with fine plant material. The breeding season runs from late April to July.

Distribution: Puerto Rico, Culebra, Vieques, St John, St Thomas, Virgin Gorda, and Tortola.

LESSER ANTILLEAN PEWEE   Plate 31
Contopus latirostris

Identification: 15 cm (6″). The ochre-colored underparts and small size distinguish this from other flycatchers.

Local Name: Bobito antillano menor

Comments: A permanent resident in Puerto Rico, but absent from the Virgin Islands. It is primarily a bird of montane forests of moderate elevation, being probably most common in coffee plantations. The species may also be found among the haystack hills and in scrubby forests and mangroves of the southwest coast. This flycatcher is not found east of Vega Alta on the north coast, Salinas on the south, and the town of Cidra in the interior.

Voice: The song is characteristic and consists of a sweet, high-pitched trill sometimes rising up the scale, reminiscent of water filling a glass.

Nesting: The nest is a well-constructed cup of mosses, lichens and other fine materials, with thin bark camouflaging the exterior. One to two cream-colored eggs with dark markings at the broad end form a clutch. Breeding occurs in the spring.

Distribution: Puerto Rico, Guadeloupe, Dominica, Martinique, and St Lucia.

GREATER ANTILLEAN PEWEE   Plate 31
Contopus caribaeus

Identification: 16 cm (6.25"). Underparts grayish buff, not as ochraceous as those of the Lesser Antillean Pewee.

Local Name: Bobito antillano mayor

Comments: Accidental. Known from a specimen taken on Mona Island (April, 1967).

Distribution: Accidental on Mona Island. Native to the other Greater Antillean islands and the northern Bahamas.

CARIBBEAN ELAENIA   Plate 31
Elaenia martinica

Identification: 16.5−18 cm (6.5−7"). The whitish wing bars help identify this from other flycatchers in the region. The call is also very distinctive.

Local Names: Pee Whistler, John Phillip, Juí blanco

Comments: A common resident in Puerto Rico and the Virgin Islands. The elaenia principally occurs in arid scrub.

Voice: This elaenia calls well into the day. It has a repetitious *jui-up, wit-churr* ⌒⁻ —   . The last syllable is softest and appears to be caused by rattling of the bill.

Nesting: A flimsy, shallow nest of twigs is constructed and two to three salmon-colored eggs with lilac and brown markings at the broad end are laid. Breeding occurs in the spring.

Distribution: Puerto Rico and the Virgin Islands and through the Lesser Antilles. Also St Andrew, Old Providence, the Caymens, and extralimital Caribbean islands.

Swallows and Martins
FAMILY: HIRUNDINIDAE

The swallows are the most distinctive family in the huge order of perching birds. Of cosmopolitan distribution, they are characterized by their short, broad bills, long pointed wings and their habit of feeding on flying insects on the wing. Swallows are very gregarious and can often be seen in numbers over fields and marshes or perched on wires. Though they resemble swifts the two families are not closely related. Swifts are distinguished by their much longer wings, shallower wing strokes and more rapid flight.

TREE SWALLOW   Plate 32
Tachycineta bicolor

Identification: 12.5–15 cm (5–6″). The pure white underparts are distinctive. The upperparts have a greenish tint. Immatures have brown upperparts.

Local Name: Golondrina vientriblanca

Comments: A very rare visitor to Puerto Rico and St Croix. There is one record for St John but it is unrecorded from the other Virgin Islands. This species is apparently increasing in the region. The Tree Swallow should be looked for among bands of other swallows.

Distribution: The Greater Antilles, St Croix, northern Bahamas, and through North America to northern Central America.

PURPLE MARTIN   Plate 32
Progne subis

Identification: 19–20 cm (7.5–8″). This is a large swallow, the male being the only form with entirely dark underparts. Females and immatures differ from the very similar Caribbean Martin by having a scaled pattern on their grayish-brown breast, light gray patches on the sides of the neck, and an indistinct border where their dark breast coloration blends into the white of the belly.

Local Name: Golondrina púrpura

Comments: Accidental. Known in Puerto Rico from a single record of a male at the Boquerón Refuge in the southwestern corner of the island (April). There are also three recent records from St Croix (March to July).

Nesting: One male bred with a martin of unverified species. They nested in June in a crevice of the Fredricksted pier and successfully raised two young.

Distribution: A transient in the West Indies from the Bahamas east to Puerto Rico. Widespread in the New World.

CARIBBEAN MARTIN   Plate 32
Progne dominicensis

Identification: 19−21 cm (7.5−8.25 "). Substantially larger than other common swallows. The male's dark head and throat and white belly are distinctive. Females and immatures have a brownish wash on the breast that blends gradually into the white of the belly.

Local Names: Swallow, Golondrina de iglesias

Comments: A fairly common breeding resident in Puerto Rico and the Virgin Islands occurring from January to September with a few records from December and October. The bird's winter range is unknown but is presumed to be in South America.

Voice: A hard, gritty *churr*.

Nesting: Nests are constructed with all sorts of materials in cavities in buildings, palms, or cliffs. Three to six white eggs are laid. Breeding occurs in late spring and early summer.

Distribution: The West Indies and western Mexico.

BANK SWALLOW   Plate 32
Riparia riparia

Identification: 12.5−14 cm (5−5.5 "). The dark band across the white breast is diagnostic.

Local Name: Golondrina parda

Comments: A fairly common spring migrant in Puerto Rico, but uncommon in the fall. A few birds regularly winter. It is rare among the larger Virgin Islands. However, the species appears to be becoming a more regular visitor to the region. Around bodies of water in southwestern Puerto Rico are the best localities for encountering the Bank Swallow.

Distribution: Widespread in the New and Old World.

BARN SWALLOW   Plate 32
Hirundo rustica

Identification: 15—19 cm (6—7.5″). The deeply forked tail is a certain field mark.

Local Names: Swallow, Golondrina de horquilla

Comments: A common spring and fall transient and uncommon winter visitor to Puerto Rico and the Virgin Islands. It occurs in open areas over fields and swamps.

Voice: A thin, unmusical *chit*.

Distribution: Throughout the West Indies and widespread in the New and Old World.

CLIFF SWALLOW   Plate 32
Hirundo pyrrhonota

Identification: 12.5—15 cm (5—6″). Distinguished by the chestnut chin, throat and side of the face, along with the buff-colored forehead and only slightly notched tail. The common Cave Swallow of this area is very similar to the Cliff Swallow, but has a deep chestnut forehead and buff-colored throat.

Local Name: Golondrina de peñasco

Comments: A rare but regular fall migrant and winter visitor to St Croix, there are several records from St John and at sea off the Virgin Islands. The species generally occurs from September to December. There are no records for Puerto Rico. The Cliff Swallow appears to be visiting the region with increasing frequency.

Distribution: Rare in the West Indies, but widespread in North, Central and South America.

CAVE SWALLOW   Plate 32
Hirundo fulva

Identification: 12.5—14 cm (5—5.5″). The rust-colored rump, only slightly notched tail, and underparts washed with rufous distinguish it from other common swallows. The Cliff Swallow, of accidental occurrence, is very similar to the Cave Swallow, but is distinguished from the latter by its chestnut-colored throat and buff-colored forehead.

Local Name: Golondrina de cuevas

Comments: A common resident in Puerto Rico, a rare visitor to St Croix and accidental among the other Virgin Islands. It is found principally over fields and bodies of water, occurring more commonly in western Puerto Rico.

Voice: A chattering or twittering is most typically heard. Also a rather musical call note, *twit*, is common.

Nesting: Nests are made of mud in cave mouths, on buildings, or under ledges and bridges. Breeding is colonial from April to June and two to five white eggs are laid with markings of various colors concentrated at the broad end.

Distribution: Puerto Rico and the other Greater Antilles. Accidental in the Virgin Islands. Also the extreme south central USA, Mexico, Ecuador, and Peru.

NORTHERN ROUGH-WINGED SWALLOW
Stelgidopteryx serripennis   **Plate 1**

Identification: 12.5−14 cm (5−5.5″). This brown-backed swallow is distinguished by its white underparts blending into pale brown on the throat.

Local Name: Golondrina de garganta palido

Comments: An extremely rare visitor to St Croix from October to March, there is one August record. The species is accidental on St John and St Thomas. There are no records from Puerto Rico. This species should be looked for among flocks of other swallows.

Distribution: The northwestern Bahamas, Cuba, Jamaica, St John and St Croix and through North and Central America.

Crows
FAMILY: CORVIDAE

Puerto Rico, like Cuba and Hispaniola, once had both a large and a small species of crow. The small one, *Corvus nasicus*, is only known from bones in Puerto Rico where it was extirpated in the nineteenth century, but it survives in Cuba. *Corvus leucognaphalus*, the large species, was extirpated from Puerto Rico in the early 1960s, but survives in Hispaniola. Crows are primarily black with strong bills and are the largest of passeriformes.

WHITE-NECKED CROW   Plate 23
Corvus leucognaphalus

Identification: 48—51 cm (19—20″). Distinguished easily by its large size and totally black appearance. The white at the base of the neck feathers that give this crow its name cannot be seen in the field.

Local Name: Cuervo pescueciblanco

Comments: The White-necked Crow was last observed in the Luquillo Mountains in 1963, its last stronghold in Puerto Rico, and is now considered extirpated from the island. In the Virgin Islands it is only known from fossil remains found in considerable numbers on St Croix. The species was previously common in Puerto Rico when the island had extensive virgin forest and was considered a valuable game bird for its good tasting flesh. Imported crows that have escaped from captivity have been observed in the wild in Puerto Rico and appear similar to the once native bird.

Voice: Wetmore describes the common call note as a high-pitched *klook*. There is also a wide variety of distinctive clucking, gurgling, bubbling and laugh-like calls and squawks, and a *caw*.

Nesting: The birds were known to nest in March, high in the tree tops.

Distribution: The species is extirpated from Puerto Rico and St Croix. It survives on Hispaniola and the adjacent islands of Gonave and Saona.

Muscicapids
FAMILY: MUSCICAPIDAE

The muscicapids are a very large and diverse family represented in this region only by the thrushes. The thrushes are a distinctive subgroup, cosmopolitan in range, of which the local species are typical. They generally have long legs, an erect posture and feed on both berries and insects, often on the ground. Many are good songsters.

AMERICAN ROBIN   Plate 31
Turdus migratorius

Identification: 24 cm (9.5″). Readily distinguished by the dull red breast and belly. The outer tail feathers are tipped with white.

Local Name: Mirlo norteamericano

Comments: Accidental. Known from a single record by the writer on 10 December 1971, at Mona Island.

Distribution: Puerto Rico (accidental), Cuba, Jamaica, the Bahamas, and throughout North America to Guatemala.

RED-LEGGED THRUSH   Plate 31
Turdus plumbeus

Identification: 28 cm (11″). The generally grayish coloration and the red bill and legs distinguish this species.

Local Names: Zorzal de patas coloradas, Zorzal azul

Comments: A common resident in Puerto Rico, but absent from the Virgin Islands. It frequents woodlands and forests at all elevations and even occurs in shrubby vegetation in gardens. This is the bird that abounds along shady mountain roads, particularly in the wee hours of the morning, and flits away in front of one's car, flashing the white tips of its outer tail feathers.

Voice: The call notes include a low *wéecha* and a rapid, high-pitched *chu-wéek, chu-wéek, chu-wéek* (Rolle), the latter being very distinctive. The song is a melodious, but monotonous series of one to three syllable phases very similar to that of the Pearly-eyed Thrasher, but a bit more musical and with shorter pauses between notes.

Nesting: Breeding occurs from January to September, but peaks in the spring. The nest is an open, bulky affair with a woven lining. Two light green eggs flecked with brown form a normal clutch.

Distribution: Confined to Puerto Rico, the Bahamas, Cuba, Hispaniola, Dominica, and the Cayman Islands.

GRAY-CHEEKED THRUSH   Plate 1
Catharus minimus

Identification: 18 cm (7″). Grayish-brown above and pale below with fine spots on the breast and throat. This thrush is distinguished by its gray cheek and the absence of an eye-ring.

Local Name: Zorzal de mejilla gris

Comments: An accidental visitor to the region, there are three records from Puerto Rico, all hand held, and one record each from Mona Island and St Croix.

Distribution: The Bahamas and Greater Antilles east to St Croix (accidental) and Martinique. Widespread in North, Central and South America.

Mockingbirds and Thrashers (Mimic Thrushes)
FAMILY: MIMIDAE

The habit of several species to mimic other birds gives this New World family its name. Mimids appear very much like thrushes, but are more slender with longer tails and more lengthy, decurved bills.

NORTHERN MOCKINGBIRD   Plate 31
Mimus polyglottos

Identification: 25 cm (10″). The gray upperparts, white underparts and the large white markings on the wings and tail, particularly conspicuous in flight, are diagnostic. The tail is long and often tilted upward. The similarly colored Gray Kingbird lacks the white wing and tail patches and does not cock its relatively short tail.

Local Names: Sinsonte norteño, Ruiseñor

Comments: A common resident in Puerto Rico and the Virgin Islands, though it was unknown from the latter islands prior to 1916. It occurs primarily in open country with scattered trees or bushes in the lowlands, but ranges into the mountains where suitable habitat is available. The species is most abundant in dry coastal scrub.

Voice: A clear, melodious series of phrases, each phrase being repeated a number of times in succession. The call note is a hard scolding *check*.

Nesting: Three to four bluish-green eggs with heavy splotches forming a ring at the thick end are laid in a well made, open nest. Breeding occurs primarily from January to July.

Distribution: In the West Indies east to the Virgin Islands. Also throughout the USA and Mexico.

PEARLY-EYED THRASHER   Plate 31
Margarops fuscatus

Identification: 28−30 cm (11−12 ″). Distinguished by the white iris, brown upperparts and white underparts marked with brown. The large white patches on the tail tips aid in identification.

Local Names: Thrush, Sour-sop Bird, Zorzal pardo, Truche, Chucho

Comments: A common resident in Puerto Rico and the Virgin Islands. It is found in thickets, woodlands and forests at all elevations from coastal palm groves to mountain tops. This is an extraordinarily aggressive species, eating the eggs and killing the young of various other birds.

Voice: The thrasher has a number of raucous call notes and a common vocalization consisting of a series of one to three syllable phrases with fairly lengthy pauses separating them. It is very similar to the call of the Red-legged Thrush, but is slower and less melodious. The thrasher often sings well into the day.

Nesting: A bulky stick nest is usually built in a cavity, though open nests are known. Two to three glossy, deep blue eggs are laid. Breeding occurs from December to September.

Distribution: Puerto Rico and the Virgin Islands, the eastern Bahamas, Beata Island, the Lesser Antilles south to St Vincent, and Bonaire.

Waxwings
FAMILY: BOMBYCILLIDAE

There are only three birds in this family, all of which have crests
and possess red, waxy structures on the tips of their secondaries.
They are arboreal and feed primarily on berries, though they
sometimes sally after insects in flycatcher fashion. Only one is
found in this area.

CEDAR WAXWING   Plate 23
Bombycilla cedrorum

Identification: 18−18.5 cm (7−7.25″). The sharp crest and the
yellow band on the tip of the tail readily distinguish this sleek
bird. Immatures are streaked on the underparts.

Local Name: Picotera

Comments: Accidental in winter, there are only three records from
Puerto Rico and one from St John. This bird apparently occurs
in a broad range of habitats from mountain rain forest to
lowland cultivated edges.

Voice: High-pitched lispy or hissing calls are frequently given.

Distribution: Rare in the West Indies, but occurs throughout
North America to Panama.

Starlings and Mynas
FAMILY: STURNIDAE

A large Old World family, a few species have been introduced
to this hemisphere. They are stocky birds with long, conical bills
and usually a somewhat iridescent plumage.

EUROPEAN STARLING   Plate 23
Sturnus vulgaris

Identification: 21.5 cm (8.5″). The glossy adult, appearing black in the field, is identified by its short tail and, in the breeding season, by its yellow bill. In other seasons the bill turns dark and the underparts of the bird are heavily flecked with white. Young are brownish-gray with fine stripes on the breast. The flight of European Starlings is straight, unlike other black birds in the region, and the wings have a typical swept-back form.

Local Name: Estornino

Comments: European Starlings were discovered in Puerto Rico in 1973 when a minimum of eight birds (including one juvenile) were found breeding just northwest of the town of Boquerón. Seven birds were immediately eliminated but in 1986 a dozen European Starlings including three juveniles were found once more in the Cabo Rojo area. Since 1982 there have been periodic reports of as many as three European Starlings on St Croix. The birds probably reached the region originally by natural means from the western Greater Antilles.

Voice: A wide variety of whistles, squeaks and raspy notes. The species is a good imitator.

Nesting: The bird breeds in the axils of coconut palms in early spring.

Distribution: Introduced in the New World where it has spread through North America, and to the Bahamas, Cuba, Jamaica, and Puerto Rico. Native to Eurasia and North Africa.

WHITE-VENTED MYNA   Plate 23
Acridotheres javanicus

Identification: 25 cm (10″). This black bird is distinguished by its crest, yellow bill and legs and white undertail coverts, tail tip and wing patch (the latter conspicuous in flight).

Local Name: Maina (Myna) vientriblanca

Comments: A very recently established introduction in Puerto Rico where it appears to be spreading from its population center in the northern outskirts of Bayamon. It is regularly seen along the newly built expressway through this area. This myna has been observed as far east as Rio Grande.

Distribution: Introduced in Puerto Rico and elsewhere. Native to Southeast Asia.

HILL MYNA   Plate 23
Gracula religiosa

Identification: 30 cm (12″). This black bird is identified by its
   brilliant orange bill, the yellow wattle on the hind neck, and
   the white wing patch.

Local Name: Maina (Myna) de colinas

Comments: Introduced in Puerto Rico, it has become established
   as an uncommon and local breeding resident along the island's
   north and east coasts. It seems to prefer open woodlands with
   dead snags. Accidental on Mona Island and Vieques.

Voice: An extremely rich, three-syllable whistle accented on the
   second note, that is somewhat plaintive ＿⌒ℒ⌒. This species
   is one of the best mimics in the bird world.

Nesting: Breeding occurs from February to June in tree cavities.

Distribution: Introduced to Puerto Rico. Native to India east
   through Southeast Asia and Indonesia.

Vireos
FAMILY: VIREONIDAE

   Vireos are typically dull olive-green birds that resemble
warblers, but have thicker bills, hooked at the tip. They are
sluggish in their movements, carefully inspecting twigs and the
undersides of leaves for insects as they move among the branches.

YELLOW-THROATED VIREO   Plate 33
Vireo flavifrons

Identification: 12.5 cm (5″). The bright yellow 'spectacles' and
   throat, and the white wing bars aid in identification. Adelaide's
   Warbler has similar markings, but the vireo has a heavier bill
   and olive-green, not gray upperparts.

Local Name: Julián Chiví gargantiamarillo

Comments: Unknown from the region prior to 1975, the species
   is an uncommon winter visitor to St John and is rare on St

Thomas and St Croix. There are two records for Puerto Rico and one for Vieques.

Distribution: A visitor in the West Indies, generally not east of Cuba. Also the eastern USA to northern South America.

WHITE-EYED VIREO   Plate 33
Vireo griseus

Identification: 12.5 cm (5″). The only vireo with white wing bars known from the region. The white iris and the yellowish lores and eye-ring give it the appearance of wearing spectacles. The immature has a brown iris.

Local Name: Julián Chiví ojiblanco

Comments: Rare in Puerto Rico and St John from November through April. There is one record from Mona Island. The species apparently is occurring more regularly in the region, all records being since 1971.

Distribution: A visitor in the West Indies, generally not east of Cuba. Also the eastern USA and Central America.

PUERTO RICAN VIREO   Plate 33
Vireo latimeri

Identification: 12.5 cm (5″). The distinctive characters are its incomplete white eye-ring and the two-toned nature of its underparts − grayish on the throat and breast and light yellow on the belly.

Local Names: Latimer's Vireo, Bien-te-veo, Julián Chiví

Comments: A fairly common resident in Puerto Rico, where it is endemic. The species does not occur east of a line between Loiza Aldea, Caguas, and Patillas. It is most common in the forests of the haystack hills of the north coast and in the more heavily forested valleys among the hills of the south coast. It also occurs commonly in the mangroves of Torrecilla-Piñones, but strangely, is known from no other mangroves on the island. Brushy pastures are also inhabited, but open areas are avoided. The Puerto Rican Vireo is an entirely beneficial species as indicated by the analysis of the contents of 43 stomachs: 86% of its food is animal material, primarily injurious species.

Voice: The common call is a melodious whistle usually of three or four syllables, that is repeated, with pauses between refrains, for several minutes. A new phrase is then adopted which is in turn sung continuously for some time. Usually at least one syllable is strongly accented. A rattling call *chur-chur-churr-rrr*, somewhat like a chattering laugh, is reported to serve in courtship and as a scolding note. Spaulding describes its contact note as *tup, tup* and states that it also issues a grating, hoarse, cat-like mew.

Nesting: Nest building begins in March and peaks in May with the young fledging in June. The nest is a deep, cup-shaped affair in the fork of a branch at a low to moderate elevation. The principal layer of nest material is lined on the inside with fine grass and camouflaged on the outside with spider egg sacks, green moss and other vegetation. Three eggs form a normal clutch and these have a roseate hue and are speckled with fine reddish-brown spots which sometimes form a ring around the broad end.

Distribution: Endemic to Puerto Rico.

RED-EYED VIREO   Plate 33
Vireo olivaceus

Identification: 15 cm (6″). The red iris and white eye stripe help identify this bird, but the absence of the black whisker stripe is critical in distinguishing it from the very similar Black-whiskered Vireo. Red-eyes also have a gray crown, whiter underparts and greener back giving the species a much less buffy appearance. The immature has a brown iris.

Local Name: Julián Chiví ojirrojo

Comments: A very rare migrant to Puerto Rico, there are single records from St John and St Croix. However, the species is probably more common than records indicate since it is easily overlooked due to its similarity with the common Black-whiskered Vireo. Red-eyes can best be found in October in sparsely wooded areas when the Black-whiskered Vireos have left the region.

Distribution: In the West Indies recorded only from Puerto Rico, the Bahamas, Cuba, Jamaica, and Barbados, but throughout the rest of the New World.

BLACK-WHISKERED VIREO   Plate 33
Vireo altiloquus

Identification: 16.5 cm (6.5″). The dark whisker stripe distinguishes this from all other vireos in the region.

Local Names: John-chew-it, John-to-whit, John Phillip, Greenlet, Julián Chiví bigotinegro, Bien-te-veo

Comments: A common breeding resident in Puerto Rico, but appears to have become less common in the Virgin Islands. Birds arrive *en masse* in early February and depart southward just as rapidly in late August or early September. There are several records from October, December, and January suggesting a few birds may remain the year round, as in Hispaniola. This species occurs in wooded areas where it is much more often heard than seen, its somewhat monotonous call being conspicuous throughout the day.

Voice: Short, melodious phrases, each a bit different and separated by a distinct pause. Numerous common names for this bird, both in English and Spanish, are renditions of its song. The species also has a thin unmusical *tsit*, and a sharp, nasal note.

Nesting: Two to three white eggs with fine spots concentrated at the broad end form a normal clutch and are laid in a deep cup-shaped nest. Breeding occurs primarily in May and June.

Distribution: Throughout the West Indies to southern Florida. A winter visitor to northern South America.

Emberizids: Wood Warblers, Blackbirds, Tanagers and Allies
FAMILY: EMBERIZIDAE

This large and diverse family unites several bird groups such as the New World wood warblers, tanagers, honeycreepers and orioles along with the blackbirds and other distinctive bird assemblages. It is by far the best represented family in the region, the subfamily of wood warblers alone being better represented than any other group of family status. The subfamilies can be detailed as follows:

Wood Warblers — Wood warblers are tiny insectivorous birds with thin, pointed bills. Most species actively hop among the tree branches gleaning their prey from leaf surfaces, but some feed on the ground or, like the Redstart, sally after flying insects. The winter plumages of many wood warblers are drab and care must be taken in the identification of these birds. Interestingly, though 31 species of wood warblers (excluding vagrants) occur in the region, only three of these species breed, the rest occurring as migrants or winter visitors.

Honeycreepers — The ubiquitous Bananaquit is the sole representative of this tropical New World group in the region. Honeycreepers typically have long, curved bills which they use to probe into flowers for nectar and insects. They have a specially adapted brush-like tongue for extracting the nectar. Soft fruits also form part of their diet.

Tanagers — The tanagers are a large New World assemblage, the males often being beautifully plumaged, but endowed with limited vocal ability (*Euphonia* in this region, sings well). *Nesospingus*, the region's only endemic avian genus, is atypical due to the male's somber coloration and the lack of sexual dimorphism. Tanagers are generally arboreal forest dwelling species that feed almost exclusively on fruits.

Grosbeaks — The grosbeaks are characterized by a thick, conical bill used for eating seeds. In appearance they resemble the finches, weavers and waxbills.

Blackbirds and Orioles — The birds of this New World group possess pointed, conical bills. Almost all of the species in the region have a significant amount of black in their plumage, and yellow or yellowish-orange is displayed in several of them.

BLUE-WINGED WARBLER   Plate 1
Vermivora pinus

Identification: 12.5 cm (5″). The all yellow body, white wing bars and dark stripe through the eye distinguish this warbler.

Local Name: Reinita aliazul

Comments: A decidedly rare visitor to some of the larger Virgin Islands from October to March. There are four records from St John, three from St Croix and two from St Thomas. The species has not been recorded from Puerto Rico. All records are since 1979 likely reflecting both an increase in observers in the Virgin Islands as well as a change in status of the bird.

Distribution: Rare in the West Indies east to St Croix and St John. Also throughout the eastern USA south through Central America.

BLACK-AND-WHITE WARBLER Plate 34
Mniotilta varia

Identification: 12.5−14 cm (5−5.5"). The entirely black and white coloration, the white striping on the crown and the absence of a white eye-ring distinguish this species. Its habit of climbing on tree trunks is also characteristic. The female is somewhat whiter than the male, particularly on the underparts. The rare Elfin Woods Warbler of the high mountain forests of Puerto Rico is the only other species with which it might be confused, but the latter differs in the characteristics mentioned above.

Local Name: Reinita trepadora

Comments: A fairly common visitor to Puerto Rico and the Virgin Islands from September through April, some individuals arriving as early as late August. Found in wooded areas at all elevations.

Voice: Frequently calls in the fall upon arrival, rarely in the spring. The call is a thin *tee-zee, tee-zee, tee-zee, tee-zee, tee-zee, tee-zee,* varying in length.

Distribution: Throughout the West Indies and much of North America to northern South America.

PROTHONOTARY WARBLER Plates 35, 36
Protonotaria citrea

Identification: 14 cm (5.5"). The golden coloration on the head, duller in the female, and the blue-gray wings are diagnostic.

Local Name: Reinita anaranjada

Comments: A decidedly uncommon winter visitor to Puerto Rico from October to March and recorded as early as August. It is rare in the Virgin Islands, being known from St Croix, St

John, and St Thomas. It no doubt occurs as well on other islands with suitable mangroves, a habitat from which the species rarely strays. These warblers appear to form small flocks before migrating north in spring.

Distribution: Throughout the West Indies and the eastern USA to Central America and northern South America.

WORM-EATING WARBLER   Plate 33
Helmitheros vermivorus

Identification: 13 cm (5.25"). The alternating stripes of black and buff on the crown are diagnostic.

Local Name: Reinita gusanera

Comments: An uncommon visitor in Puerto Rico and St John, rare on the other large Virgin Islands. The species occurs from October to April and frequents the heavy forests of the interior mountains. It is very rarely seen on the coast.

Distribution: Throughout the Greater Antilles, Bahamas, the eastern USA, Mexico, and Central America.

SWAINSON'S WARBLER   Plate 1
Limnothlypis swainsonii

Identification: 15 cm (6"). This is a plain warbler, olive-brown above and pale below. It is distinguished by its rusty crown and conspicuous white eye stripe.

Local Name: Reinita de Swainson

Comments: An accidental visitor, there are three records from St John (Jan., Feb., Mar.) and one from Puerto Rico (Feb.). The species generally prefers dense forest undergrowth.

Distribution: In the West Indies east to St John and through the southeastern USA to Belize.

GOLDEN-WINGED WARBLER   Plate 35
Vermivora chrysoptera

Identification: 12.5 cm (5"). The yellow wing patch and the black (♂) or gray (♀) throat are diagnostic.

Local Name: Reinita alidorada

Comments: A rare but regular winter visitor to Puerto Rico. There are single records from St Croix and St John. This species prefers the high mountain forests of the interior, but has been seen on the coast.

Distribution: In the West Indies east to Puerto Rico and through the eastern USA to Central America.

NORTHERN PARULA   Plate 35
Parula americana

Identification: 10.5—12 cm (4.25—4.75″). The white wing bars, the bluish-gray upperparts with the yellowish wash on the back, and the yellow breast and throat help identify this warbler. Adult males have a distinct breast band. The similar Adelaide's Warbler can be distinguished by its yellow spectacles.

Local Names: Parula Warbler, Reinita pechidorada

Comments: The most common wintering warbler in the region, it occurs infrequently as early as August and as late as June. In late March and April these birds are often in song. Parulas occur from coastal thickets and scrub into mountain forests.

Voice: The call note is a sweet *toip*. The song is an ascending insect-like buzz with a sharp note or warble at the end, *bzzzzzzit-tit* ∫ — .

Distribution: East in the West Indies to Guadeloupe and from eastern North America to Costa Rica.

YELLOW WARBLER   Plates 35, 36
Dendroica petechia

Identification: 12.5—14 cm (5—5.5″). This warbler has more yellow in its plumage than any other (though immatures have varying amounts of white). The yellow spots in the tail are diagnostic. Males have rust-colored streaks on the breast; these are faint or lacking in females and immatures.

Local Names: Canary, Mangrove Canary, Canario de mangle

Comments: A very common permanent resident in the region. It primarily inhabits mangroves, but also occurs on the coast in freshwater swamps, dry scrub and shade trees usually near water.

Voice: The call notes include a hard *chip*, more melodious than Adelaide's Warbler, and also a thin *zeet*. The song is variable, but a typical version would be *tsú, tsu, tsu, tsuk-a-tsu*.

Nesting: Three heavily spotted greenish-white eggs are laid in a finely woven open nest. Breeding is primarily from February to June, but occurs in other months.

Distribution: Throughout the West Indies and North America to northern South America.

MAGNOLIA WARBLER   Plates 34, 36
Dendroica magnolia

Identification: 11.5—12.5 cm (4.5—5″). The white tail markings distinguish it in all plumages.

Local Name: Reinita manchada

Comments: An uncommon and irregular visitor to Puerto Rico and rare on St Thomas, St John and St Croix. It has not been recorded from elsewhere in the Virgin Islands. This warbler occurs from September to April.

Distribution: In the West Indies east to St John and Barbados. Widespread in North America south to northern South America.

CAPE MAY WARBLER   Plates 34, 36
Dendroica tigrina

Identification: 12.5—14 cm (5—5.5″). In all plumages the heavy striping on the breast and the yellowish rump help identify this bird. Usually a diagnostic yellow patch is present behind the ear. Males have a distinctive chestnut-colored cheek.

Local Name: Reinita tigre

Comments: A fairly common winter visitor to Puerto Rico from November to March, with some birds occurring as early as

September and as late as May. It is uncommon in the Virgin Islands. The species prefers mountain forests, but also occurs in thickets, mangroves and even gardens on the coast.

Voice: It rarely sings its whispery, unmusical single-pitched song *tseet-tseet-tseet-tseet*, before migrating north.

Distribution: Throughout the West Indies and much of North America into Central America.

BLACK-THROATED BLUE WARBLER Plates 35, 36
Dendroica caerulescens

Identification: 13 cm (5.25"). The blue-backed, black-faced male is unmistakable. The female can be distinguished by the white wing spot. Immatures sometimes lack this and can be identified by the light eye stripe and dark brownish upperparts extending onto the cheek.

Local Name: Reinita azul

Comments: A common winter visitor to Puerto Rico occurring as early as September and as late as May. It is uncommon on St John, and even scarcer among the other Virgin Islands which have less extensive forests. Surprisingly, there are no reports as yet from Tortola where doubtless the bird occurs at high elevations. This species prefers heavy forests of the interior.

Voice: Before migrating north it rarely sings a wheezy, rising *zur, zur, zree*.

Distribution: Throughout the West Indies and eastern North America to Central America.

YELLOW-RUMPED WARBLER Plates 34, 36
Dendroica coronata

Identification: 14 cm (5.5"). In any plumage the combination of the yellow rump and white throat are distinctive.

Local Names: Myrtle Warbler, Reinita coronada

Comments: Fairly common in an extremely limited number of locales in Puerto Rico, but decidedly uncommon over most of the island as well as in the Virgin Islands. This is one of the last warblers to reach the region; the first birds normally only begin to arrive in November. By March they are heading north again, a few remaining into early April. This species inhabits forests and open thickets. It is only found with regularity around the mangrove thickets at Boquerón Refuge and the Cabo Rojo Lighthouse.

Voice: The call note is a hard, characteristic *check*.

Distribution: Throughout the West Indies and North America into Central America.

BLACK-THROATED GREEN WARBLER   Plates 34, 36
Dendroica virens

Identification: 12.5 cm (5″). In all plumages the cheek is yellow or surrounded by a yellow band which is characteristic.

Local Name: Reinita verdosa

Comments: A very rare visitor to Puerto Rico, St Croix, St John, and Water Island. The species occurs from late September to early May. It should be looked for in forested areas.

Distribution: Throughout the West Indies and much of North America to Central America.

BLACKBURNIAN WARBLER   Plates 35, 36
Dendroica fusca

Identification: 13 cm (5.25″). The brilliant throat and facial markings, orange in the male and yellower in the female and fall birds, readily identify adults. Immatures have much less distinctive facial markings and can easily be confused with young Black-throated Green Warblers. They can be differentiated from the latter by their yellow throat and breast and the whitish stripes on their back.

Local Name: Reinita de fuego

Comments: A very rare visitor to the region, there are three records from Puerto Rico and four from St John. Records range from December to March, but the species likely occurs from September through November as well. This warbler has a decided preference for conifers and more intensive observations in Honduras Pine plantations will no doubt turn up more records.

Distribution: Rare in the West Indies. Also eastern North America, Central America and northeastern South America.

YELLOW-THROATED WARBLER   Plate 34
Dendroica dominica

Identification: 13 cm (5.25 "). The yellow throat, white eye stripe and white neck patch are diagnostic in all plumages.

Local Name: Reinita gargantiamarilla

Comments: An uncommon visitor to Puerto Rico from September to April. There are a few records from St Thomas, St John and St Croix. It inhabits the crowns of palms near the sea, sometimes entering adjacent mangroves. The species also occurs among Spanish moss (*Tilandsia*) and similar epiphytes, particularly in southeastern Puerto Rico.

Voice: The call note is a soft, high-pitched slightly metallic *tsip*.

Distribution: Throughout the West Indies and the eastern USA south through Central America.

ADELAIDE'S WARBLER   Plate 35
Dendroica adelaidae

Identification: 12.5 cm (5 "). Distinguished, particularly from the similar Northern Parula, by the eye marking, yellow above, and either yellow or white below.

Local Name: Reinita mariposera

Comments: A common permanent resident in Puerto Rico, but unknown from the Virgin Islands. This species favors the lowlands, being most common in the dry scrubland of the south coast, but also occurring in thickets on the north coast, the haystack hills, and sparingly into the mountains. It is absent from the extreme eastern end of the island.

Voice: The call note is a *chick*, of medium strength. The song is quite variable, typically consisting of a loud trill that either ascends, descends, remains on the same pitch, or is a combination of these. It may slow at the end or have other minor modifications.

Nesting: Three or four white eggs flecked with reddish-brown spots, particularly at the broad end, are laid in a finely woven, cup-shaped nest located in a tree or dense thicket from 6 inches to over 20 feet above the ground. Breeding occurs from March to June.

Distribution: Puerto Rico, Vieques, Barbuda, St Lucia.

CHESTNUT-SIDED WARBLER   Plates 34, 36
Dendroica pensylvanica

Identification: 12.5 cm (5″). In winter plumage it is identified by its white underparts and eye-ring, the wing bars, and yellowish-green upperparts. Immatures lack chestnut on the sides and flanks. In breeding plumage the cap is yellow.

Local Name: Reinita costadicastaña

Comments: A very rare visitor through the winter in Puerto Rico, being known from ten sight records between October and April. It has been observed five times on St John and twice on St Croix. The species generally occurs in well-forested areas. This warbler is apparently becoming a more regular visitor to the region.

Distribution: Rare in the West Indies east to St John. Also throughout eastern North America and Central America.

BAY-BREASTED WARBLER   Plates 34, 36
Dendroica castanea

Identification: 14 cm (5.5″). In winter plumage it is similar to the Blackpoll Warbler, but buff-colored undertail coverts, black legs and feet, and a faint bay wash on the sides and flanks (absent in immatures and some adults), distinguish it from the latter. Summer plumaged males are chestnut on the head, throat and sides. Females are much paler.

Local Name: Reinita castaña

Comments: Accidental from October to May. There are three sight records from Puerto Rico, a sight record from Mona Island and two specimens from St Croix.

Distribution: Rare in the West Indies east of Cuba. Also through much of North America to northern South America.

BLACKPOLL WARBLER   Plates 34, 36
Dendroica striata

Identification: 12.5—14 cm (5—5.5″). The winter plumaged Blackpoll is difficult to distinguish, but it is identified by the white wing bars and undertail coverts and particularly the pale yellowish legs. In summer plumage the black cap and white cheeks of the male are diagnostic; females are similar to winter plumaged birds.

Local Name: Reinita rayada

Comments: A fairly common fall migrant in Puerto Rico in October and November, uncommon in September and December, and rare from January to May. The species is uncommon on St John, St Thomas, and St Croix in the fall. Low branches in sparsely wooded areas are its typical haunts.

Distribution: Widespread in the Western Hemisphere.

PRAIRIE WARBLER   Plates 34, 36
Dendroica discolor

Identification: 12 cm (4.75″). Identified in all plumages by its yellow underparts with blackish streaks on the sides, and its tail-bobbing habit.

Local Name: Reinita galana

Comments: A common visitor to Puerto Rico and only fairly so in the Virgin Islands from as early as late August to April. It prefers scattered thickets in dry areas.

Voice: The call note is a hard *chick*.

Distribution: Throughout the West Indies and the eastern USA.

PALM WARBLER   Plates 34, 36
Dendroica palmarum

Identification: 12.5—14 cm (5—5.5″). The tail-bobbing habit is a major field mark. It is distinguished in winter plumage by the yellowish undertail coverts, olive rump, faint eye stripe, and brownish back. In summer plumage, the cap is chestnut-colored.

Local Name: Reinita palmera

Comments: An uncommon winter visitor to Puerto Rico, St Croix and at Caneel Bay, St John. It is rare on St Thomas and Tortola and undoubtedly occurs irregularly on the other islands. The bird is found from September to April primarily inhabiting mangrove fringes and thickets near water. The species is locally fairly common at the Boquerón Refuge in western Puerto Rico.

Distribution: East in the West Indies to the Virgin Islands and throughout much of North America to Mexico.

ELFIN WOODS WARBLER   Plate 34
Dendroica angelae

Identification: This black and white plumaged warbler is very similar to the migrant Black-and-white Warbler, but is distinguished by its incomplete white eye-ring, entirely black crown, thin white stripe above the eye, and conspicuous white patches on the ear coverts and side of the neck. Immatures are similarly patterned to adults, but the black is replaced by grayish-green on the back and yellowish-green on the head and stripes on the underparts. This species does not creep over the trunks of trees as does the Black-and-white Warbler, but gleans insects from the leaves and thinner branches.

Local Name: Reinita de bosque enano

Comments: The Elfin Woods Warbler is an endemic resident in Puerto Rico, where it is uncommon and local in distribution. In the eastern part of the island it is known only from the Luquillo Mountains, where it primarily inhabits the elfin woodland or dwarf forest on the ridges and mountain summits, sometimes ranging down as far as the colorado zone; in the west it is restricted to the upper elevations of Maricao State Forest. This is an extremely active warbler, moving among the dense vines of the forest canopy, sometimes in small parties, in an incessant search for insects and allowing one to only glimpse its presence. It is no doubt a combination of this bird's great activity, well concealed habitat, restricted range, and similarity to the common Black-and-white Warbler that allowed it to go undiscovered by science a full 45 years longer than any other bird species in the West Indies. In fact, Drs Cameron and Kay Kepler, who discovered in the bird in 1971, had resided and worked extensively in the Luquillo Mountains for over two years before they were certain that they had encountered a new species. Persons specifically interested in observing this unusual warbler might most readily do so by hiking the El Toro trail (check at the La Mina Recreation Area on El Yunque for directions to the trail) for several hundred meters until the first extensive patch of dwarf forest is reached. Of course, this is no guarantee you'll see the bird!

Voice: The song is a series of short, rapidly uttered, rather unmusical notes on one pitch, swelling in volume, and terminating with a short series of distinct double (iambic) syllables sounding slightly lower in pitch. There is also a contact note similar to the song but lacking the terminal iambic syllables. The above vocalizations are very similar to the buzzy call of the ubiquitous Bananaquit. The call note, infrequently given, is a single, short metallic chip similar in quality and duration to that of the Black-throated Blue Warbler (Kepler and Parkes).

Nesting: The nest is unknown.

Distribution: Endemic to Puerto Rico.

OVENBIRD
Plate 33

Seiurus aurocapillus

Identification: 15 cm (6"). The orange crown bordered with black stripes and the heavily streaked underparts are diagnostic.

Local Name: Pizpita dorada

Comments: A fairly common visitor to Puerto Rico and St John from October to April, some birds arriving in September. It is uncommon in the other Virgin Islands which have less extensive forests. This species dwells principally among the leaf litter of forests in the interior where it is silent and easily overlooked. It also occurs in dry thickets and even in mangroves.

Distribution: Throughout the West Indies and widespread in North America south to northern South America.

NORTHERN WATERTHRUSH   Plate 33
Seiurus noveboracensis

Identification: 12.5—15 cm (5—6″). The buff-colored eye stripe
and the streaked underparts with flecks on the throat identify
this warbler. Like the Louisiana Waterthrush, this species
characteristically bobs its tail.

Local Name: Pizpita de mangle

Comments: A very common visitor to Puerto Rico and the Virgin
Islands from September to April. It primarily inhabits
mangroves where it is found on the ground or in low vegetation.
However, particularly in the Virgin Islands, it may occur up
mountain streams, a habitat dominated by the Louisiana
Waterthrush in Puerto Rico. It is easily attracted by a 'swishing'
noise.

Voice: The call note is a sharp, emphatic *tchip*.

Distribution: Throughout the West Indies and North America
to northern South America.

LOUISIANA WATERTHRUSH   Plate 33
Seiurus motacilla

Identification: 15—16 cm (6—6.25″). The white eye stripe and
unflecked throat and the heavily streaked whitish underparts
are distinctive. The constant tail-bobbing of waterthrushes helps
identify them.

Local Name: Pizpita de río

Comments: A fairly common visitor to Puerto Rico from
September to April with some birds arriving as early as August
and remaining as late as May. The species is very uncommon
in the Virgin Islands. The borders of freshwater streams in
mountain forests are its typical habitat.

Voice: A sharp *tchip*, of higher pitch than that of the Northern
Waterthrush.

Distribution: Throughout the West Indies and the eastern USA
south to northern South America.

KENTUCKY WARBLER   Plates 35, 36
Oporornis formosus

Identification: 14 cm (5.5″). The black facial mark and the
yellow eye stripe and eye-ring are diagnostic. Immatures show
only a sign of the black facial mark. Their entirely yellow
underparts and light olive upperparts help identify them.

Local Name: Reinita de Kentucky

Comments: A very rare visitor to Puerto Rico and St John from
September to March. There are single records from St Thomas
and St Croix. The species inhabits forested areas with thick
underbrush and consequently is difficult to observe.

Distribution: Rare in the West Indies east to Guadeloupe. Also
from the southeastern USA to northern South America.

CONNECTICUT WARBLER   Plates 35, 36
Oporornis agilis

Identification: 14—14.5 cm (5.5—5.75″). In all plumages there
is a complete white eye-ring and at least a suggestion of the
hood, gray in adults and olive in immatures. Females and
immatures are duller than males.

Local Name: Reinita de Connecticut

Comments: A decidedly rare fall migrant to Puerto Rico, there
is one winter record. This warbler has been observed with
greater frequency in recent years. There is one fall record for
St Croix and one questionable spring sighting from St John.
The species, like the similar Mourning Warbler, favors areas
of heavy brush.

Distribution: A rare migrant in the West Indies. Throughout
much of the New World.

MOURNING WARBLER   Plates 35, 36
Oporornis philadelphia

Identification: 12.5 cm (5″). The black bib of the male is
diagnostic. In winter plumage, the female and immature have
a distinct buff-colored band across the breast, a very yellow

belly and an incomplete eye-ring. The very similar Connecticut Warbler has a complete eye-ring.

Local Name: Reinita enlutada

Comments: Accidental. Known from a specimen (March 1912) and three sight records from Puerto Rico (Oct., Mar., Dec.) and a sight record from Vieques (Dec.). It prefers thickets and brush.

Distribution: Accidental in the West Indies. Through much of North America to northern South America.

COMMON YELLOWTHROAT   Plate 35
Geothlypis trichas

Identification: 12.5 cm (5″). The male's black mask is distinctive. The female is identified by her bright yellow throat and breast and dull white belly.

Local Name: Reinita pica tierra

Comments: A fairly common visitor to Puerto Rico from October to April occurring as early as September and as late as June. The species is rare in the Virgin Islands where it is known from St Croix, St John, St Thomas, Tortola, and Anegada. Yellowthroats frequent wet grassy areas usually on the edges of freshwater swamps, ponds, or canals. They appear to congregate and pair in spring before migrating north.

Voice: The call note is distinctive, sounding like a stone being thrown into a pile of gravel. The clear song *witchity, witchity, witchity, witch* is heard only in May and even then only rarely.

Distribution: Throughout the West Indies and North and Central America.

HOODED WARBLER   Plates 35, 36
Wilsonia citrina

Identification: 14 cm (5.5″). The male, with its black hood, is unmistakable. The white outer tail spots, which are constantly flashed, are a good character for the species. Females have a distinctive yellow cheek and usually a yellow forehead. Immatures have a yellow eye stripe.

Local Name: Reinita de capucha

Comments: A decidedly uncommon winter visitor to Puerto Rico and the Virgin Islands from October to March. It prefers forest undergrowth and mangrove swamps. In the latter it is easily overlooked due to its similarity to the common Yellow Warbler.

Distribution: Throughout the West Indies and the eastern USA south to Panama.

CANADA WARBLER
Wilsonia canadensis

Plates 34, 36

Identification: 13 cm (5.25″). In all plumages there is at least some sign of the black 'necklace'. The yellow 'spectacles' and entirely gray upperparts also aid in identification.

Local Name: Reinita de Canadá

Comments: Accidental. There are three records from Puerto Rico, two from Mona Island and one each from St Thomas and St Croix. Records range from October to April.

Distribution: Accidental in the West Indies. Through eastern North America south well into South America.

AMERICAN REDSTART
Setophaga ruticilla

Plate 35

Identification: 12.5 cm (5″). The primarily black male with its large orange wing and tail patches is unmistakable. The lighter female is easily identified by her large yellow wing and tail markings, the latter being quite apparent as the tail is regularly flicked.

Local Name: Candelita

Comments: A common visitor to Puerto Rico and the Virgin Islands from September to April with records from August and early May. It prefers forested areas and occurs from the mountains to the mangroves.

Voice: The call note is a sharp *tschip*.

Distribution: Throughout most of the Western Hemisphere.

BANANAQUIT   Plate 33
Coereba flaveola

Identification: 10–12.5 cm (4–5″). The white eye stripe and wing spot, the gray throat and the yellow breast, belly and rump easily identify this bird.

Local Names: Yellow Breast, Bahaman Honeycreeper, Reinita común

Comments: An abundant resident in the region, it is found in virtually every habitat.

Voice: A thin, ascending insect-like buzz that tumbles into a short warble. The call note is an unmusical *tsip*.

Nesting: Globular nests of grasses and fine plant fibers are constructed and many go unused. The entry hole is in the bottom or side and two to four whitish eggs with a ruddy tint and brown flecks are laid in any season.

Distribution: Throughout the West Indies, except Cuba. Also Central and South America.

ANTILLEAN EUPHONIA   Plate 38
Euphonia musica

Identification: 11.5 cm (4.5″). The sky-blue crown and nape are distinctive.

Local Names: Blue-hooded Euphonia, Canario del país, Jilguero

Comments: This small tanager is common in Puerto Rico, but is unknown from the Virgin Islands. It is much more often heard than seen due to its preference for thick mountain forests where it flits about in the dense vegetation of the canopy. The species occurs from the dry hills of the south coast to the rainy dwarf forest high in the Luquillo Mountains, being most common in the former habitat.

Voice: A variety of distinctive call notes including a rapid, mild, almost tinkling *ti-tit* (sometimes one or three syllables), and a hard, metallic *chi-chink*. Also a plaintive *whee* like the Puerto Rican Flycatcher, but more melodious. It also has a jumbled, tinkling song mixed with explosive notes.

Nesting: Breeding is from January to July. Four spotted eggs are laid in a domed nest which is often well concealed among tree epiphytes.

Distribution: Puerto Rico, Hispaniola, and the Lesser Antilles.

STRIPE-HEADED TANAGER   Plate 38
Spindalis zena

Identification: 16.5 cm (6.5 ″). In the adult male the white markings on the black head are diagnostic. The head markings show faintly in females and immatures.

Local Names: Puerto Rican Spindalis, Reina mora

Comments: A common permanent resident in Puerto Rico, but not known from the Virgin Islands. The species frequents woodlands and forests at all elevations, but is more common in the mountains.

Voice: Its thin, but distinctive song can be heard commonly during the breeding season *zeé-tit-zeé-tittit-zeé*. The *zee* syllable often seems like an inhaling sound. This basic call has many variations. A thin trill like the beating of a tiny hammer is rarely heard as is a short twittering call. The call note is a soft *teweep*.

Nesting: Two to three heavily spotted white eggs are laid in a very bulky, open nest. Breeding occurs primarily from April to June, but sometimes begins in December.

Distribution: The Greater Antilles, Bahamas, Grand Cayman, and Cozumel Island.

SCARLET TANAGER   Plate 38
Piranga olivacea

Identification: 18 cm (7 ″). Good field marks of adults in winter dress are the yellowish-green plumage, notched tanager bill and, in the case of the male, the black wings. The red plumaged male in summer dress might be observed in late spring.

Local Name: Escarlatina

Comments: A very rare spring and fall migrant. It is known in the region from Puerto Rico, Mona Island, St Croix and St John. The species apparently occurs most regularly on St Croix where it has been observed nearly each year for the past 10—15 years.

Distribution: Rare in the West Indies. Also eastern and central North America south to northwestern South America.

PUERTO RICAN TANAGER   Plate 38
Nesospingus speculiferus

Identification: 18—20 cm (7—8 "). A distinctive bird, primarily olive-brown above and white below with dusky stripes on the breast and a conspicuous white spot in the wing. Immatures lack the wing spot and have brownish underparts.

Local Name: Llorosa

Comments: The endemic Puerto Rican Tanager is common in many, but not all, of Puerto Rico's higher mountain forests, including those of the Luquillo Mountains, the western mountains around Maricao (including adjacent coffee plantations) and in the Carite-Guavate State Forest. The species even occurs locally in disturbed second growth forest at moderate altitude near Cidra. Inexplicably this tanager does not occur in the vicinity of Toro Negro in the heart of the Central Mountains, where appropriate habitat appears to be plentiful. The absence of the Puerto Rican Tanager at this locality and among the haystack hills, where it formerly occurred, gives this species one of the most puzzling distributions among the island's forest birds.

The Puerto Rican Tanager is normally found in noisy flocks foraging in the dense forest canopy where its feeding methods and general behavior are very variable. At night the birds retreat to communal roosts in palms or bamboo clumps. Interestingly, the Cuban naturalist Juan Gundlach, who is credited with the discovery of the Puerto Rican Tanager in 1868, was unaware that a specimen he had of this bird, in a collection received from a friend and forwarded to the Smithsonian Institute, represented a species new to science. Gundlach was incredulous when he saw his name in the original species description and had to be convinced that he personally had prepared the specimen tag.

Voice: This noisy bird has a harsh call note *chuck* or *chewp* which is frequently run into a chatter of varying length *chi-chi-chit*.

It uncommonly sings a sweet, warbling courtship song with the quality of a hummingbird call, also a soft, short twitter, and a thin sigh like a heavy exhale.

Nesting: Breeding extends from January through August. The nest is cup-shaped and situated from 7 feet to 30 feet above the ground. A clutch contains two to three cream-colored eggs heavily speckled with dark brown. Only three nests have been found.

Distribution: Endemic to Puerto Rico.

ROSE-BREASTED GROSBEAK   Plate 39
Pheucticus ludovicianus

Identification: 19−20 cm (7.5−8″). The rose-colored breast of the male is distinctive. The female is distinguished by her large size, heavy bill and white crown stripes.

Local Name: Piquigrueso rosado

Comments: A very rare visitor in the region from October to May. Known from ten records including Puerto Rico proper, Mona Island, St Thomas, St John, and St Croix. This species appears to be visiting the region with greater regularity than formerly.

Distribution: Rare in the West Indies, but through much of North America to northern South America.

BLUE GROSBEAK   Plate 39
Guiraca caerulea

Identification: 16.5−19 cm (6.5−7.5″). The blue male with rust-colored wing bars is distinctive. The brown female can be identified by her large size, heavy bill and rust-colored wing bars.

Local Name: Azulejo

Comments: A decidedly rare visitor to Puerto Rico where it is only seen with any regularity in the coastal scrub of the southwest. The species is very rare elsewhere in the region having been recorded from Mona Island, St John, and St Croix. It occurs from October to April. The Blue Grosbeak appears to be occurring with increasing frequency in the region.

Distribution: Rare in the West Indies east to St John. Also through the southern USA into Central America.

INDIGO BUNTING   Plate 39
Passerina cyanea

Identification: 14 cm (5.5 ″). The all blue male is only seen in spring. His plumage is brown in fall and winter when he can be identified by tints of blue in his wings and tail. The female is completely dull brown with very light breast stripes. She has no conspicuous markings.

Local Name: Gorrión azul

Comments: A visitor in the region from November through early May, it is common on St John and fairly common on Tortola. The species is uncommon on Virgin Gorda and St Croix and rare on St Thomas. It is unrecorded from the less forested and smaller of the Virgin Islands. In Puerto Rico this bird occurs in small numbers locally during winter and spring migration. Agricultural stations and grassy road edges bounded by heavy thickets, particularly near the coast, are favorite habitats.

Voice: The call note is an emphatic *twit* and the bird sometimes gives its thin song, usually of paired phrases.

Distribution: Through the Bahamas and Greater Antilles (excluding Hispaniola) to the Virgin Islands. Also the eastern USA to Central America.

DICKCISSEL   Plate 39
Spiza americana

Identification: 15−18 cm (6−7 ″). There is a yellowish wash on the breast, paler in the female, and a dull yellow eye stripe. The male has a black patch in the center of the throat, which in winter is reduced or absent. A rust-colored patch at the base of the wing helps identify this species.

Local Name: Sabanero americano

Comments: Accidental. Known by one bird photographed in Puerto Rico (Sept. 1972).

Distribution: Accidental in Puerto Rico, normally only occurring in the islands of the western Caribbean northeast of Cuba. Also through the central and eastern USA to northern South America.

PUERTO RICAN BULLFINCH   Plate 39
Loxigilla portoricensis

Identification: 16.5—19 cm (6.5—7.5 "). Adults are black with a rufous band around the crown, on the throat and on the undertail coverts. Immatures are dark olive-green with only the undertail coverts rufous.

Local Names: Puerto Rican Grosbeak, Come ñame de Puerto Rico, Come gandul, Capacho, Gallito

Comments: The Puerto Rican Bullfinch is an endemic permanent resident in Puerto Rico. There is a single record from St John, apparently of an escaped bird. It is very common in the woodlands of Puerto Rico, particularly the heavy forests of the mountains where it is far more often heard than seen. However, it occurs in dry coastal thickets and infrequently in mangroves. The only apparently suitable habitats from which this bullfinch appears to be absent are the coastal thickets of the extreme eastern tip of the island from Fajardo to Ceiba.

The Puerto Rican Bullfinch was not always endemic to this island. A larger, thicker-billed subspecies was known to inhabit the higher mountain slopes of St Kitts in the Lesser Antilles where it was not uncommon, at least until 1888. However, the St Kitts bird, which was locally called Mountain Blacksmith, was last collected in the 1920s and is now presumed extinct. The cause of extinction of the St Kitts form is not known with certainty. Some experts speculate that introduced Green Monkeys were responsible. However, there are a number of strong objections to the monkey hypothesis, one being that the monkeys were there for over 200 years while the bullfinches survived. A more plausible explanation is that a devastating hurricane eliminated the St Kitts bullfinch from its limited range.

On Puerto Rico proper there is an impending threat to the bullfinch. It is in the form of the innocuous Lesser Antillean Bullfinch which recently crossed the broad Anegada Passage and became established on St John. Presently, this is the only naturally established breeding landbird in the Virgin Islands that is absent from Puerto Rico, and it can be expected that the Lesser Antillean Bullfinch will easily expand its range and in only a few decades arrive on Puerto Rico's shores. Here it will probably attempt to occupy a niche very similar to that already filled by the closely related Puerto Rican Bullfinch. Which species will suffer as a result, and to what degree, will only become clear after many years of interaction. It will be a situation well worthy of careful observation.

Voice: A very distinctive series of from two to ten rising whistles followed by a buzz. The call is much louder and more forceful than the similar call of the Lesser Antillean Bullfinch. A second call is whistled *coochi, coochi, coochi*. The call note is a medium strength *check* like hitting two stones together. This bird sings much of the day, particularly from February to June.

Nesting: The nest is either open or domed with an entrance in the side. Usually three eggs with a dull green hue and dark spots are laid. Breeding is primarily from February to June, but occurs sporadically in other seasons.

Distribution: Endemic to Puerto Rico. Formerly, also on St Kitts.

LESSER ANTILLEAN BULLFINCH   Plate 39
Loxigilla noctis

Identification: 14—15 cm (5.5—6″). The primarily black male has a rufous mark above and forward of the eye, as well as a rufous throat and undertail coverts. Females and immatures are identified by the tawny undertail coverts.

Local Name: Come ñame antillano menor

Comments: Fairly common and widespread on St John and now local but breeding on St Croix. It was also reported from Norman and Peter Islands but has not been seen there recently. This species arrived in the Virgin Islands around 1960, apparently by natural means, and can be expected to extend its range to nearby islands. It primarily inhabits areas of dry scrub.

Voice: Five to ten *seep* notes sometimes followed by a buzz.

Nesting: A domed nest is constructed with a hole in the side. Two spotted brown eggs are laid. Breeding is from January to February.

Distribution: From St John and St Croix through the Lesser Antilles with the exception of the Grenadines.

YELLOW-FACED GRASSQUIT   Plate 39
Tiaris olivacea

Identification: 11.5 cm (4.5″). The male has a distinctive yellow throat and eye stripe, and a black breast. Care must be taken in identifying the olive-colored female and immature grassquits; they usually have some yellowish markings around the eye.

Local Names: Gorrión barba amarilla, Chamorro bello

Comments: A common permanent resident in Puerto Rico, but unknown from the Virgin Islands. It prefers open grassy areas, being narrower in its habitat tolerances than the Black-faced Grassquit.

Voice: The call note is usually a soft *tek*, imitated by removing one's tongue from against the upper palate. The song is a distinctive, thin trill, sometimes uttered sequentially on different pitches.

Nesting: Generally three bluish-white eggs, heavily flecked at the broad end, are laid in a domed nest of fine grass with the entrance in the side. The nest is low off the ground and breeding occurs the year round.

Distribution: The Greater Antilles and the Cayman Islands. Also Mexico to northwestern South America.

BLACK-FACED GRASSQUIT   Plate 39
Tiaris bicolor

Identification: 11.5 cm (4.5″). The black head and underparts of the male are distinctive. The female is of drab olive coloration and can be identified by her total lack of markings.

Local Names: Sinbird, Grass Sparrow, Carib Grassquit, Gorrión negro, Chamorro negro

Comments: An abundant permanent resident in Puerto Rico and the Virgin Islands. It occurs in almost all open areas and road edges, or clearings in forests.

Voice: An extremely emphatic buzz that often gets a second effort which makes it louder. The call note is a soft, musical *tsip*.

Nesting: The nest is domed with a hole in the side or the bottom. Usually three whitish eggs, heavily flecked at the broad end, are laid in any season.

Distribution: Through the West Indies (except Cuba) to northern South America.

SAFFRON FINCH   Plate 38
Sicalis flaveola

Identification: 14 cm (5.5″). This medium-sized yellow finch, the adult having an orange crown, is quite distinctive. Immatures can usually be distinguished by a yellow band across the breast. Its preference for lawns, as much as its larger size and thicker bill, help distinguish it from the somewhat similar Yellow and Prothonotary Warblers.

Local Name: Gorrión azafrán

Comments: Introduced probably about 1960 in Puerto Rico, the Saffron Finch is now a well established resident. The species is found in Old San Juan and Santurce, being abundant in the Naval Reserve at Isla Grande. It has gradually expanded its range to Sabana Seca and should be looked for in adjacent areas. This bird is restricted to cultivated lawns with scattered trees.

Voice: The call note varies from a soft to a loud, sharp *pink*. Also a whistled *wheat* on one pitch. The song is a fairly loud, melodious, but slightly harsh *chit, chit, chit, chi-chit*, with variations of differing lengths.

Nesting: A bulky nest is built among palm fronds, or in a building cavity and two to three eggs are laid. Breeding occurs from August to October.

Distribution: Introduced in Puerto Rico, Jamaica, and elsewhere. Native to South America.

GRASSHOPPER SPARROW   Plates 39, 40
Ammodramus savannarum

Identification: 12.5 cm (5″). The eye stripe is golden near the bill and it has a central crown stripe which is whitish. Young lack the mark by the bill and have fine streaks on the breast and flanks. It is best distinguished from the very similar brown plumaged Red Bishop and Yellow-crowned Bishop by the single central crown stripe.

Local Names: Chingolo chicharra, Gorrión chicharra

Comments: A common but very local resident in Puerto Rico, not known from the Virgin Islands. It inhabits weedy fields and pastures with long grass, where it is much more frequently heard than seen.

Voice: Two distinct calls. A long, thin buzz like an insect, followed by what sounds like a hiccup *zzzzzzz-hic*. Also a very thin, high-pitched twitter or tinkling song like fairy bells. The call note is a high-pitched, gritty *kr-r-it*, sounding very much like an insect.

Nesting: Three heavily marked white eggs are laid in a domed nest in the grass. Breeding is primarily in spring and summer.

Distribution: Through the eastern Caribbean to Puerto Rico. Also widespread in North America to northwestern South America.

WHITE-THROATED SPARROW   Plate 39
Zonotrichia albicollis

Identification: 17 cm (6.75″). The white throat patch, yellow lores, and black and white striped crown identify this sparrow.

Local Name: Chingolo gargantiblanco

Comments: Accidental. Known from two sightings by the writer of apparently the same bird in San Juan, Puerto Rico (Jan., Feb. 1971).

Distribution: The above sightings are the only West Indian records. Widespread in North America.

SHINY COWBIRD   Plate 37
Molothrus bonariensis

Identification: 18–20 cm (7–8″). The medium body size and tail length, and the conical bill help identify this species. Males are glossy black; females are grayish-brown, much lighter below and with a light stripe above the eye. Immatures are much like females.

Local Names: Glossy Cowbird, Tordo lustroso

Comments: A common resident in Puerto Rico, but a rare breeder in the Virgin Islands where it has been recorded from St John, St Thomas, Tortola, St Croix and Anegada. Native to South America, the species was first found in Puerto Rico in numbers in 1955. (There is a record of a single bird collected on Vieques from 1859 or 1860; this was probably a stray, or escaped cage bird.) It is now common throughout the lowlands and occurs in the mountains where there is appropriate habitat. The species ranges in open country favoring dairies and agricultural areas where grains are grown. It has extended its range rapidly in recent years and doubtless will increase in numbers in the Virgin Islands.

Voice: A soft unmusical *ka-wúk* ⎯ ╱ and a longer musical call with whistles followed by a trill.

Nesting: A nest is not built, rather the female lays her eggs in the nests of other species to be hatched and the young raised by the foster parents. In this region the Shiny Cowbird most heavily parasitizes the Yellow-shouldered Blackbird.

Distribution: Native to tropical and subtropical zones of South America, but since 1891 has extended its range north in the Lesser Antilles to Antigua as well as to the Virgin Islands, Puerto Rico and Hispaniola.

GREATER ANTILLEAN GRACKLE   Plate 37
Quiscalus niger

Identification: 25—30 cm (10—12″). The grackle is identified by its glossy black coloration, V-shaped tail and narrow, gently curved bill. The similar Smooth-billed Ani is also black, but has a broad bill, flat tail and is larger.

Local Names: Mozambique, Chango

Comments: An abundant permanent resident in Puerto Rico and fairly common on Vieques. The species was introduced on St Croix about 1917, but was soon extirpated. This bird occurs primarily in the lowlands in every type of open area including pastures, residential zones, crop lands and along swamp and mangrove edges. It is uncommon in the mountains in unforested localities. Grackles roost in large flocks and show a decided preference for using electrical substations for this purpose.

Voice: The call note is a *chuck*. The species also has a wide variety of other notes including clear musical ones and wheezy gasps.

Nesting: Nesting is colonial with bulky open nests being constructed in a variety of habitats from low mangrove thickets to the tops of palms. Three to four olive-colored eggs with markings of various colors are laid. Breeding occurs from February to September but peaks from April to August.

Distribution: Throughout the Greater Antilles and the Cayman Islands.

BLACK-COWLED ORIOLE   Plate 37
Icterus dominicensis

Identification: 20–22 cm (8–8.75″). The yellow on the wings, rump and undertail coverts is distinctive. The similar Yellow-shouldered Blackbird only has yellow in the wings. Immatures are a dull yellow below and olive above with black wings. They sometimes have black or ruddy coloring on the neck and head.

Local Names: Puerto Rican Oriole, Calandria capuchinegra

Comments: A fairly common permanent resident in Puerto Rico, absent from the Virgin Islands. It frequents forests and forest edges, particularly where palms are available for nest sites.

Voice: The call note is a hard, sharp *keek* or *check* sometimes sounding as if the bird had a cold. Rarely heard, the beautiful song is given after dawn. It consists of high-pitched whistles, some seeming exclamatory and others querulous.

Nesting: Breeding is primarily from March to June, but occurs irregularly through the rest of the year. Three white eggs with a blue hue are laid in a hanging nest of plant fibers, usually under a palm frond.

Distribution: The Greater Antilles (except Jamaica), the Bahamas, and Central America into Mexico.

NORTHERN ORIOLE   Plate 37
Icterus galbula

Identification: 20 cm (8"). The medium size and limited white
in the wing distinguishes the male from the similar Troupial.
Females and immatures are identified by their white wing bars
and deep orange underparts. The Troupial, significantly larger,
has no gold tail marks and has a bare eye patch.

Local Names: Baltimore Oriole, Calandria del norte

Comments: An uncommon but regular visitor to St John and rare
on Puerto Rico and St Croix. It is extremely rare on the other
large Virgin Islands. In Puerto Rico the species occurs primarily
in the dry southwest. It should be looked for from September
to May.

Distribution: Rare in the West Indies east to the Virgin Islands.
Widespread in North America occurring to northern South
America.

TROUPIAL   Plate 37
Icterus icterus

Identification: 25 cm (10"). This large orange-yellow and black
bird with its extensive white wing patch is quite distinctive.

Local Names: Bugler Bird, Turpial

Comments: A common permanent resident in southwest Puerto
Rico from Ponce to Boquerón. It also occurs uncommonly
around San Juan and Bayamón and is periodically recorded
elsewhere. The species is uncommon on Mona Island, Culebra,
St Thomas (where it occurs along the south and east coasts)
and Water Island, while strays have been observed on St John.
The Troupial is believed to have been introduced into the
region; it has been here for over a century.

Voice: A clear series of whistles reminding one of its name, *troup,
troup, troup*, or *troup-ial, troup-ial, troup-ial.*

Nesting: A pendant nest is constructed, often in thorny scrub or
cacti, in which three to four spotted eggs are laid.

Distribution: Apparently introduced on Puerto Rico, Culebra,
Mona Island, St Thomas, Water Island, St John, Antigua,
Dominica, Grenada, and Jamaica. Native to South America.

YELLOW-SHOULDERED BLACKBIRD   Plate 37
Agelaius xanthomus

Identification: 20—23 cm (8—9 "). This species is entirely glossy
black with yellow epaulets. The similar Black-cowled Oriole
is more extensively marked with yellow. Immature Yellow-
shouldered Blackbirds are a duller black than adults and possess
a brown abdomen.

Local Names: Mariquita, Capitán

Comments: The Yellow-shouldered Blackbird is endemic to
Puerto Rico, being observed with any regularity only along the
coast in the southwest and on Mona Island. The bird is
decidedly uncommon elsewhere on the coast and inland where
it wanders in winter in search of food. The principal habitats
in which it is encountered are open mangrove areas and arid
scrublands. Outside the breeding season these birds usually
roost in flocks on offshore mangrove islets, dispersing during
the day over inland areas. Previously common island-wide in
coastal areas, the Yellow-shouldered Blackbird has undergone
a dramatic decline in recent decades. The apparent reason for
this decline is nest parasitism by the Glossy Cowbird, a recent
colonizer from South America. Rather than build its own nest,
the cowbird lays its eggs in the nests of other birds and the
cowbird nestlings out-compete the host's own offspring for food.
In Puerto Rico the principal host of the Glossy Cowbird is the
Yellow-shouldered Blackbird and it has suffered accordingly.
Blackbird numbers on Puerto Rico proper as of February 1988
were between 200 to 300. Such is the case despite years of study
and efforts to control cowbird numbers and devise cowbird-
proof nest boxes. A stable population of several hundred
blackbirds survives on Mona Island.

Voice: A wide variety of calls including a raspy *tñaaa* ⌐___
accented at the beginning; a whistled *tsuu*, ↘ starting with
an accent and descending the scale; a melodious *eh-up*, ⌐↘_
the second syllable one note lower and slightly accented; a *chuck*,
and when disturbed a sharp, nasal, squeaky *chink* and *check*,
and sharp staccato scolding notes around the nest.

Nesting: Yellow-shouldered Blackbirds nest primarily in small
aggregates in May and June, but breeding has been observed
as early as March and as late as September. The eggs, two to
four of which form a clutch, have a bluish luster and are covered

with brown splotches or fine squiggles sometimes concentrated at the broad end. A variety of sites are used for nesting including various portions of the mangrove, particularly fairly open flats with scattered, small trees, also the axils of palms, hollow stumps, thorny scrubland trees, and on Mona Island crevices in the precipitous coastal cliffs.

Distribution: Endemic to Puerto Rico and Mona Island.

BOBOLINK   Plate 37
Dolichonyx oryzivorus

Identification: 18.5 cm (7.25″). Adults in winter plumage can be distinguished by the black and buff-colored stripes on the crown. Males in summer dress are black below with white patches above. The Grasshopper Sparrow, and the Napoleon Weaver and Red Bishop in nonbreeding plumage appear similar to the Bobolink, but they are all significantly smaller. They also lack streaks on the sides and flanks (except for immature sparrows).

Local Name: Chambergo

Comments: A migrant, uncommon and very local in the fall and rare in the spring in Puerto Rico, St Thomas, St John, and St Croix. This species normally occurs in flocks in fields where grass is seeding.

Voice: A very distinctive *pink*.

Distribution: Throughout the West Indies and much of the New World.

Finches
FAMILY: FRINGILLIDAE

The finches are characterized by a conical bill for eating seeds. In appearance they resemble the Ploceidae, Estrildidae and grosbeaks of the Emberizidae. The males of most species are colorful, at least during the breeding season, and many species flock following nesting. The nest is usually cup-shaped. Flight is undulating.

YELLOW-FRONTED CANARY   Plate 38
Serinus mozambicus

Identification: 11.5 cm (4.5″). Distinguished by the yellowish breast, rump and eye stripe, its thick bill and the dark moustache stripe.

Local Names: Green Singing-Finch, Verdón cantador

Comments: Introduced probably about 1960 in Puerto Rico, this finch is possibly established very locally along the northeast coast. The species had been recorded in small numbers in coastal sea grape forests at Ramey, Vacia Talega and Punta Mameyes, but has not been observed recently. It may occur in similar habitat elsewhere. Whether it nests has not been determined.

Voice: A clear, whistled warble.

Distribution: Introduced in Puerto Rico and elsewhere. Native to much of Africa.

RED SISKIN   Plate 38
Carduelis cucullata

Identification: 10 cm (4″). The small size, black hood and extensive orange-red markings of the male are distinctive. The female is dark gray above and light gray below with an orange rump, wing bar and wash on the breast.

Local Name: Cardenalito

Comments: Introduced in Puerto Rico probably 50 or more years ago, the Red Siskin is established, but appears to be rare and very local between Coamo, Aibonito and Guayama. It inhabits fairly thick scrubby areas of the dry hills. This species was so heavily collected for the pet trade in its native land that it is endangered there.

Voice: A high-pitched twitter and a distinctive *chi-tit* like that of the Silverbill.

Nesting: Birds were observed carrying nesting material in June.

Distribution: Puerto Rico (introduced). Native to Venezuela, Colombia, Trinidad, Monos Island, and Gasparee Island.

Old World Sparrows
FAMILY: PASSERIDAE

A family of drab birds with conical finch-like bills represented in the New World only by introduced species.

HOUSE SPARROW   Plate 40
Passer domesticus

Identification: 15 cm (6″). The black bib on the male readily distinguishes him. The female has a buff-colored eye stripe and underparts and brown upperparts streaked with black.

Local Names: English Sparrow, Gorrión inglés

Comments: An uncommon and extremely local introduced resident in Puerto Rico, it appears to be extirpated from St Thomas. On the former island it is known only from Playa de Ponce (where it probably became established in the late 1960s) to Yauco, its range apparently expanding. In the early 1950s the bird inhabited the area of Miller Manor Hotel in Charlotte Amalie, St Thomas, but it has not been recorded recently. This species probably reached the islands on boats shipping grain. A flock of 60 birds was found on Mona Island in 1987. House Sparrows generally flock and should be looked for in lots and weedy edges along city streets.

Voice: The call note is a distinctive *chirp*.

Nesting: In St Thomas the House Sparrow nested in a date palm, but a nest has not been found in Puerto Rico.

Distribution: Introduced virtually around the world. Native to Eurasia and Africa.

Weaver Finches
FAMILY: PLOCEIDAE

This is a large Old World family that consists primarily of heavy billed seed-eating birds similar to the finches. Many species are very colorful and make popular pets. As a result of extensive importations into the Western Hemisphere, numbers have escaped and become established. This is the case for the three species in the region and all appear to have arrived in the last two decades. Ploceids generally build domed nests.

PIN-TAILED WHYDAH   Plate 40
Vidua macroura

Identification: Breeding male 30—33 cm (12—13"), female 11.5 cm (4.5"). In breeding plumage the long-tailed male is unmistakable. Females and nonbreeding males are mottled rusty-brown having a distinctive red bill and black and white facial stripes. Immatures are more grayish-brown and have buff-colored, rather than white eye stripes. Their bill is blackish but a pinkish-red coloration can be noted at the base.

Local Name: Viuda colicinta

Comments: A recently introduced but well established exotic in Puerto Rico, it now occurs uncommonly around the entire coast. The species only frequents areas of short grass such as lawns and some fields where it may be found in large flocks when not breeding.

Voice: A distinctive twittering call sometimes intermixed with loud chattering notes and plaintive whistles. The call note is an emphatic *sweet*.

Nesting: A nest is not constructed, but rather the female lays her eggs in the nests of other birds, primarily those of waxbills of the genus *Estrilda*. Two species of waxbills have been introduced to Puerto Rico and no doubt serve as hosts for the whydah. Breeding occurs as early as April through November.

Distribution: Introduced in Puerto Rico and elsewhere. Native to much of Africa.

YELLOW-CROWNED BISHOP   Plate 40
Euplectes afer

Identification: 11.5—12.5 cm (4.5—5″). The yellow and black breeding male is unmistakable. Females and nonbreeding males are brown sparrow-like birds very similar to Red Bishops and Grasshopper Sparrows. They can be distinguished from the former by the presence of yellow in the eye stripe which contrasts sharply with the dark brown eye line. They differ from the sparrow by the absence of a central white crown stripe.

Local Names: Napoleon Weaver, Golden Bishop, Napoleón tejedor

Comments: Recently introduced to Puerto Rico, probably in the 1960s this escapee is apparently established. However, it is still uncommon and local being known from marshes both east and west of San Juan, fields around the Ponce airport and the Lajas Agriculture Experimental Station where it has not occurred of late. The species inhabits areas of high grass near bodies of water.

Voice: A series of *sweet* and *chuck* notes similar to the call of the Red Bishop.

Nesting: Breeding occurs in summer and fall. However, a nest has yet to be found on the island.

Distribution: Introduced to Puerto Rico. Native throughout much of Africa.

RED BISHOP   Plate 40
Euplectes orix

Identification: 12.5 cm (5″). Males in their orangish-red and black breeding plumage can be confused with no other bird. Females and nonbreeding males are mottled brown with a buff-colored eye stripe and underparts, the latter being finely striped. They can be distinguished from the Grasshopper Sparrow by the absence of a yellow spot on the lores and the very fine series of crown stripes rather than a single, central stripe. They are known from the very similar Yellow-crowned Bishop by the absence of yellow in the eye stripe and by the pale brown rather than dark brown eye line.

Local Names: Orange Bishop, Grenadier Weaver, Obispo colorado

Comments: A recently escaped exotic in Puerto Rico, probably in the 1960s, the Red Bishop is now well established locally on the north coast from San Juan to Vega Baja. The species is uncommon inland at Gurabo and in the southern part of the island west to Ponce. Its range is still expanding. Large concentrations of Red Bishops occur at the Rio Piedras Agriculture Experimental Station (north side) and in the cane fields east of Dorado. Numbers appear to be declining in recent years. Three individuals have been observed on St Croix. The species primarily occurs in sugar cane fields bordered by grassy edges. Flocks form outside the breeding season.

Voice: Breeding males sing a sputtering series of *sweet* notes interspersed with a few harsh *chuck* notes, while in their bobbing nuptial flight, or while sitting atop a cane stalk or wire.

Nesting: Breeding occurs from March to November, the male having as many as four to five mates. A bulky globular nest with the entrance in the side is built in which two to four glossy blue eggs are laid (nests have been found but not studied in Puerto Rico).

Distribution: Introduced to Puerto Rico and elsewhere. Native to Africa.

Waxbills and Allies
FAMILY: ESTRILDIDAE

Eight species of this Old World family of finch-like birds have been introduced into the region.

ORANGE-CHEEKED WAXBILL   Plate 41
Estrilda melpoda

Identification: 10 cm (4″). The reddish bill and uppertail coverts, and particularly the orange cheek patch distinguish this mite. The similar Black-rumped Waxbill lacks the red patch on the uppertail coverts and has a red stripe through the eye rather than an orange cheek. Immatures of both species lack diagnostic facial markings and appear similar for a short period after fledging.

Local Name: Veterano mejillianaranjado

Comments: A common resident along most of Puerto Rico's coastal plain. Initially introduced from Africa, probably with the importation of slaves, the species was long confined to the southwest corner of the island. Apparently a second recent introduction around the late 1950s enabled this waxbill to establish itself along the entire coast. Orange-cheeked Waxbills normally occur in flocks where tall grasses are in seed such as at agricultural stations, sugar cane borders, road edges and the like.

Voice: The call note is a clear *pee* or a series of the same. Flocking birds have a characteristic twittering call. The song is rarely heard and is apparently quite variable.

Nesting: Three to four white eggs are laid in a domed nest with a funneled entranceway and an interior lined with fine grasses. The nest is usually on the ground, but one has been found ten feet high in vines. One of two recently examined nests apparently contained a Pin-tailed Whydah egg.

Distribution: Introduced in Puerto Rico and elsewhere. Native to central West Africa.

BLACK-RUMPED WAXBILL   Plate 41
Estrilda troglodytes

Identification: 10 cm (4″). The red line through the eye is diagnostic. Immatures have a pale pinkish bill and no red eye line.

Local Names: Red-eared Waxbill, Pink-cheeked Waxbill, Gray Waxbill, Veterano orejicolorado

Comments: This is a broadly established exotic species in Puerto Rico. An escapee, probably in the 1960s, it is found spottily along the entire coastal plain. Areas of high grass by cane fields are the preferred habitat of the Black-rumped Waxbill. There are recent records from Vieques and St Thomas.

Voice: Call note *pit*, *cheww* or *chit-cheww*; the latter sounds like a bullet ricocheting off a rock. There is also a nervous twittering call.

Nesting: The nest has not yet been found in Puerto Rico. Observations of young birds suggest breeding occurs in the fall.

Distribution: Introduced in Puerto Rico and elsewhere. Native to central Africa.

RED AVADAVAT   Plate 41
Amandava amandava

Identification: 10 cm (4″). Breeding plumaged males are primarily a deep red with white spots on the wings, flanks and sides. Adult females and nonbreeding males can be distinguished by the red uppertail coverts and bill, and the white spots on the wing. Immatures are similar to females, but the red color is lacking and the wing spots are buff-colored. They are most readily identified by virtually always being in association with adults. Brown plumaged birds can be distinguished from the similar Black-rumped Waxbill by the white wing spots and the nearly black, rather than red, line through the eye.

Local Names: Strawberry Finch, Amadavat, Chamorro fresa

Comments: A recently introduced escapee in Puerto Rico that is now a common, established resident in the lowlands. It is not known from the Virgin Islands. The species thrives in the grassy margins of freshwater swamps around the island, sometimes occurring in adjacent sugar cane fields and along weedy drainage canals.

Voice: The call notes are a musical *sweet* and *sweet-eet*. The species has a variety of appealing songs including melodious whistles and warbles.

Nesting: Males are in breeding plumage from June to November and young have been seen, but the nest has not been found.

Distribution: Introduced in Puerto Rico and elsewhere. Native from Pakistan through southeastern Asia to Indonesia.

WARBLING SILVERBILL   Plate 41
Lonchura malabarica

Identification: 11.5 cm (4.5″). Distinguished by its overall light coloration and white uppertail coverts.

Local Names: Indian Silverbill, White-throated Munia, Gorrión picoplata

Comments: Probably introduced in the 1960s, this recent escapee is common in metropolitan San Juan, occurring west to

Dorado. The species is abundant in the arid scrub along the coast in the southwest from La Parguera to the Cabo Rojo Lighthouse and north to Boquerón. Silverbills are uncommon elsewhere on the south coast. There is a recent record of this species from Mona Island and of two individuals on St Croix. Arid pastures and gardens where grass is in seed are the primary habitats of this bird.

Voice: A medium strength *chit* or series, but usually a quick, two syllable *chit-tit*. Rarely, a loud, musical song.

Nesting: A nest of grasses with an entrance hole in the side is constructed in a tree or even on a window sill. Four to six tiny white eggs are a normal clutch. Breeding is primarily from June to November, but also occurs in other months.

Distribution: Introduced in Puerto Rico and elsewhere. Native to India, Sri Lanka, the Arabian Peninsula, and central Africa.

BRONZE MANNIKIN   Plate 41
Lonchura cucullata

Identification: 10 cm (4″). The distinctive black hood, the dark grayish-brown back, and the white belly with ringlets confined to the sides and flanks distinguish this species. Immatures lack the hood, but have dark coloration on the back like that of adults. They are darker and smaller than young of related species.

Local Names: Hooded Weaver, Hooded Mannikin, Diablito

Comments: A common, established resident in Puerto Rico, believed to have been brought from Africa in the era of the slave trade. A small flock has been observed on St Croix. The species normally occurs in flocks in fields, on lawns, and virtually in every habitat where grass is in seed along the coast. It becomes less common with increased elevation and is rare over 300 m.

Voice: The call note is a coarse *crrit*. There is much chattering within the flocks.

Nesting: Three white eggs are laid in a loose, domed nest with the entrance in the side. Breeding occurs from March to October.

Distribution: Introduced in Puerto Rico. Widespread in Africa.

NUTMEG MANNIKIN   Plate 41
Lonchura punctulata

Identification: 11.5 cm (4.5 "). In adults the cinnamon-colored hood and the scaled underparts are distinctive. Immatures lack the markings of the adults and can be confused with a number of other species. Their heavy, blackish bills and light cinnamon coloration distinguish them.

Local Names: Spice Finch, Nutmeg Finch, Scaly-breasted Munia, Ricebird, Spotted Munia, Gorrión canela

Comments: Recently introduced, probably in the 1960s, this escapee has become fairly common in Puerto Rico along the coast from Ceiba to Vega Baja though it occurs sparingly around the entire coast. Numbers appear to be declining in recent years. A flock has been recorded from St Croix and the species has been observed on Mona Island. The Nutmeg Mannikin occurs in lowland habitats where there are seeding grasses.

Voice: A soft, plaintive, whistled *péet* dropping in pitch and fading away at the end.

Nesting: An extremely bulky nest of grasses with a fine lining is built at a moderate to high elevation in a tree. There is an entrance hole in the side or near the bottom. The breeding season appears to center during summer and fall, but some years nests have been found in the spring, suggesting that the cycle varies from year to year. Six white eggs form a normal clutch.

Distribution: Introduced in Puerto Rico and elsewhere. Native from India to southeastern Asia, Taiwan, and the Philippines.

CHESTNUT MANNIKIN   Plate 41
Lonchura malacca

Identification: 11.5 cm (4.5 "). The black hood distinguishes it from all finch-like birds except the Bronze Mannikin. It is known from the latter by the large black patch on its belly and its cinnamon-colored back. Immatures are light brown, darker above.

Local Names: Black-headed Nun, Tricolored Mannikin, Chestnut Munia, Monja tricolor

Comments: A common recently introduced species in Puerto Rico, it occurs around the entire coast. This bird prefers high grass bordering sugar cane fields, swampy areas, or canals.

Voice: The call note is a thin, nasal honk *ñeat*, less plaintive, clear, and melodious than that of the Spice Finch.

Nesting: A bulky nest with the entrance hole in the side is built 3 to 9 feet up in dense sugar cane. Four to five white eggs form a normal clutch. Breeding occurs through the summer.

Distribution: Introduced in Puerto Rico and elsewhere. Native from India through southeastern Asia to Taiwan, Indonesia, and the Philippines.

JAVA SPARROW   Plate 40
Padda oryzivora

Identification: 15—16.5 cm (6—6.5″). This generally gray plumaged bird is easily distinguished by its broad, red bill, white cheek, and black crown. Immatures have a duller bill, buff-colored cheek and a brownish body color.

Local Names: Java Finch, Ricebird, Java Temple Bird, Pinchón arrocero

Comments: An introduced escapee in Puerto Rico which is now well established in the San Juan metropolitan area. It is not known among the Virgin Islands. The species frequents areas of short grass such as athletic fields and large lawns where grass is going to seed. Here it can often be found in large flocks numbering as many as 100 birds. The species is most abundant in Old San Juan and the Isla Grande Naval Reserve. Numbers appear to be declining in recent years.

Voice: The call note is a very hard, metallic *chink*.

Nesting: Breeding is from July to as late as February. The nest is usually built of grasses in a crevice or window ledge of a building.

Distribution: Originally from Java, Sumatra, and Bali, it has become established all over southeastern Asia, the Philippines, and adjacent areas as well as in Puerto Rico.

Vagrants, Unestablished Exotics and Hypothetical Species

VAGRANTS

Northern Fulmar *Fulmarus glacialis:* Aug. 1975, from boat among VIs.

Herald Petrel *Pterodroma arminjoniana:* July 7 1986 (photo), Cayo Lobito near Culebra.

Sooty Shearwater *Puffinus griseus:* May 29 1954 and Oct. 17 1958, PR.

Manx Shearwater *Puffinus puffinus:* Sept. 5 1975, PR; fossil, St Croix.

Little Shearwater *Puffinus assimilis:* Jan. 30 1977, PR.

Little Egret *Egretta garzetta:* Late May to early June 1986, Culebra.

Canada Goose *Branta canadensis:* Nov. 10 1984, PR.

White-faced Whistling-Duck *Dendrocygna viduata:* fossil, PR.

Eurasian Wigeon *Anas penelope:* Feb. 22 1958, PR.

Garganey *Anas querquedula:* Jan.–Mar. 1978, PR.

Greater Scaup *Aythya marila:* Dec. 23 1984 to Feb. 17 1985, Nov. 8 & 27 1985, St Croix.

Bald Eagle *Haliaeetus leucocephalus:* Oct. 8 1975, PR; Feb. 21 1977, St John.

Ridgway's Hawk *Buteo ridgwayi:* Apr. 1984 (3 days), Culebra.

Virginia Rail *Rallus limicola:* Jan. 28 1976, PR.

Northern Jacana *Jacana spinosa:* 1870s PR. (Blanco received a specimen that could not be preserved.)

Long-billed Curlew *Numenius americanus:* Sept. 20 1981, St Croix.

Bar-tailed Godwit *Limosa lapponica:* May 19–28 1987, St Croix.

Buff-breasted Sandpiper *Tryngites subruficollis:* Sept. 28 1983 and Sept. 18 1984, St Croix.

Red-necked Phalarope *Phalaropus lobatus:* Dec. 30 1977 and Apr. 24 1980, PR.

Parasitic Jaeger *Stercorarius parasiticus:* July 17 1988, Tortola.

Franklin's Gull *Larus pipixcan:* Jan. 1970 and Jan. 1972, PR.

Boneparte's Gull *Larus philadelphia:* Apr. 29 1966, PR.

Black-legged Kittiwake *Rissa tridactyla:* Feb. 2 1984, salvaged from waters of British VIs.

White-winged Tern *Chlidonias leucopterus:* Sept. 23 1986, St Croix.

Black-billed Cuckoo *Coccyzus erythrophthalmus:* Drawing by Bello of specimen, PR.

White-tailed Nightjar *Caprimulgus cayennensis:* Nov. 23 1974, PR.

Common Potoo *Nyctibius griseus:* Dec. 5 1974, Mona Island; Oct. 24 1987, Desecheo Island.

White-collared Swift *Streptocrocne zonaris:* July 21 1971, Vieques.

Antillean Palm Swift *Tachornis phoenicobia:* July 12 1969, PR.

Alpine Swift *Apus melba:* July 20 1987, Desecheo Island.

Green-breasted Mango *Anthracothorax prevostii:* Mar. 9 1976, PR.

Purple-throated Carib *Eulampis jugularis:* Apr. 17 1987, St John; May 3 1987, St Croix.

Vervain Hummingbird *Mellisuga minima:* Mar. 1976, PR.

Ringed Kingfisher *Ceryle torquata:* 1960, PR.

Hairy Woodpecker *Picoides villosus:* Mar. 27 1974, Mona Island.

Eastern Wood-Pewee *Contopus virens:* Oct. 9 1986, St Croix.

Great Crested Flycatcher *Myiarchus crinitus:* One winter sighting (*ca* 1960), PR.

Eastern Kingbird *Tyrannus tyrannus:* Two records (*ca* 1847 and 1960), PR.

Scissor-tailed Flycatcher *Tyrannus forficatus:* Dec. 1960 (two records), PR.

Gray Catbird *Dumetella carolinensis:* Feb. 25 1985 (netted), PR.

Northern Wheatear *Oenanthe oenanthe:* Sept. 22 1966, PR.

Veery *Catharus fuscescens:* Mar. 23 1978, St John.

Wood Thrush *Hylocichla mustelina:* Drawing by Bello of specimen, PR.

Trembler *Cinclocerthia ruficauda:* March 4 1976, St Thomas.

Pine Warbler *Dendroica pinus:* Sept. 29 1987, Mona Island.

Cerulean Warbler *Dendroica cerulea:* Oct. 22 1987, Mona Island.

Tennessee Warbler *Vermivora peregrina:* Mar. 17 1986 (photo), St John.

Nashville Warbler *Vermivora ruficapilla:* Sept. 18 1987, Mona Island.

Wilson's Warbler *Wilsonia pusilla:* Jan. 6 1978 (netted), Mona Island.

Dark-eyed Junco *Junco hyemalis:* Oct. 16 1963, PR; Nov. 11 1928, St Thomas.

Lincoln's Sparrow *Melospiza lincolnii:* Dec. 14 1923 and Apr. 23 1980, PR.

UNESTABLISHED EXOTICS

Mute Swan *Cygnus olor:* Dec. 11 1968, VIs; swans seen in the winters in 1969 and 1970 in the VIs were probably also this species.

Black Swan *Cygnus atratus:* May 1988, Culebra, had last six primaries missing, obviously a recent escapee.

Ring-necked Pheasant *Phasianus colchicus:* Feb. 6 1974, and other unidentified pheasants, PR; intentionally introduced on St Thomas decades ago without success. A flock was released on St Croix in Mar. or Apr. 1988.

Common Peafowl *Pavo cristatus:* Semi-feral, breed around estates on St Croix.

Crested Bobwhite *Colinus cristatus:* Intentionally introduced on St Thomas well over a century ago. This species did well for a time, but is now extirpated.

California Quail *Callipepla californica:* Intentionally introduced on St Croix in 1958 without success.

Rainbow Lorikeet *Trichoglossus haematod:* Sept. 8 and 22 1974, PR.

Cockatiel (?) *Nymphicus hollandicus:* A small flock, probably of this species, reported from 1972–1974 in Arecibo, PR.

African Gray Parrot *Psittacus erithacus:* Feb. 24 1973, Mar. 1973, PR.

Rose-ringed Parakeet *Psittacula krameri:* One to two birds at two localities from June 21 1979 to present, PR.

Mitred Conure *Aratinga mitrata:* Breeding at Interamerican University campus in San German, May 1986, PR; four birds observed the past 4 to 6 years on St Croix.

Blue-and-yellow Macaw *Ara ararauna:* Aug. 25 1972 and Sept. 1972, PR.

Parrotlet *Forpus* sp.: Sept. 6 1974, PR.

Scaly-headed Parrot *Pionus maximiliani:* Feb. 17 1971 and subsequently (a single bird), PR.

White-fronted Parrot *Amazona albifrons:* Small, scattered flocks from Oct. 1978 and subsequently, PR.

Turquoise-fronted Parrot *Amazona aestiva:* Scattered observations of one to three birds from May 31 1971 and subsequently, PR.

Lilac-crowned Parrot *Amazona finschi:* Jan. 1 1983 and subsequently that year (a single bird), St Croix.

Toucanets *Ramphastidae:* Nov. or Dec. 1973, PR.

Red-billed Blue Magpie *Urocissa erythrorhyncha:* One sighting in 1972, PR.

Crow *Corvus* sp.: Jan. 1973, May 29 1973, PR.

Red-crested Cardinal *Paroaria coronata:* Single sightings in 1973 and 1976, a pair at Dorado Beach Hotel since Aug. 1987 (observed constructing a nest), PR; Dec. 15 1982, St Croix.

Paradise Whydah *Vidua paradisaea:* Sept. 8 1974, Jan. 15 1975, PR.

HYPOTHETICAL

Curlew Sandpiper *Calidris ferruginea:* Early 1970s, Virgin Gorda.

Blue-headed Quail-Dove *Starnoenas cyanocephala:* Comment of hunters to Biaggi, PR.

Townsend's Warbler *Dendroica townsendi:* Bond considered a report from Puerto Rico to be questionable.

Golden-cheeked Warbler *Dendroica chrysoparia:* Nov. 23 1939 and Jan. 8 1940, St Croix.

Bachman's Warbler *Vermivora bachmanii:* Oct. 21 1982, St Croix.

Pine Warbler *Dendroica pinus:* Dec. 1984, PR.

Places to Bird

The seven localities presented here were chosen for their avifaunal diversity and uniqueness, as well as their accessibility and distribution so that portions of the region are represented. Some localities are more thoroughly studied than others, therefore, you should not be surprised if you find species not marked as occurring on the checklist for a particular locality. The status abbreviations are based upon known records from each site and not on speculation.

The final column is a regional checklist for your personal records.

El Yunque, Puerto Rico

The Luquillo Mountains, of which El Yunque is the best known peak (1065 m (3494 ft)), receive more rain than any other locality in Puerto Rico or the Virgin Islands. As a result, a lush rain forest covers these mountain slopes and this supports a number of unique local birds. Most noteworthy of these is the endangered Puerto Rican Parrot found nowhere else in the world. A good site to look for this parrot is around the La Mina Recreation Area. The local subspecies of the Broad-winged Hawk is also most readily observed at La Mina. To locate the elusive Elfin Woods Warbler, it is best to search along the higher mountain ridges, in the habitat commonly known as dwarf forest, where the trees are extraordinarily stunted. The trail to El Toro peak passes through suitable habitat for this bird. You can inquire from a forest ranger as to how to locate this trail. The Green Mango is regularly seen by Coca Falls. Most of the other bird species found in the Luquillo Mountains occur throughout the forest, but are more common and more easily seen at the lower elevations where the vegetation is sparser. Interestingly, the total avian diversity is not as high in this forest as in others such as Guánica and Maricao. Species of the open pastures surrounding the mountains have not been included in the checklist.

Directions

From San Juan, proceed east on Route 3 (approximately 30 km (19 miles)) and turn right onto Route 191 at the large El Yunque sign. Pass through Palmer and continue on 191 up the mountain to the La Mina Recreation Area, where there is a large map of the various trails.

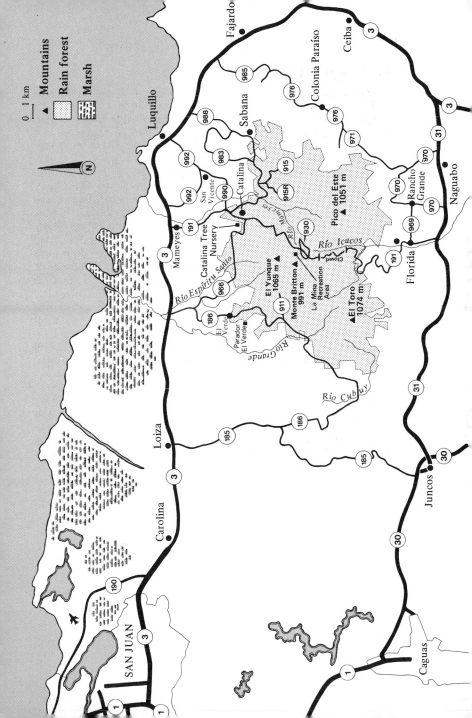

Cartagena Lagoon, Puerto Rico

The finest freshwater swamp in Puerto Rico is Cartagena Lagoon. About half of Puerto Rico's avian species have been recorded from the Lagoon and the adjacent hills to the south. Though deteriorating due to eutrophication, Cartagena still remains the best locality in Puerto Rico for observing waterbirds. Outside the hunting season (December to January), it is the prime swamp around which to search for Glossy Ibis, Yellow-breasted Crake, Purple Gallinule, West Indian and Fulvous Whistling-Ducks, and other freshwater denizens. The western half of the lagoon is generally more productive than the eastern half; however, the northeast corner is a favorite haunt of the uncommon Short-eared Owl. One word of warning: though the snail that carries bilharzia (a tropical and subtropical fluke — see: *Introduction*) has not been recorded from Cartagena Lagoon, it is not recommended that the water be entered without hip waders. Besides, Cartagena has some very large leeches.

Directions

Cartagena Lagoon is located in a rather remote portion of Puerto Rico's southwest coast near the town of Lajas, and though the resourceful and daring can come within 1 km of the lagoon by 'público', access to Cartagena is only truly practical by car. The lagoon is approximately a 3-hour drive from San Juan by way of Caguas and Ponce. Cartagena is marked on road maps and once one gets to Route 101 or 303, the map opposite will help. The entrance to the lagoon from Route 303 by way of Maguayo is often very rough and it should not be attempted by any vehicle with a low chassis. Entering on the cane road passing south from Route 101 at km 16.0 is much safer (but do not get caught at Cartagena during a rain; this road becomes as slippery as glass and has ditches on both sides). It is opposite the turnoff to Route 306 marked 'París Palmarejo'.

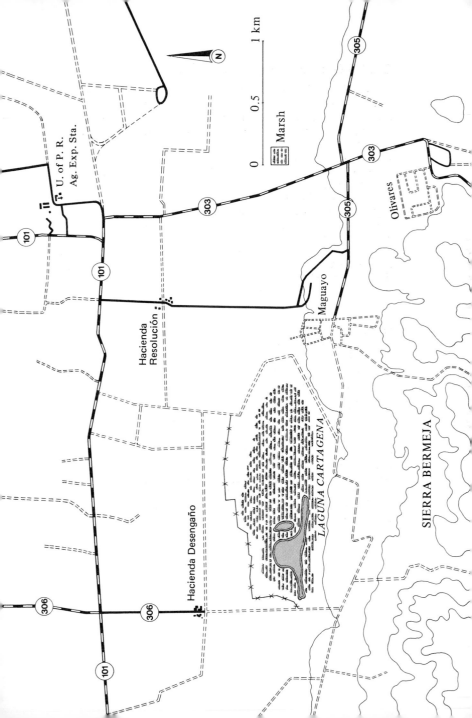

Cabo Rojo Saltflats, Puerto Rico

The most outstanding feature of this locality is the large number of shorebirds it sustains in its numerous shallow salt ponds. Principal among these birds is the Snowy Plover which occurs regularly nowhere else on the island. The coastal mangroves are excellent for herons and warblers, while the cliffs below the lighthouse are regularly frequented by resting Brown Boobies.

Directions

About 3 km (2 miles) east of the town of Boquerón, at km marker 16.6, take Route 301 south. As you approach this turnoff from either direction along Route 101 you will see a green sign labeled 'El Combate' and a standard highway sign with the route number (301) and an arrow. Stay on Route 301, bypassing the turnoffs to 'Cuevas' (km 3.5) and 'El Combate' (km 7.8). (At the El Combate turnoff you *do not* follow the highway sign indicating '301 Ramal'.) Near km 9.7 the road curves sharply to the right at the first salt pond. If you do not mind a good walk and getting your feet wet, you can park off the road at this point and head down the embankment and to the left around the salina to an excellent mangrove (particularly to the east) which features herons and sometimes waterfowl. Continuing along Route 301 the highway turns to a dirt road and is lined with numerous salt ponds. Near the end of the ponds two cement tracks lead to the lighthouse and the cliffs.

If you have difficulty finding the locality, ask for directions to 'El Faro'.

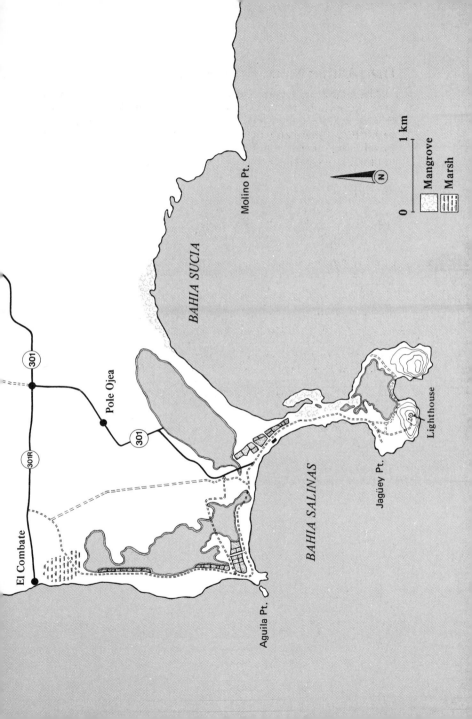

El Combate

301

30R

Pole Ojea

301

BAHIA SUCIA

Molino Pt.

BAHIA SALINAS

Aguila Pt.

Jagüey Pt.

Lighthouse

N

0   1 km

Mangrove

Marsh

Isla Grande Naval Reserve, Puerto Rico

The Isla Grande Naval Reserve, a large portion of which has been turned over to the Commonwealth (Dept. of Public Works — Motor Vehicles Section), is one of the few extensive green areas within San Juan. While its athletic fields and large lawns are not particularly attractive to many native birds, they harbor a large number of the exotic forms now established in Puerto Rico. Easily reached by bus or car, this locality boasts some of the most beautiful exotics and will possibly continue to attract new ones that have recently escaped. Be sure to check areas with both long and short grass and keep your ears open for new sounds, particularly parrots. Marine birds, such as pelicans and frigatebirds that can be seen by viewing the bay, are not in the checklist.

Directions

Although the Naval Reserve is in Santurce, by car it must be approached from Old San Juan. From Old San Juan, follow the 'Santurce' or 'Fernández Juncos' signs. Immediately after crossing the bridge into Santurce there is a sign for the Isla Grande Airport. Pass the airport entrance and follow the next road to the right. The main gate of the Naval Reserve is on the right about 100 m down this road.

Practically all of the buses leaving Old San Juan pass by the reserve (with the exception of a few buses that go to the Condado). Any bus that goes to Old San Juan passes within easy walking distance of the reserve. Stop 10 is closest, but buses passing through the Condado will have to leave you at Stop 9.

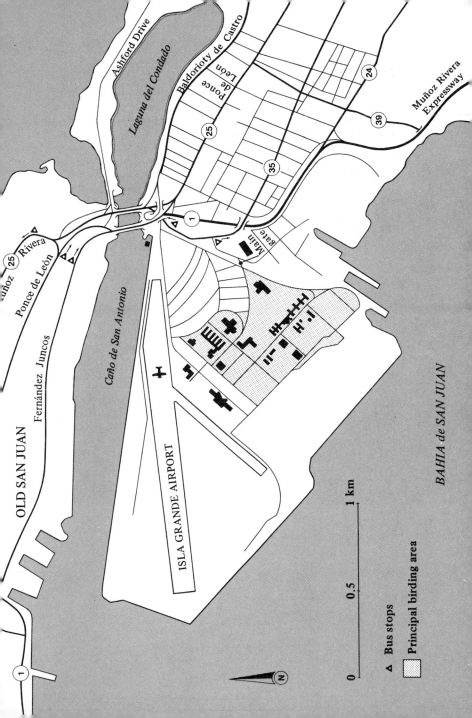

Mangrove Lagoon, St Thomas
by Robert Norton

Located on the southeast coast of St Thomas, among a bewildering assortment of human developments, is the island's largest and most diverse habitat for resident and migratory avifauna. The Mangrove Lagoon in Jersey Bay offers an opportunity to study shorebirds, ducks, herons, the White-crowned Pigeon and a variety of other land birds.

After scanning the mudflats for shorebirds, a panoramic view of the Lagoon, Jersey and Benner Bays will provide an overall sense of the ecology of the area. A visit to Long Point can also prove exciting during late summer to fall when several species of otherwise pelagic terns can be seen and the opportunity of a visiting Peregrine Falcon is not to be discounted.

Directions

Drive east from Charlotte Amalie on Frenchman's Bay Road and turn left at the intersection marked by the sign 'Havensight Hills' — the first major left after the Sheraton Marina Hotel. Continue on this major coastal road south passing Antilles School (1.3 km (0.8 miles)) and the Bolongo Bay Beach Hotel (2.4 km (1.5 miles) past the school) and just 1.1 km (0.7 miles) beyond the hotel is a gas station on the left and a drag strip directly opposite on the right. Take the right turn and follow the strip turning left at the end and negotiate your way to the flats located off to the left of the paved road. Should you miss the drag strip, you will see a racetrack on your right indicating you must turn back.

Though the northwest corner of the lagoon is marred by a land fill and car dump, do not be discouraged. After walking the solid ground of the mudflats, continue on the paved road past the land fill and the car dump to Long Point where the view will improve.

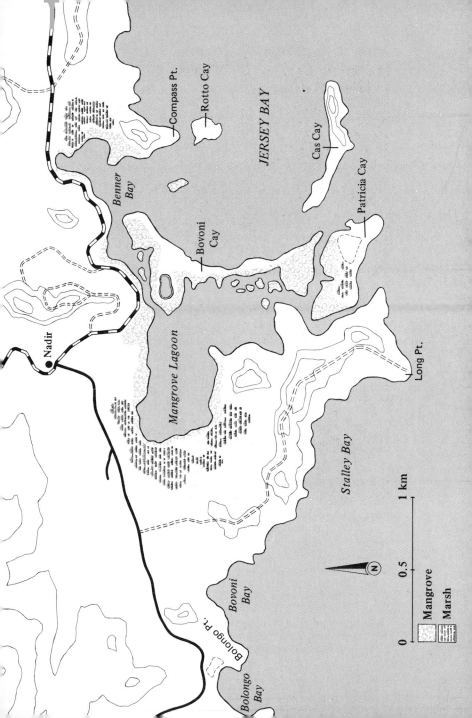

Compass Pt.

Rotto Cay

JERSEY BAY

Cas Cay

Patricia Cay

Benner Bay

Bovoni Cay

Mangrove Lagoon

Long Pt.

Nadir

Stalley Bay

Bovoni Bay

Bolongo Pt.

Bolongo Bay

N

0   0.5   1 km

Mangrove

Marsh

Mary Point Pond, St John
by Jim Riddle, Robert Norton and Thelma Douglas

Nestled behind Mary Point, the northernmost point of St John is one of the island's most productive birding spots. This pond, the nearby forest and the Francis Bay shoreline provide the observer with a great variety of birdlife at any time of the year. The brackish pond is rimmed by mangroves and other salt tolerant vegetation, which harbor migrants and local specialties such as Mangrove Cuckoo, Scaly-naped Pigeon, White-cheeked Pintail and Smooth-billed Ani. There also are opportunities for good views of a variety of waterfowl, herons, shorebirds and warblers. Along the beach and rocky shoreline, Brown Booby, Brown Pelican, Magnificent Frigatebird and various terns can be seen offshore.

A bird checklist is available at the National Park Visitor Center in Cruz Bay and in winter, weekly birds walks are sponsored by the National Park Service.

Directions
From the town of Cruz Bay, take the North Shore Road (Route 20) to the Annaberg turnoff. At Leinster Bay make a left toward Mary Point Pond rather than a right to the Annaberg Historic Area. Continue on this road to a small parking area on the right next to a reconstructed stone warehouse. A sign marks the beginning of the trail. Along the trail, the National Park Service is constructing an overlook to the pond and bay. Beyond that a boardwalk is planned to transit the mangrove area with overlooks to the pond to provide views of shorebirds and waterfowl. The trail continues to the beach at Francis Bay. Just inland from the beach, a narrow trail leads along the shore of the pond with views through the mangroves at various points. This part of the trail ends at the gravel road. Heading inland along this road will return you to your starting point.

Other places in this area to look for birds
Head of Mary Creek   As you leave the Mary Point Pond parking area toward Annaberg, there is a small unmarked opening that permits you to go down from the paved road on to the mudflats.
Annaberg Mangroves   At the Annaberg intersection, continue toward Annaberg Historic Area and bird the mangroves on both sides of the road for warblers such as Prothonotary, Worm-eating, Yellow and Northern Waterthrush.
Leinster Bay Pond   When the Annaberg road climbs the hill to the Historic Area, continue straight ahead instead on a very narrow dirt road along Leinster Bay. At the dead end, there is another small pond for shorebirds and herons.

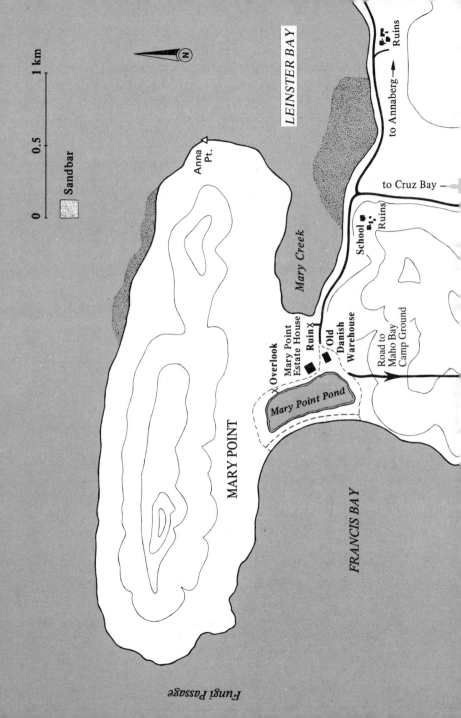

Little Dix Bay, Virgin Gorda

The bird life of Little Dix Day is typical of the Virgin Islands. Habitats one should survey include the ornamental plantings around the hotel facilities for warblers and hummingbirds, Pond Bay Salt Pond for rails and shorebirds, the freshwater sewage treatment plant for White-cheeked Pintails, and rocky promontories by the sea for American Oystercatchers.

Directions

No directions are needed for Little Dix Bay. To reach Pond Bay Salt Pond, hike the Savana Bay Trail from the east end of Little Dix Bay to Savana Bay and then follow the seashore (a total of about 3 km (2 miles)) or drive to the pond along North Sound Road.

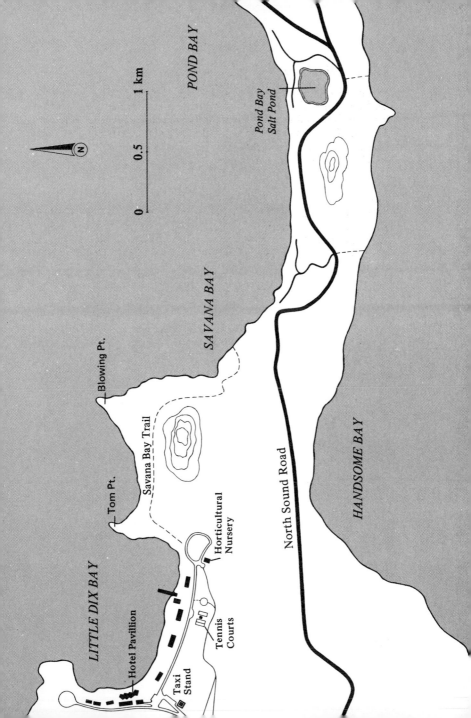

Locality Checklist

Locality Checklist

Locality Checklist

Site Abbreviations: CL: Cartagena Lagoon; CR: Cabo Rojo Saltflats; EL Y: El Yunque; IG: Isla Grande; ML: Mangrove Lagoon; MPP: Mary Point Pond Area; LDB: Little Dix Bay; Pl./P: Plate and Page.
Status Abbreviations: VC: Very Common; C: Common; UC: Uncommon; R: Rare; VR: Very Rare; A: Accidental (only 1 record at site); EXT: Extirpated; * Domestic

SPECIES	Pl./P	CL	CR	EL Y	IG	ML	MPP	LDB	√
Grebes PODICIPEDIDAE									
Least Grebe	23/16	R					VR		
Pied-billed Grebe	24/16	C					UC		
Shearwaters PROCELLARIIDAE									
Audubon's Shearwater	3/25								
Greater Shearwater	1/25								
Black-capped Petrel	3/26								
Storm-Petrels HYDROBATIDAE									
Leach's Storm-Petrel	3/26								
Wilson's Storm-Petrel	3/27								
Tropicbirds PHAETHONTIDAE									
Red-billed Tropicbird	2/28					UC			
White-tailed Tropicbird	2/28		R			R			
Boobies SULIDAE									
Masked Booby	2/29		C			C	C	C	
Brown Booby	2/30		VR			C	C	C	

Species	No.						
Pelicans PELECANIDAE							
American White Pelican	2/32		C		C	C	C
Brown Pelican	2/32						
Cormorants PHALACROCORACIDAE							
Double-crested Cormorant	16/33	VR					VR
Olivaceous Cormorant	16/34						
Frigatebirds FREGATIDAE							
Magnificent Frigatebird	2/35	UC	C		C	C	C
Herons, Egrets and Bitterns ARDEIDAE							
Great Blue Heron	7/36	UC	C		UC	UC	R
Green-backed Heron	8/36	C	C		C	UC	UC
Little Blue Heron	7/37	UC	C		C	C	C
Cattle Egret	7/38	VC	C		C	UC	C
Reddish Egret	7/39	A	C	R			
Great Egret	7/39	C	C				
Snowy Egret	7/40	C	C	VR			
Tricolored Heron	7/40	UC	UC				
Black-crowned Night-Heron	8/41	C	C		UC	R	R
Yellow-crowned Night-Heron	8/42	R	UC	R	UC	R	UC
Least Bittern	8/42	C			UC	VR	
American Bittern	8/43	R				UC	
Ibises and Spoonbills THRESKIORNITHIDAE							
Glossy Ibis	9/44						
White Ibis	9/44	UC			UC		
Roseate Spoonbill	9/44						

SPECIES	Pl./P	CL	CR	EL Y	IG	ML	MPP	LDB	✓
Flamingo PHOENICOPTERIDAE									
Greater Flamingo	9/45								
Ducks, Geese and Swans ANATIDAE									
Tundra Swan	16/47								
Snow Goose	16/47								
Fulvous Whistling-Duck	17,18/47	UC							
Black-bellied Whistling-Duck	19/48	A							
West Indian Whistling-Duck	17,18/48	VR							
Mallard	19/49	A							
American Black Duck	19/49								
Northern Pintail	17,18/50	R	R			C	C	UC	
White-cheeked Pintail	17,18/50	VR				VR	C	R	
Green-winged Teal	17,18/51	R				C			
Blue-winged Teal	17,18/51	C	UC						
Cinnamon Teal	1/52								
American Wigeon	17,18/52	R				R	UC		
Northern Shoveler	17,18/52	R							
Wood Duck	19/53								
Ring-necked Duck	17,18/53	R							
Canvasback	19/54								
Lesser Scaup	17,18/54	R							
Bufflehead	19/54								
Ruddy Duck	17,18/55	C							

Masked Duck	17,18/55					
Hooded Merganser	19/56					
Red-breasted Merganser	19/56					
American Vultures CATHARTIDAE						
Turkey Vulture	20/57	C			C		C
Hawks and Harrier ACCIPITRIDAE						
Sharp-shinned Hawk	20/58			UC	UC		UC
Red-tailed Hawk	20/58	C	VR	C			R
Broad-winged Hawk	20/59	R	R		C		
Northern Harrier	20/59				UC		
Osprey	20/60	UC	UC		R	R	R
Falcons FALCONIDAE						
Peregrine Falcon	20/60	R	UC	VR	R	R	C
Merlin	20/61	R	UC	UC	R		
American Kestrel	20/61	UC	UC	R	UC		C
Junglefowl and Quail PHASIANIDAE						
Northern Bobwhite	23/62						
Red Junglefowl	23/63						
Guineafowl NUMIDIDAE						
Helmeted Guineafowl	23/64		C*				
Rails, Gallinules and Coots RALLIDAE						
Clapper Rail	15/65	UC	C		UC	R	
Sora	15/65	UC			UC	UC	
Yellow-breasted Crake	15/66						UC

SPECIES	Pl./P	CL	CR	EL Y	IG	ML	MPP	LDB	√
Black Rail	15/66	A							
Purple Gallinule	15/67	C							
Common Moorhen	15/67	VC	UC			C	C	R	
American Coot	15/68	UC				R	UC		
Caribbean Coot	15/68	UC					R		
Limpkin ARAMIDAE									
Limpkin	9/69								
Plovers CHARADRIIDAE									
Northern Lapwing	10/70								
Semipalmated Plover	10/70	UC	C			C	UC		
Piping Plover	10/71		UC						
Snowy Plover	10/71		C						
Wilson's Plover	10/72	VR	C			UC	UC		
Killdeer	10/72	C	UC		UC	UC		C	
Lesser Golden Plover	10/73	VR	R					C	
Black-bellied Plover	10/73	R	C			UC	UC	C	
Oystercatchers HAEMATOPODIDAE									
American Oystercatcher	13/74					UC	R	R	
Stilts and Avocets RECURVIROSTRIDAE									
Black-necked Stilt	14/75					C	C		
American Avocet	14/75		C					C	

Turnstones, Snipes and Sandpipers

SCOLOPACIDAE

Species							
Ruddy Turnstone	11/76		C		C	C	C
Common Snipe	14/77	UC	R		UC	R	R
Whimbrel	13/77		VR		R		
Eskimo Curlew	13/77			R			
Upland Sandpiper	14/78		C				
Spotted Sandpiper	12/78	UC			C	C	C
Solitary Sandpiper	12/79	UC	VC		UC	R	C
Lesser Yellowlegs	14/79	C	C		VC	C	C
Greater Yellowlegs	14/79	UC	UC		C	C	R
Willet	13/80	VR	UC		R		R
Red Knot	11/81	VR					
Dunlin	13/81						
Least Sandpiper	12/82	R	C		UC	C	
Baird's Sandpiper	1/82						
White-rumped Sandpiper	12/83	R	UC		R		R
Pectoral Sandpiper	11/83	UC	UC		UC		R
Semipalmated Sandpiper	12/83	UC	VC		VC		R
Western Sandpiper	12/84	R	C		UC		
Sanderling	12/84		C		UC		
Short-billed Dowitcher	11/85		UC		UC	UC	
Long-billed Dowitcher	11/85					UC	
Stilt Sandpiper	11/86	R	C		C		
Marbled Godwit	13/86		A				
Hudsonian Godwit	13/87	A					
Ruff	11/87		A		VR		
Wilson's Phalarope	14/87		A				

SPECIES	Pl./P	CL	CR	EL	Y	IG	ML	MPP	LDB	√
Gulls, Terns and Allies LARIDAE										
Lesser Black-backed Gull	1/89									
Great Black-backed Gull	4/89									
Herring Gull	4/89	A					UC			
Ring-billed Gull	4/90									
Common Black-headed Gull	4/90	VR					VR			
Laughing Gull	4/91	R	C				VC	C		
Gull-billed Tern	6/91									
Forster's Tern	5/92		C							
Common Tern	5/92						R	UC	R	
Roseate Tern	5/93						UC			
Arctic Tern	1/94									
Bridled Tern	6/94		R				C	UC		
Sooty Tern	6/95		R				C	UC		
Least Tern	6/95		C				UC	R		
Royal Tern	5/96		C				C	C	C	
Cayenne Tern	5/96									
Sandwich Tern	5/97	VR	R				UC	R		
Caspian Tern	5/97									
Black Tern	6/98	R	R				C	C		
Brown Noddy	6/98		R							
Pomarine Jaeger	3/99									
Skua	3/99									
Black Skimmer	4/100									

Pigeons and Doves COLUMBIDAE							
White-crowned Pigeon	25/100	R	VR	VR		C	R	R
Scaly-naped Pigeon	25/101			C			C	
Plain Pigeon	25/102							
Rock Dove	25/103	UC	C*					
Mourning Dove	25/103	UC						
Zenaida Dove	25/104		UC	R	C	C	C	C
White-winged Dove	25/105		R		C			
Ringed Turtle-Dove	25/106				C	C	C	C
Spotted Dove	25/106						VR	
Common Ground-Dove	25/107	VC	C	UC				
Ruddy Quail-Dove	25/107							
Key West Quail-Dove	25/108						R	
Bridled Quail-Dove	25/109							
Parrots and Parakeets PSITTACIDAE								
Budgerigar	26/110				UC	UC		
Orange-fronted Parakeet	26/110							
Brown-throated Parakeet	26/111				R	R		
Hispaniolan Parakeet	26/112				C			
Monk Parakeet	26/112				C			
Canary-winged Parakeet	26/113							
Red-crowned Parrot	26/113							
Yellow-crowned Parrot	26/114							
Orange-winged Parrot	26/114							
Hispaniolan Parrot	26/115							
Puerto Rican Parrot	27/116			R				
Black-hooded Parakeet	26/117							

SPECIES	Pl./P	CL	CR	EL Y	IG	ML	MPP	LDB	√
Cuckoos and Anis CUCULIDAE									
Mangrove Cuckoo	21/118	UC	UC	R		UC	UC	C	
Yellow-billed Cuckoo	21/119	UC	UC	C			R		
Puerto Rican Lizard-Cuckoo	22/119	R							
Smooth-billed Ani	21/120	C	UC	VR	C	UC	C	C	
Barn-Owls TYTONIDAE									
Common Barn-Owl	21/121								
Typical Owls STRIGIDAE									
Puerto Rican Screech-Owl	21/122			C					
Short-eared Owl	21/123	R							
Goatsuckers CAPRIMULGIDAE									
Chuck-will's-widow	28/125			R				R	
Puerto Rican Nightjar	28/125								
Common Nighthawk	28/127					VR			
Antillean Nighthawk	28/127	UC	R						
Swifts APODIDAE									
Black Swift	28/129	VR							
Short-tailed Swift	28/129			UC					
Chimney Swift	1/130								
Hummingbirds TROCHILIDAE									
Puerto Rican Emerald	29/130	R	R	C					
Antillean Mango	29/131	UC	C	VR					

Species	No.							
Green Mango	29/132	R		C		UC	C	C
Green-throated Carib	29/133			C			C	C
Antillean Crested Hummingbird	29/134							
Ruby-throated Hummingbird	1/135							
Todies TODIDAE								
Puerto Rican Tody	30/136	C		C		C	C	
Kingfishers ALCEDINIDAE								
Belted Kingfisher	23/137	C	R	C		R	UC	UC
Woodpeckers PICIDAE								
Puerto Rican Woodpecker	24/138	UC		C		C	UC	
Yellow-bellied Sapsucker	23/139			R		R		
Tyrant Flycatchers TYRANNIDAE								
Gray Kingbird	31/139	UC	C	R	C	VC	C	C
Loggerhead Kingbird	31/140	UC		R			R	
Puerto Rican Flycatcher	31/141	C	UC	R		R		
Lesser Antillean Pewee	31/142	UC	R	R				
Greater Antillean Pewee	31/143					C	C	C
Caribbean Elaenia	31/143							
Swallows and Martins HIRUNDINIDAE								
Tree Swallow	32/144		R					
Purple Martin	32/144	R	C					
Caribbean Martin	32/145	UC	UC		UC	UC		R
Bank Swallow	32/145	VC	C		C	C		
Barn Swallow	32/146	C	C		C	UC	UC	R

SPECIES	Pl./P	CL	CR	EL Y	IG	ML	MPP	LDB	√
Cliff Swallow	32/146	VC	C	R	C				
Cave Swallow	32/146								
Northern Rough-winged Swallow	1/147								
Crows CORVIDAE									
White-necked Crow	23/148			EXT					
Muscicapids MUSCICAPIDAE									
American Robin	31/149		C		C				
Red-legged Thrush	31/149	R		C					
Gray-cheeked Thrush	1/150								
Mockingbirds and Thrashers MIMIDAE									
Northern Mockingbird	31/150	VC	C	VR	C	UC	UC	C	
Pearly-eyed Thrasher	31/151	UC	R	C	UC	C	C	C	
Waxwings BOMBYCILLIDAE									
Cedar Waxwing	23/152			VR					
Starlings and Mynas STURNIDAE									
European Starling	23/152								
White-vented Myna	23/153								
Hill Myna	23/154								
Vireos VIREONIDAE									
Yellow-throated Vireo	33/154						R		
White-eyed Vireo	33/155								

Species	No.	1	2	3	4	5	6	7	8
Puerto Rican Vireo	33/155	R							R
Red-eyed Vireo	33/156			R					
Black-whiskered Vireo	33/157	C	C	UC	C	C	UC	UC	
Emberizids EMBERIZIDAE									
Blue-winged Warbler	1/158								
Black-and-white Warbler	34/159	UC	UC	UC	UC	UC	C	C	
Prothonotary Warbler	35,36/159			R			R	R	
Worm-eating Warbler	33/160				UC				
Swainson's Warbler	1/160								
Golden-winged Warbler	35/160		VR	VR	R				
Northern Parula	35/161	C	C	UC	R	C	C	C	
Yellow Warbler	35,36/161	C	C	C	C	C	C	C	C
Magnolia Warbler	34,36/162	R	R		R		R	R	UC
Cape May Warbler	34,36/162	UC	UC	UC	UC	UC	UC	UC	R
Black-throated Blue Warbler	35,36/163				C				
Yellow-rumped Warbler	34,36/163	R		R	R		R		
Black-throated Green Warbler	34,36/164		R		VR				
Blackburnian Warbler	35,36/164				VR				
Yellow-throated Warbler	34/165				VR				
Adelaide's Warbler	35/165	C	C						
Chestnut-sided Warbler	34,36/166		R	R	VR				
Bay-breasted Warbler	34,36/166	C			A				
Blackpoll Warbler	34,36/167	UC	UC		UC	UC	UC	UC	
Prairie Warbler	34,36/167		C	C	UC	UC	C	UC	
Palm Warbler	34,36/167			UC	UC			UC	
Elfin Woods Warbler	34/168						R	R	
Ovenbird	33/169	VR	VR		UC				

SPECIES	Pl./P	CL	CR	EL Y	IG	ML	MPP	LDB	√
Northern Waterthrush	33/170	C	C			C	C		
Louisiana Waterthrush	33/170	R		C					
Kentucky Warbler	35,36/171			R					
Connecticut Warbler	35,36/171	A	A						
Mourning Warbler	35,36/171	UC							
Common Yellowthroat	35/172	VR							
Hooded Warbler	35,36/172	A							
Canada Warbler	34,36/173								
American Redstart	35/173	C	UC	C	UC	UC	UC		
Bananaquit	33/174	C	C	C	C	C	VC		
Antillean Euphonia	38/174	R		C	UC			C	
Stripe-headed Tanager	38/175	R		C					
Scarlet Tanager	38/175								
Puerto Rican Tanager	38/176	C		C					
Rose-breasted Grosbeak	39/177			A					
Blue Grosbeak	39/177								
Indigo Bunting	39/178								
Dickcissel	39/178							R	
Puerto Rican Bullfinch	39/179		R	C					
Lesser Antillean Bullfinch	39/180						R		
Yellow-faced Grassquit	39/181	C		R	C				
Black-faced Grassquit	39/181	C	C	R	C	C	C	C	
Saffron Finch	38/182				C				
Grasshopper Sparrow	39,40/182								
White-throated Sparrow	39/183	UC							

Species							
Shiny Cowbird	37/183	C	UC		UC	C	
Greater Antillean Grackle	37/184	C	UC	R	C		
Black-cowled Oriole	37/185	R	R	UC	UC		R
Northern Oriole	37/186	VR			UC	UC	
Troupial	37/186	C	C				
Yellow-shouldered Blackbird	37/187	C	C			R	
Bobolink	37/188						
Finches FRINGILLIDAE							
Yellow-fronted Canary	38/189				C		
Red Siskin	38/189						
Old World Sparrows PASSERIDAE							
House Sparrow	40/190				C		
Weaver Finches PLOCEIDAE							
Pin-tailed Whydah	40/191				C		
Yellow-crowned Bishop	40/192						
Red Bishop	40/192	R					
Waxbills and Allies ESTRILDIDAE							
Orange-cheeked Waxbill	41/193	C	UC		C		
Black-rumped Waxbill	41/194	R					
Red Avadavat	41/195						
Warbling Silverbill	41/195		UC		UC		
Bronze Mannikin	41/196	C		UC	C		
Nutmeg Mannikin	41/197				C		
Chestnut Mannikin	41/197	UC			UC		
Java Sparrow	40/198				C		

Index

References to specific birds, families, localities, and environmental factors have been indexed.

Bold numbers specifically refer to the plate(s) where illustrations of the birds appear.

Italic numbers correspond to the page(s) where detailed descriptions of the birds are given.

Map of Puerto Rico

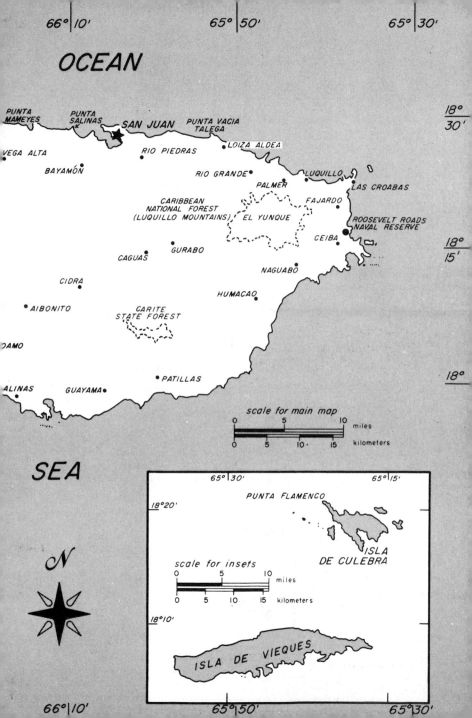

Map of the Virgin Islands

The Virgin Islands

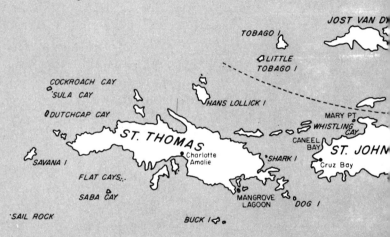

ATLANTIC OCEAN

65°   50'

18°
30'

JOST VAN DY

TOBAGO I

LITTLE
TOBAGO I

COCKROACH CAY
SULA CAY

HANS LOLLICK I

DUTCHCAP CAY

MARY PT

WHISTLING
CAY

CANEEL
BAY   ST. JOHN

ST. THOMAS

SAVANA I

Charlotte
Amalie   SHARK I

Cruz Bay

20'

FLAT CAYS

SABA CAY

MANGROVE
LAGOON   DOG I

SAIL ROCK

BUCK I

FRENCHCAP CAY

10'

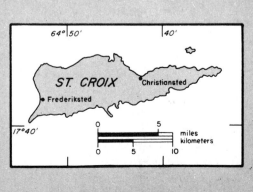

64° 50'   40'

ST. CROIX

Christiansted

Frederiksted

17°40'

0   5
                        miles
                        kilometers
0   5   10

CARIBBEAN

65°   50'

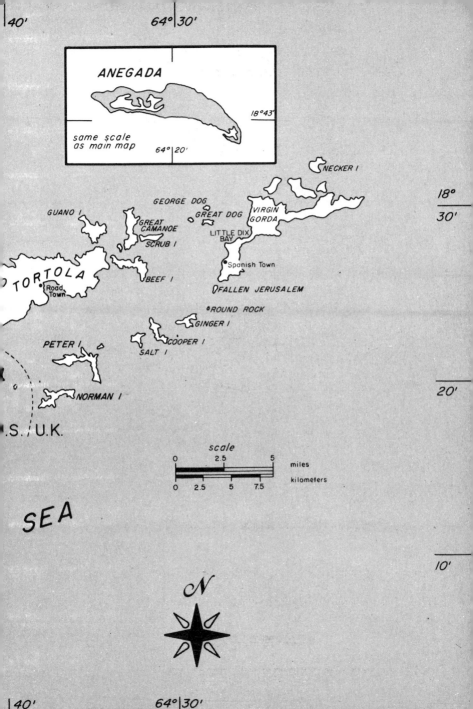

Library of Congress Cataloging-in-Publication Data

Raffaele, Herbert A.
  A guide to the birds of Puerto Rico and the Virgin Islands /
Herbert A. Raffaele: illustrated by Cindy J. House. John
Wiessinger. — [revised ed.]
      p.   cm.
  Includes index.
1. Birds—Puerto Rico—Indentification. 2. Bird—Virgin Islands of
The United States—Identification.   I. Title.
QL688.P6R33   1989
598.297295—dc20   89-34781
                                                              CIP

ISBN 0-691-08554-4
ISBN 0-691-02424-3 (pbk.)